Aging
Societies

Aging Societies

The Global Dimension

BARRY BOSWORTH
GARY BURTLESS
Editors

1998

Brookings Institution Press
Washington, D.C.

Library of Congress Cataloging-in-Publication Data

Aging societies : the global dimension / Barry Bosworth and Gary
Burtless, editors.
   p.   cm.
Includes bibliographical references and index.
ISBN 0-8157-1026-7
ISBN 0-8157-1025-9 (pbk.)
   1. Aging—Economic aspects.   2. Aged—Economic conditions.
3. Retirees—Economic conditions.   4. Aged—Government policy—
Economic aspects.   5. Age distribution (Demography)—Economic aspects.
I. Bosworth, Barry, 1942–   II. Burtless, Gary T., 1950–
   HQ1061 .A4845   1998
   305.26—ddc21   98-8944
                                     CIP

9 8 7 6 5 4 3 2 1

The paper used in this publication meets the minimum
requirements of the American National Standard for
Information Sciences—Permanence of Paper for Printed Library
Materials, ANSI Z39.48-1984

Typeset in Palatino

Composition by Harlowe Typography, Inc.
Cottage City, Maryland

Printed by R. R. Donnelley and Sons Co.
Harrisonburg, Virginia

Foreword

INDUSTRIALIZED COUNTRIES are in the middle of a momentous demographic transition. Low fertility rates and increasing life expectancy will soon produce populations that are older and more dependent on government transfers than they have ever been. Although the expansion of public pensions and other programs has dramatically improved the well-being of the elderly, the increasing ratio of retirees to active workers will also bring ever heavier tax burdens. Maintaining the structure and present generosity of programs that help the elderly threatens intolerably large government deficits or major increases in tax rates. Even though all industrial countries confront this problem, there are significant differences among them in the magnitude and timing of expected demographic change. There are also important differences in the generosity of programs providing income support and medical care to the aged.

The papers in this volume compare the structure of public programs for the elderly in the five largest industrialized economies, evaluate forecasts of cost trends, and discuss options for policy change in each country. The studies were undertaken in 1996–97 by the five member institutions of the Tokyo Club Foundation for Global Studies: the Brookings Institution (United States), IFO–Institut für Wirtshaftsforschung (Germany), Institute Français des Relations Internationales (France), Royal Institute of International Affairs (United Kingdom), and Nomura Research Institute, Ltd. (Japan). The authors find that the fiscal implications of population aging are surprisingly diverse. Aging is an important and immediate problem in Germany and Japan, where it is proceeding rapidly and where public pensions are comparatively generous. The pace is slower and less dramatic in France, but the complex and generous public pension system there will face very large cost increases unless it is reformed soon. Major demographic change is smallest and most delayed in the United States because of high American fertility rates and immigration. The generosity of U.S. public pensions is also comparatively modest, but the United States more than other countries faces an enormous future bill for providing health care to a growing aged population. The fiscal challenge associated with population aging is astonishingly small in the United Kingdom. Unlike the other major industrialized countries, Britain has already significantly scaled back its public pension commitments.

The ultimate effects of population aging on public spending and national policies toward the elderly will not be known for many years, but the papers presented here offer a preview of the difficult policy challenges that voters in major industrial countries will confront.

The research in this volume was generously supported by the Tokyo Club Foundation for Global Studies.

James Schneider edited the manuscript, Carlotta Ribar proofread it, and Sherry Smith prepared the index. Sheryl Zohn and J. J. Prescott provided research assistance, and Mark Steese provided staff assistance.

The views expressed in this book are those of the authors and should not be ascribed to the persons or organizations acknowledged above or to the trustees, officers, or other staff members of the Brookings Institution.

Michael H. Armacost
President

March 1998
Washington, D.C.

Contents

Chapter 1

Population Aging and Economic Performance

Barry Bosworth and Gary Burtless

ALL OF THE MAJOR industrial countries will experience significant aging of their populations over the next several
decades. In Germany and Japan, one in three persons will be older
than age 64 by 2030 and two out of five persons in France and Great
Britain. Although the projected rate is lower for the United States, it
will still represent a sharp increase from today's level. The cost of
providing income transfers and medical care for the elderly will put
major pressure on public sector budgets at a time of reduced growth
or actual shrinkage in the size of the work force. The aging of the
population also raises concerns about declining rates of private saving
in the advanced industrialized economies and the economic effects of
international flows of capital between aging rich countries and younger
developing countries. But although population aging is a matter of
common concern, there are significant differences among the G-5
countries in the magnitude and timing of the demographic changes,
and for some it goes beyond aging to actual population decreases. The
implications for public sector budgets also vary among these countries
because of large differences in the structures of public transfer programs for the elderly.

For most of the G-5 countries the projected public sector costs of
population aging are so large that they will be forced to make significant changes in the structure of programs that provide income and
health care support for the elderly. The purpose of this study is to
review the outlook for these countries and compare the policies that

We gratefully acknowledge the research assistance of J. J. Prescott.

have been adopted (or proposed) to deal with population aging. How similar are the problems and the proposed policy reforms? Can important lessons be drawn from the policy debate in the five countries? Finally, are there important implications for the global economy? How will a large change in the age distribution of the population in the industrial countries affect national saving, capital requirements, and international capital flows?

In this overview we survey the expected demographic changes over the next fifty years, the current living conditions of retirees in the G-5 countries, and the projected impact of aging on the costs of their public programs. We also summarize the categories of the policy responses that could be undertaken: raising taxes to maintain programs in their current form, increasing the age of eligibility for the programs, reducing benefits, and prefunding a portion of the added future costs. Finally, we briefly discuss the implications of aging for saving, economic growth, and other aspects of macroeconomic performance.

Demography

One simple measure of the age structure of a population is the aged dependency rate, the ratio of persons past the typical retirement age of 65 to the number of working-age persons (15 through 64). During the next several decades the aged dependency rate among the G-5 countries will increase most in Germany and Japan. This reflects both a large increase in the number of elderly persons and a striking decrease in the working-age population (table 1-1).[1] In fact, the total populations of both countries are expected to shrink substantially in the next forty years. The fertility rates of Germany and Japan are currently far below the rate needed to maintain a constant population (the replacement rate), which is currently about 2.1 children per woman (table 1-2). Although official Japanese projections assume the fertility rate will gradually recover to a level consistent with population replacement, official projections for Germany assume the total fertility rate will remain close to the current level of 1.4. The German demographic forecasts also assume significant but dwindling immigration,

---

1. Estimates in table 1-1 are based on official population projections of national statistical or social welfare agencies. Alternative estimates based on consistent population projections from the World Bank are displayed in appendix table 1A-1.

TABLE 1-1. *Aged Dependency Rates and Index of Elderly and Working-Age Populations in G-5 Countries, Selected Years, 1960–90, and Projected to 2050*

Characteristic	1960	1990	2000	2010	2020	2030	2050
Aged dependency rate[a] (percent)							
France	18.8	20.8	23.6	24.6	32.3	39.1	43.5
Germany	15.9	21.4	24.3	30.1	35.0	47.1	51.3
Japan	8.9	17.3	25.1	34.1	43.2	43.5	50.2
United Kingdom	17.9	24.2	24.2	25.5	30.5	38.3	40.9
United States	15.2	18.7	18.7	19.1	24.8	31.9	33.5
Population aged 65 and older (1990 = 100)							
France	69	100	118	127	161	187	198
Germany	51	100	115	139	153	180	164
Japan	36	100	146	186	220	215	211
United Kingdom	67	100	103	112	132	157	161
United States	54	100	111	124	165	213	233
Population aged 15–64 (1990 = 100)							
France	76	100	104	107	104	99	95
Germany	68	100	101	99	94	82	68
Japan	70	100	101	95	88	86	73
United Kingdom	91	100	103	106	105	99	96
United States	66	100	110	121	125	125	130

Sources: National sources. Data for France are from Bos and others (1994).
a. The dependency rate is the ratio of the number of persons older than age 64 to the number of persons aged 15–64.

projecting an annual rate of about 2 immigrants per 1,000 residents compared with an average net rate of 5.6 during the first half of the 1990s.[2] For Japan, immigration is assumed to be negligible. Thus for Germany and Japan the economic issues raised by population aging are compounded by a broader concern with the possibility of significant population decreases. The rise in their dependency rates reflects both a steep expansion in the number of people age 65 and older and an absolute decline in the number of people younger than 65.

France and the United Kingdom also face significant population

2. This estimate of immigration is the midpoint of a high and low projection, but even the high projection is significantly below the rate of recent years.

TABLE 1-2. *Fertility Rates, Immunization, and Male Life Expectancy in G-5 Countries, Selected Years and Periods, 1960–95*

Country	Total fertility rate 1990–95[a]	Net migration 1990–95[b]	Male life expectancy					
			At birth			At age 60		
			1960	1990	Annual percent change	1960	1990	Annual percent change
France	1.8	1.2	67.0	72.7	0.3	15.6	18.7	0.7
Germany	1.3	5.6	66.9	71.8	0.3	15.5	17.5	0.5
Japan	1.5	0	65.5	75.9	0.5	14.8	19.8	1.0
United Kingdom	1.8	0.9	68.3	73.0	0.2	15.3	17.3	0.4
United States	2.1	4.4	66.6	72.0	0.3	15.8	18.2	0.5

Source: Bos and others (1994); and OECD Health Data (1996).
a. The number of children that a woman would have in her lifetime if, at each year of age, she experienced the age-specific birthrate occuring in the general population.
b. Per thousand resident persons.

aging, but the trend is expected to be less dramatic than in Germany or Japan. Although French and British fertility rates have fallen, recent rates are not as far below the replacement rate as they are in Germany and Japan. The total populations of France and Britain are expected to grow through the next quarter century, and the working-age population will remain virtually unchanged. The increase in their dependency rates is thus fully explained by the increase in the number of the elderly.

The United States has the largest projected increase in the size of the aged population but for several reasons will experience the smallest increase in the aged dependency rate. First, the total fertility rate is close to the replacement rate, and second, the country is expected to accept relatively large numbers of immigrants. Thus the working-age population will continue to grow, although the official projections imply a sharp slowdown in its growth rate.[3]

The demographic projections for all five countries assume a greatly reduced rate of improvement in life expectancy (table 1-2).[4] The projections for Japan and the United States, for example, assume that life expectancy will increase over the next three decades at one-sixth and one-half, respectively, of the rates of the past three. Projections for Germany assume life expectancy will be constant after 2000. Many demographers believe the predicted improvement in longevity is unrealistically slow, implying that the projections may seriously understate the potential increase in the aged dependency rate.

Relative Income of the Aged

Before turning to the costs and burdens associated with population aging, it is worth noting the enormous accomplishments of the G-5 countries in improving the well-being and reducing the poverty rates of their elderly. Since World War II, changes in public retirement sys-

3. The demographic projections of the U.S. Social Security Administration imply a significantly smaller increase in the aged dependency rate than those of the World Bank (compare tables 1-1 and 1A-1). That is because the SSA assumes a higher fertility rate, a smaller increase in life expectancy, and continuation of the current high rate of immigration.

4. The table shows only the male life expectancy. The life expectancy of women shows the same trend and consistently exceeds that of men by 6 to 8 percent.

tems have generally been directed toward boosting the real value of retirement benefits to support living standards among the elderly that are comparable to those of the working-age population. By the mid-1980s the five countries had largely achieved this goal. Poverty rates among the elderly were sharply reduced, and on average the countries had reached rough parity in the disposable incomes received by their aged and non-aged populations. Although significant differences remain in the gross incomes of elderly and nonelderly families, these are mostly offset by the smaller households of the elderly and the more favorable tax treatment of their incomes. The comparison is complicated in the case of Japan because a large proportion of the elderly live with their children. In the United States a large part of the public benefits provided to the elderly is in the form of in-kind assistance, such as health insurance, that is not provided to younger households. Most of these benefits are excluded from money income measures, so the relative well-being of elderly U.S. households is understated by comparisons of money incomes.

There are important differences among the G-5 countries in the extent to which public programs provide benefits to the elderly. Public pensions account for about 70 percent of the total reported income of aged households in Germany and France but 50 to 60 percent in Japan and the United Kingdom and only about 45 percent in the United States.[5]

Current Pension Costs

The costs of public pensions measured as a percentage of GDP vary among these five countries by more than would be expected from considering their dependency rates. But dependency rates do not necessarily indicate actual program costs because there are significant differences in the generosity of public pensions among the countries. For example, although the current old-age dependency rate is similar in Japan and the three European countries, the cost of the pension

---

5. There are some serious questions about the accuracy of these data. The United States is often cited for a low rate of household saving relative to Japan and Germany, but American retirees appear to derive a larger portion of their retirement income from the accumulation of private wealth. It may be that there are important differences in the magnitude of underreporting of income in the various household surveys.

system as a share of GDP is much higher in France and Germany than it is in Japan or the United Kingdom (table 1-3). In part, this reflects differences in the generosity of the pension programs as shown by the higher ratio of average benefits to net wages (the net replacement rate). In addition, costs have been driven up in France and Germany by the practice of using the pension or quasi-pension programs to finance early retirement among the long-term unemployed. The result has been a sharp rise in the *program* dependency rate in comparison with the *old-age* dependency rate. This is reflected by the low labor force participation rates of those over age 54 (table 1-3). In contrast, Japanese labor force participation rates remain high even after age 65.

Among the five countries the United States spends the smallest proportion of national income on public pensions. Its aged dependency ratio is, of course, the lowest of the five. In addition, however, its public pensions are comparatively modest when measured as a percentage of workers' average wages (table 1-3, row 2), and its labor force participation rate is, along with Japan's, the highest among the five countries.

A brief overview of each country's basic pension system is helpful in understanding differences among their program costs.

France

The French pension system is unusually fragmented, consisting as it does of several hundred pay-as-you-go plans. The major plan (the basic régime général) offers an initial benefit equal to 50 percent of a reference wage calculated over a worker's 10 highest-earning years, but truncated at the social security ceiling. This initial pension is available to workers retiring at age 60 who have at least 37.5 years of contributions. Pensioners who have contributed to the system for less than 37.5 years receive a reduced pension. The pension is then indexed on prices. People benefiting from this basic pension generally also get benefits from two major complementary schemes, ARRCO and AGIRC, that are more strictly contributive (pensions are proportional to the cumulative amounts of past contributions). In addition to this two-pillar structure covering approximately two-thirds of the total population, there are many small plans with rules applying to specific socioeconomic groups.

TABLE 1-3. *Public Sector Financing of Programs for the Elderly in G-5 Countries, Selected Years, 1993–95, and Projected to 2050*

Characteristics	France	Germany	Japan	United Kingdom	United States
1. Public pension costs, 1995 (percent of GDP)	10.6	11.1	8.6	6.5	5.1
2. Net replacement rate[a] (percent)	78.0	63.0	55.0	50.0	50.0
3. Labor force participation rate, 1993–94 (percent)					
Male					
Total	74.5	78.0	90.6	72.7	87.0
55–64	42.1	51.5	85.0	64.3	65.5
65 and older	2.8	3.9	37.6	7.4	16.8
Female					
Total	59.6	60.8	62.1	52.8	71.4
55–64	30.1	26.8	48.1	39.7	48.9
65 and older	1.4	1.8	15.9	3.5	9.2
4. Pension cost projections (percent of GDP)					
1995	10.6	11.1	8.6	6.5	5.1
2000	11.5	11.4	10.5	6.3	5.1
2010	12.6	12.0	14.0	6.2	5.3
2020	14.8	13.3	14.8	6.0	6.1
2030	17.2	14.1	15.5	6.2	6.8
2040	20.4	14.2	na	5.7	6.8
5. Present value of net pension liabilities (percent of GDP)	115	110	105	5	25

6. Health care spending (percent of GDP)				
Total (public plus private)	9.1	8.5	6.6	13.7
Public spending	6.1	6.1	5.5	6.1
7. Age distribution of health care costs				
Ratio of spending on old relative to young[b]				
Total (public plus private)	3.0	2.7	3.9	4.8
Public spending	3.0	3.0	3.9	12.0
8. Effects of aging on public health costs[c] (percent of GDP)				
1990	6.1	6.1	5.5	6.1
2000	6.3	6.2	5.5	6.1
2010	6.3	6.6	5.6	6.3
2020	6.7	6.8	5.9	7.2
2030	7.0	7.4	6.3	8.2
2050	7.2	7.5	6.4	8.5

Sources: 1. Roseveare and others (1996) for France and Germany; Tanaka (1996) for Japan; Franco and Munzi (1996) for the United Kingdom; and Board of Trustees (1996) for the United States. Includes public employees. 2. Rates for Europe are averages of data shown in column 3, table 3.1 of Davis (1996). The net rate is the after-tax benefit as a percent of the after-tax average wage. Comparable rates for the United States were computed using an average gross replacement rate of 42 percent, and an employee tax rate of 15 percent. The 42 percent is the average retiree benefit in 1994. The estimate for Japan is based on a gross replacement rate of 45 percent and a 16 percent average tax rate. 3. OECD Labor Force Statistics (August 1995). 4. Compiled by authors on the basis of national estimates, as explained in text. 5. IMF (1996). Net liabilities are projected benefits less contributions out to 2050. 6. OECD Health Data File. All the data are for 1991 except for the United States, which is 1994. 7. Sturm (1996). The age distribution of costs for public spending is assumed to be the same as that for national spending in all countries except for the United States and Germany, where separate data are available. 8. Calculations based on the age distribution of medical care cost shown in item 7.
a. After-tax value of public pension as a percentage of after-tax wage while at work for average-wage worker.
b. Ratio of health care spending on average person aged 65 and older to spending on average person younger than 65.
c. Estimated public medical care spending on the elderly assuming that ratio of public spending per aged person to public spending per younger person remains unchanged and health spending per younger person rises at the rate of per capita income growth.

Reforms have thus far focused on the régime général. They have consisted of raising the number of years used to compute a worker's average wage to 25 years (from 10) and increasing the period of contribution needed for full participation to 40 years (from 37.5). Unlike the other G-5 countries, however, France has no immediate plans to raise the normal retirement age. The age of eligibility for pensions will remain 60 for both men and women.

Germany

Germany operates a pay-as-you-go pension plan in which the basic benefit is determined by the number of years a worker contributes to the plan and his or her relative wage in each of those years. For a worker earning the average wage in each year for forty-five years of contribution, the pension would be 70 percent of the average net wage in the year of retirement.[6] Workers earning less than half the average wage receive a small extra benefit. Benefits in later years of retirement are indexed to reflect annual changes in the economywide average *net* wage (the gross wage minus income taxes and social insurance contributions). The retirement age is currently 63 for men and 60 for women, but is scheduled to rise to 65 by 2005. There is, however, extensive use of early retirement pensions as a substitute for unemployment compensation. The pension system is financed with a proportional tax on earnings up to maximum taxable level. Dependent spouses without covered employment can make voluntary contributions to the system and can receive pension credits for years they devote to child rearing. Similar credits are provided to university students.

Japan

Japan has a two-tier public system composed of a flat-rate basic benefit and an earnings-related pension. The basic benefit is available

6. This is computed as 1.5 percent for each year of contribution multiplied by a worker's average real wage over the period of contribution. Past wages are adjusted using an index of economywide wage changes. Thus thirty-five years of contributions would provide a worker with an initial pension equal to 53 percent of his average wage.

to all citizens of Japan and currently covers about 80 percent of the work force. In 1995 it provided a maximum pension of ¥65,000 a month at age 65 for a person who has contributed for forty years. It offers separate pensions to dependent wives of employees. The actual average first-tier pension was closer to ¥45,000, or about 12 percent of the average wage. Workers can retire as early as age 60 but will receive a reduced pension. The first-tier benefit amount is adjusted to reflect consumer price inflation. If real wages continue to rise, the first-tier pension will decrease over time relative to the economywide average wage. The financing scheme for the first-tier pension is unusual: a flat tax on each insured person (equal to ¥12,300 a month in 1996) plus a subsidy from the general fund.

The second-tier system is fragmented because businesses can choose not to participate in part of the public program if they provide their own pension program.[7] Benefits are paid beginning at age 60 on the basis of each worker's average lifetime real wages. The pension consists of a component related to the number of months of the worker's coverage under the system plus a component that accrues at the rate of 0.75 percent of the average wage for each year of contribution. A worker with 40 years of service would receive an earnings-related pension equal to 30 percent of the average lifetime wage. In the computation of the initial benefit, past earnings are adjusted for inflation using an index of the economywide average wage. Pension payments in later years of retirement are adjusted to reflect price inflation. In addition, the second-tier program pays the first-tier national pension for those who retire before age 65 and are not yet eligible for the flat-rate benefit. Thus, most workers can retire at age 60 with a full pension. This concession to early retirees is to be phased out early in the next century, when the first-tier pension will be limited to those who have attained age 65. The earnings-related pension is financed by a premium that is proportionate to the after-tax wage.

United Kingdom

Like Japan, the United Kingdom has a two-tier pension system, but the second-tier pension is much smaller than it is in Japan, and the

---

7. Public employees are covered by mutual aid associations that provide earnings-related pensions.

firms and workers can opt out of the second tier into privately managed programs. The U.K. retirement age is 65 for men and is being increased from 60 for women. The basic flat-rate pension has declined over time to about 18 percent of the average wage. The second-tier earnings-related pension pays 1.25 percent of average real covered wages for each year of contribution up to a total of twenty years. Thus, a worker with twenty years of contributions would have a total replacement rate of about 43 percent. Current legislation will scale back the earnings-related public pension by about 20 percent. Benefits will decrease even further relative to the average wage because both the basic benefit and the upper limit for defining covered wages rise with the general price level rather than with average wages. The erosion in the second-tier component has led more than two-thirds of employees to leave the program. In effect, the United Kingdom is gradually reducing the scope of its public pension. The retired do, however, receive significant income support through other programs. From the point of view of public spending on pensions, Britain will not face the financing problem that confronts the other G-5 countries.

United States

The United States operates a single plan for all private sector workers and the overwhelming majority of public sector workers. The system covers about 97 percent of the work force. The public program is a pay-as-you-go defined-benefit plan in which the initial benefit is linked to a worker's average real wage in the best thirty-five years of his career. An index of changes in the economywide average wage is applied to earnings in past years to reflect inflation. After a person's pension begins, benefits are adjusted annually in line with changes in the consumer price index. The system is intentionally redistributive and heavily favors low-wage workers. The benefit formula provides significantly higher benefits relative to wages for workers with low lifetime earnings than it provides for workers with high average earnings. Benefits are financed with a proportional payroll tax imposed on wages and net self-employment income up to a maximum annual amount ($62,700 in 1996).

An American worker who earns the economywide average wage during each year of his career will receive a retirement benefit at age

65 equal to about 43 percent of his real final wage. Because wages are more heavily taxed than public pension benefits, on an after-tax basis the net replacement rate for an average-wage worker is about 50 percent. The U.S. system provides a benefit for dependent spouses equal to one-half of the breadwinner's pension, so a typical benefit for a married couple with only one earner would be 64 percent of the average pretax wage. The gross replacement rate is much lower in the more common case in which marriage partners both work.[8] The earliest age at which workers can receive unreduced pensions (or the normal retirement age) is 65 in the U.S. system, although workers can retire as early as age 62 with a reduced benefit. Under a reform passed in 1983 the normal retirement age is scheduled to rise to 66 by 2009 and to 67 by 2027, although the early retirement age will remain unchanged.

Projected Pension Costs

The projected costs of public pension programs vary widely across the G-5 countries (row 4 in table 1-3). France, Germany, and Japan will encounter serious problems in financing their existing pension systems within a few decades. Without reform of the systems, the share of national income devoted to spending on public pensions will double in France and Japan by 2040. Germany is also faced with a substantial increase in an already large program. The United Kingdom stands out by the absence of a significant financing problem in its public pension system. Through a series of legislative changes, it has already moved to scale back its public pension system, choosing to rely increasingly on a basically private system of providing retirement income. And the financing problems faced by the United States also seem surprisingly small compared with those faced by France, Germany, and Japan. The United States will experience a smaller increase in the dependency rate, its basic public pension is relatively modest, and it has refrained from using the pension system to provide unemployment compensation to jobless workers nearing retirement age.

8. The large benefit for spouses in the U.S. system is an unusual feature not shared by most other countries' systems. It makes the United States appear generous in international comparisons of married couples with one earner, although the country is less generous to unmarried earners and dual-earner couples.

The differences among the five countries can be highlighted by computing the present value of the net pension liability (future pension benefits less projected future contributions). For France, Germany and Japan, estimated unfunded liabilities exceed current GDP (row 5 in table 1-3). In contrast, the net liabilities of the U.S. public system are about one-fourth of GDP, and those in the United Kingdom are near zero.

Medical Care

Cost projections that focus solely on the public pension system significantly understate the fiscal burden associated with an aging population because they exclude the public cost of providing health care to the elderly. In the United States, for example, spending on medicare, the health care program for the aged, is expected to exceed spending on the public pension program by 2020. In all of the G-5 countries, medical care needs increase sharply with age, particularly after age 70. Per capita medical care spending on persons older than 65 typically exceeds spending for those age 0–64 by a ratio of between 3:1 and 5:1. The cost of medical care will thus be an important area in which population aging can be expected to push up public sector costs.

The impact of aging on public medical care spending is shown in table 1-3. The table displays projections to 2050 based on the current age distribution of public medical spending. The cost estimates are obtained by combining information about the age pattern of spending with the basic population projections of table 1-1. These are conservative estimates because they assume no further increase in health care costs relative to the growth in per capita income. In most countries, and especially in the United States, medical care cost inflation has substantially exceeded income growth.

The impact of aging on public medical care spending is especially pronounced for the United States because of the sharp division between privately financed programs for those younger than 65 and publicly financed health insurance for the aged. Per capita public spending on the U.S. elderly population is twelve times the spending for those younger than 65 (table 1-3). Thus, even though the United States is expected to experience the smallest amount of aging, it has the largest projected increase in public health care spending costs.

These costs may increase one-third by 2030. In view of the extraordinarily high levels of health care spending in the United States, the projected public cost of its program for the aged may exceed the public cost of providing medical care for the *entire population* in other G-5 countries. Yet the cost increases due to aging alone are less than half the growth anticipated by official government projections that incorporate continued medical care inflation.

For the other G-5 countries, the public cost of medical care for the aged adds 1 to 2 percent of GDP to the public budgetary costs associated with aging. The cost increases are smallest for the United Kingdom because medical care spending is such a low percentage of that nation's total output. Even taking account of medical care costs, the United Kingdom does not face a major fiscal problem in financing public programs for the aged. Medical care costs add to the problems faced by France, Germany and Japan, but they do not represent such a serious problem as they do for the United States.

Proposals for Reform

Public pension, health insurance, and assistance programs have been an outstanding success in meeting basic needs and alleviating poverty among the elderly of the G-5 countries. But as we have shown, the future costs of the programs will be daunting. Continued reliance on employment taxes to pay for these costs will impose serious disincentives on future workers and their employers. Governments have therefore begun to focus on proposals for long-term budget saving that range from modest curtailment of existing benefits to thorough reconsideration of the public role in ensuring retirement income.

The main proposals can be grouped into four categories for dealing with the budgetary challenge. Within the pay-as-you-go framework, benefits can be cut, taxes increased, or the age of eligibility for retirement benefits delayed. A fourth option is to reorient the financing of pensions to rely more on advance funding of future retirement obligations. This reorientation could be achieved either within the current public pension system or through an expansion of privately owned and managed funds. Each of the four reforms would have far-reaching effects on active and retired workers and would need to be introduced gradually. A politically acceptable package of reforms will probably involve elements of at least two and possibly all four approaches. A reform package that relies exclusively on benefit cutbacks or contribution increases, for example, is unlikely to be politically acceptable.

Benefit Reductions

In many countries the public retirement program was designed to supplement private retirement resources. In practice, however, the public system now provides the dominant source of income for most retirees: public benefits account for 40 percent of total retirement income in the United States and up to 70 percent in Germany.[9] Despite the success of public programs in reducing poverty among the elderly, many old people receive modest incomes and frequently incomes that are not far above the national poverty line. Consequently, for most of the G-5 countries there is limited scope for reducing the amount of the basic or minimum pension without causing a sizable increase in poverty. Many proposals for scaling back benefits therefore focus on introducing more means testing or modifying the formula that keeps benefits in line with inflation.

Japan, the United Kingdom, and the United States already offer public pensions under a formula that favors low-wage workers at the expense of workers with moderate or high lifetime earnings. The U.S. formula is explicitly redistributive with respect to the average lifetime wage, while Japan and the United Kingdom provide part of the public pension in the form of a flat-rate benefit that is unrelated to average earnings. France and Germany offer public pensions that are generally proportional to workers' average wages over a major portion of their careers.

Greater emphasis on flat-rate benefits could significantly reduce public pension costs. Retirees who earned high lifetime wages would receive reduced benefits while those who earned low average wages would be assured of at least a minimal public pension. This way of scaling back benefits carries significant risks, however. In a flat-rate pension scheme there is no link between average wages during a working life (and average tax contributions) and the pension a worker

9. Even in the United States the social security pension provides more than 70 percent of family cash income for retirees who are in the bottom 60 percent of the income distribution.

receives in retirement. By eliminating the link between average contributions and benefits, the reform would convert pension contributions into a pure tax on labor earnings, creating a significant disincentive to work and a major incentive for workers to evade taxes.[10]

If this approach to benefit reduction is adopted, it is important to maintain a strong link between receipt of the full flat-rate pension and the number of years of contribution. For some countries there may also be a strong political risk in transforming the public pension system into a flat-rate pension scheme. This type of system often arouses opposition among high-wage workers, who would be asked to pay a tax proportional to their wage but who could expect to receive only a minimum, flat-rate pension. To keep the contribution rate modest, these workers may use their political influence to reduce the basic pension to a very low level, possibly threatening the ability of the pension system to keep old people out of poverty.

Some advocates of pension reform propose means testing public pensions on the basis of retirees' current income rather than lifetime wages. This action can achieve large budgetary savings, mainly at the expense of retirees who have substantial incomes apart from their public pensions. But means testing on the basis of current income would create a major disincentive to private saving and might encourage greater reliance on public pensions among middle-income workers. Workers affected by means testing would achieve a financial advantage from consuming all of their wage income rather than saving for retirement. Unlike disability, retirement is a predictable event. Rational workers will take account of the retirement income test when deciding how to allocate their income. If nothing else, a means test would induce many retirees to avoid reporting their retirement assets and would encourage others to transfer assets to their children before retirement.

Benefits could also be scaled back by reducing the extent of indexation for general inflation. In all of the G-5 countries, a worker's initial public pension is determined by current and past wages but, except

10. The link between contributions and benefits is not eliminated completely. In most flat-rate pension schemes, workers are required to contribute to the program for a minimum number of years before they become eligible to receive old-age pensions. In addition, many flat-rate systems provide higher benefits to workers who have contributed longer than the minimum period.

in Germany, benefits during later years in retirement are adjusted only to reflect price increases. Retirees' pensions are held constant in real terms, but they do not rise in step with the real wages of workers.[11] To justify a lower level of indexation, some observers have suggested that the nonmedical consumption needs of the elderly decrease with age. In the United States, it is also argued that the official measure of consumer price inflation overstates increases in the cost of living. In effect, American pensioners receive an annual adjustment in their benefits that overcompensates them for changes in the cost of living; they receive a benefit whose real value rises as they age. Because biases in the measurement of price inflation may be similar in all the G-5 countries, the same argument might be valid outside the United States. One option would be to reduce the annual cost of living adjustment to the rate of increase in the consumer prices less some fixed percentage, perhaps 1 percent. This would have no effect on workers' initial benefits, which would continue to be indexed to past wage growth, but it would progressively reduce the real benefit of retirees as they age. If continued during every year of retirement, a 1 percent reduction in the cost of living adjustment would reduce the pension of an 80-year-old by 15 to 20 percent of what it would have been under current rules.

Reduced indexation has an immediate impact on budget outlays. In fact, it can have a larger immediate effect than a cut in the initial benefit because it affects all of the currently retired. But its effects are less attractive over the long term. Few other forms of retirement income are indexed, so the curtailment of indexation in the public pension system would reinforce a pattern in which the real income position of the elderly deteriorates as they age. Most of the available evidence suggests that poverty and low income are already more serious problems among the very old than they are among new retirees.

Increased Revenues

Employment tax rates are already high in several G-5 countries, and the increase needed to bridge the future funding gap seems prohibi-

---

11. The German system adjusts postretirement incomes to keep them in line with the incomes of workers. But the system was recently reformed to use net, aftertax wages rather than the pretax wage rate.

tively great.[12] In most countries, however, the high tax rates apply to a tax base that is limited to a fraction of total labor compensation. There are often limitations on the maximum wages subject to taxation, and noncash wage supplements are usually not taxed. In the United States the long-term shift of labor compensation into untaxed benefits accounts for more than a third of the projected retirement fund deficit. In Japan wage bonuses were not taxed before 1994, even though they often account for an important percentage of worker incomes. Some of the pension financing gap could obviously be closed by broadening the tax base to include fringe benefits and untaxed bonuses. However, under existing benefit formulas some of the extra revenues would ultimately be offset by higher pension payments to workers who would be credited with higher average wages. Another difficulty is that many forms of noncash labor compensation (health insurance and free company meals, for example) are difficult to value at the level of the individual worker, making it hard to assess pension contributions.

Revenues might also be increased by broadening the tax base to include sources of income in addition to labor compensation. This would represent a fundamental shift in the philosophy of the retirement system in some countries, where benefit payments have long been tied to workers' past contributions from wages. However, a broader base certainly makes sense for supporting some transfers targeted on the elderly, especially public medical insurance. Medical care costs at the individual level are not related to past contributions, so there is little reason to exclude the recipients of capital income from paying for the benefits.

Alternatively, countries might focus on increasing the number of contributors to the system by allowing more immigration, providing incentives for having children, or providing inducements to greater labor force participation among people who are younger than the retirement age. Immigration is far less popular in Europe than it was in the earlier postwar period, in part because of high rates of unemployment. And in the United States, although immigration continues at a high rate, it has become more controversial and substantially less

---

12. Current tax rates for public pensions (employer plus employee rates) are about 19 percent in France, 18.6 percent in Germany, about 11 percent in Japan, about 18 percent in the United Kingdom, and 12.4 percent in the United States. Some countries provide additional funding for public pensions through general revenues.

popular during the past decade. Major increases in U.S. immigration seem unlikely in the immediate future. Massive immigration has never been considered a serious policy option in Japan.

Both Germany and Japan could avoid a major part of the financial burden associated with aging if they boosted their fertility rates to a level closer to the population replacement rate. Unfortunately, public policies that might accomplish this are not obvious. Germany has experimented with a large tax allowance for having children and a longer period of pension fund credits for child raising, but it is too early to tell if these inducements have had a noticeable effect on the birthrate. It should also be noted that some incentives for childbearing provide powerful incentives for young women to withdraw from the labor force, either temporarily or for prolonged periods. A lower female participation rate will obviously reduce the number of contributors to the pension system, partially offsetting the benefits of a higher birthrate.

To increase contributions and hold down the contribution rate, it also makes sense to increase the percentage of working-age adults who are employed in pension-covered jobs. In the past two decades, high unemployment in the general population and declining labor force participation among men older than 50 have caused more serious financing problems for European pension programs than has the aging of the population. The labor force participation rate for men between ages 55 and 64 is about 50 percent in France and Germany compared with 85 percent in Japan. Female labor force participation rates have increased in all G-5 countries, but they remain 15 to 20 percentage points below the comparable rates for men. Some of the financing problems of public pension systems could thus be alleviated, at least temporarily, by increasing the labor force participation rate. Increases in the female participation rate would produce the greatest financial benefit to the public pension programs in Japan and the United States because these two countries provide substantial subsidized benefits to dependent spouses. If dependent spouses became employed, the financing of public pensions would improve.

Increasing the Retirement Age

The contribution rate needed to finance old-age pensions could eventually be stabilized through periodic increases in the eligibility age. If the retirement age were raised enough to hold constant the proportion of the expected lifespan that is devoted to retirement, the long-term imbalance in public pension systems would be significantly reduced. Since 1960, expected longevity at age 60 has increased about one-fifth in the G-5 countries, yet the official retirement age has hardly changed. In some countries, such as the United States, the pension system has been liberalized to permit earlier retirement (although early retirees must accept reduced pensions).[13] Other countries have made it easier for the long-term unemployed to retire with an early pension. In some countries the retirement age for women is being raised to match that for men. Germany is attempting to restore 65 as the normal age of retirement, that is, the earliest age for receiving a full benefit. The United States is committed to raising the normal retirement age to 67, but this policy will not become fully effective until 2027.[14] Japan also plans to increase the eligibility age for receiving the first-tier flat-rate benefit to 65 for all employees. The U.S. experience since 1975 suggests that most workers will retire at the earliest possible age that they are eligible for benefits. Increases in the normal retirement age without any change in the early retirement age are thus equivalent to a benefit reduction.

Increases in the early and normal retirement age can have a significant effect on the long-term cost of public pensions. Raising the German retirement age by one year would reduce the required contribution rate by two percentage points. The entire long-term deficit in the U.S. public pension system could be eliminated if the scheduled increases in the retirement age began immediately, if increases continued until the normal retirement age reached 70 in 2030, and if the early retirement age were raised from 62 to 67.

Raising the retirement age does have drawbacks. Although life expectancy has increased, evidence of commensurate improvements in the health status of the elderly—and in their ability to continue work-

---

13. In 1961 the U.S. public pension law was changed to permit men aged 62 to 64 to draw early social security benefits. Previously the earliest age of entitlement for public pensions was 65.

14. When the normal retirement age reaches 67, workers will continue to be eligible for an early pension at age 62 but with a permanent actuarial reduction in benefits equal to 30 percent of the full pension. The actuarial reduction at age 62 is presently just 20 percent.

ing—is more controversial. An increase in the early retirement age also implies that workers with short life expectancies will be forced to accept disproportionate reductions in lifetime benefits. A higher retirement age may be more acceptable to white-collar workers, who hold sedentary jobs and enjoy longer life expectancies, than it is to manual workers in physically demanding jobs. Some public concerns about the fairness of raising the retirement age could be alleviated if the disability insurance system were liberalized at the same time the retirement age is increased. Workers who reach age 60 and find it physically difficult to continue working could apply for disability insurance under more lenient eligibility rules. It would, of course, be important to restrict liberalized disability benefits to workers who are fairly old. But some countries have found it difficult to control access to the disability programs; and if young workers also become eligible to draw these liberalized benefits, the cost reduction from increasing the retirement age could disappear.

Advance Funding

Proposals to address the future problems of financing public pension systems through some combination of benefit reduction and tax increase are inherently divisive. The policy problem is that the financial security of the retired generation and the after-tax incomes of active workers are both reduced. These solutions do not change the fundamental nature of the financing problem, because the size of the future retired population and its needs remain the same. The debate over policy then focuses on which generation or income class is going to make the larger sacrifice in the fiscal adjustment that is inevitably needed. People who are already old naturally favor a solution that requires contributions from active and future workers, either in the form of payroll tax increases in the short run or benefit cuts in the distant future. People at the top of the income distribution favor solutions that emphasize benefit cuts and greater reliance on workers' own resources. Workers with more modest incomes may favor greater means testing in the benefit formula.

This kind of discussion diverts attention from alternative policies that could increase the total amount of future income out of which the consumption needs of both future workers and future retirees could be financed. The most straightforward policy of this kind is increasing the saving of the current generation to finance an increased percentage of its own retirement consumption. The current generation of workers could accumulate retirement saving at a faster rate than would occur under present retirement and fiscal policies. This could be accomplished by boosting the rate of accumulation in the nation's public or private retirement system by increasing the payroll tax or requiring active workers to contribute to private retirement accounts. The effect of larger accumulations in the retirement system would be to raise the nation's capital stock over the medium and long terms. If national investment and saving were larger, national output would be higher in the future. In the next century the nation would be paying for greater spending on old-age pension programs, but paying for it out of a larger economic pie, leaving a bigger slice of the future pie for future workers.

The current system of financing public pensions does not yield any increase in national saving. The G-5 countries finance their pension programs on a pay-as-you-go basis. Payroll contributions from the current generation of workers are almost entirely used up to pay for public pensions to the current generation of retirees. This financing method has important advantages for countries with steadily increasing populations and healthy productivity growth. Paul Samuelson and Henry Aaron have shown that under such circumstances, the expected real rate of return on contributions in a mature pay-as-you-go pension system will be the sum of the growth rate in the labor force and the growth rate in average real wages.[15] An alternative to pay-as-you-go financing is advance funding for each generation's own retirement (either through public or private saving). Each generation accumulates enough assets to pay fully for its own retirement consumption. The rate of return on contributions in that kind of system is simply the rate of return on capital investment.

In all the G-5 countries, pay-as-you-go financing looked very attractive in the 1950s and 1960s. The labor force was growing at a healthy rate and real wages were climbing between 2 and 5 percent a year. The internal rate of return on contributions under a pay-as-you-go system was expected to be 4 to 7 percent a year, even when the public

15. Samuelson (1958); and Aaron (1966).

pension system reached maturity. Ordinary workers in most G-5 countries could earn far less on their own savings. Most of them probably believed their investment alternatives were restricted to bank or postal savings accounts, government bonds, or insurance policies, which offered real returns ranging between -1 and 2 percent a year. Under those circumstances, workers and policymakers found the logic of a pay-as-you-go system very appealing.

Declining labor force growth (and the impending shrinkage of the work force in Germany and Japan) and the dramatic slowdown in labor productivity growth in all G-5 countries have reduced or eliminated the advantages of pay-as-you-go financing. The internal rate of return in a mature pay-as-you-go system has fallen below 2 percent a year in most of the countries, and may become negative early in the next century. Meanwhile, workers and pension fund managers now have access to private investment alternatives that yield real returns exceeding 3 percent a year. Many young and middle-aged workers could earn higher returns if they saved for their own retirement rather than contributed to a pay-as-you-go program. If today's workers and young voters were offered the choice that was available to policymakers when current pension systems were established, many would choose prefunded retirement accounts.

Unfortunately, present and future generations of workers cannot escape the consequences of the pay-as-you-go financing system that was adopted in the past. Huge liabilities have been accumulated under that system, obligations to workers who are already retired or who are approaching retirement age. The governments of G-5 countries are unlikely to default on the liabilities. Current and future workers will pay for public pensions to today's retirees and old and middle-aged workers over the next several decades, regardless of whether the governments establish advance-funded pension systems that will pay for pensions when they reach old age. This obligation makes it costly for younger workers to move cleanly from pay-as-you-go financing to advance funding. They would be required to pay off some or all of the accumulated liabilities of the existing system while accumulating enough assets to pay for their own retirement. This double burden would make it difficult to shift completely from the existing pay-as-you-go system to funded pensions.

Nonetheless, the current generation of workers could increase the percentage of retirement income it expects to derive from capital income and reduce the percentage it receives as a result of payroll contributions from future workers. Partial funding of future retirement obligations could be accomplished through either a modification of the current public retirement system or by its full or partial conversion into a private retirement system. In either case it is reasonable to ask whether the increment to funding would really add to national saving and capital formation and boost future national income. Would the added retirement saving be offset by reduced saving in other accounts of the public sector or in reductions in private saving?

PUBLIC FUNDING.   Advance funding would be simplest to implement within the existing public programs because accrued benefit claims would be left intact. The financing reform requires only some combination of an increase in the contribution rate or reduction of benefits to create a reserve and a firm commitment to separate the surplus from other government accounts. From the perspective of the economic benefits to the nation, it is of little consequence whether the reserve is invested in public or private securities. The economic benefits flow from the increased investment in real capital. If the public pension fund purchased government debt, a larger proportion of private saving would go to finance private investment. If the public fund were invested instead in private debt or equities, a larger percentage of private saving would be used to purchase public sector debt.

Investment of the increased public reserves in private securities might be advantageous for several reasons, however. First, if the reserves were invested solely in public debt, there is some risk that the additional retirement saving would simply be appropriated by national legislatures to finance spending in other government accounts.[16] If the added funds were invested in private securities, governments might find it more difficult to appropriate them. Many proposals to invest public pension reserves in private assets are based on the assumption that the money would be invested in large index funds and that fund managers would not be permitted to influence the operation of individual corporations.

16. There is little reason to anticipate a change in private saving behavior because the promised future retirement benefit remains unchanged.

Second, if the fund is restricted to investing in government securities, most of the economic benefits of a high-saving program would be concentrated in private incomes. The public pension reserves would earn the comparatively low (but safe) return on public debt, whereas a larger percentage of private saving would be held in high-return private debt and equities. The added private capital formation would boost the incomes of future workers, but it is doubtful whether they would recognize that their improved living standard was partly the result of increased saving and investment by past generations of workers and savers. Most of the increase in future capital income will accrue to private investors who bear the risk. If the additions to the social security reserves were invested instead in a portfolio that included a substantial fraction of high-return private securities, the trust fund would earn a much higher future return, reducing the need for future payroll tax increases. Of course, this strategy would also increase the riskiness of the public pension portfolio. However, concentrating all public retirement saving in government debt is itself a highly skewed investment strategy that fails to take advantage of the benefits of portfolio diversification.

PRIVATIZATION.   Public management of a huge retirement fund raises difficult political issues. Investment decisions might be skewed by political criteria rather than guided by purely economic considerations. Public officials might use accumulations in the reserve to offset deficits in other government accounts. Private retirement accounts can reduce these political risks. They also offer workers flexibility in managing their own retirement savings. Partial privatization can occur within a two-pillar system such as the one successfully introduced in Chile during the early 1980s. The system could comprise a public program that provides modest benefits—perhaps a flat benefit amount or one related to the number of years a worker participates—and a second, defined-contribution pension with no redistributional element. Participants' funds in the individual accounts would be invested in a range of capital market assets, presumably directed by the individual contributors.

Privatization carries both political and economic risks. There is a danger that the explicit separation of the redistributional component could result in strong pressure to reduce or eliminate it. Some observers doubt that a two-pillar, partially privatized system would provide adequate old-age income security for workers with low lifetime earnings. Many workers may be poorly qualified to make good investment decisions.[17] Individual accounts also raise the problem of how to manage the conversion of the accounts into annuities when workers retire, become disabled, or (for those who leave survivors) die. If individuals are given the option of accepting lump-sum cash-outs, a private system for converting assets into annuities will encounter problems of adverse selection. The price of annuities would therefore have to rise. This is not a problem faced by a national system of defined-benefit pensions, in which, by definition, there is universal and mandatory conversion to annuities. Substantial privatization would also involve higher administrative costs. The administrative costs of universal public systems are a modest percentage of annual benefit payments. No private insurance or investment management company has administrative costs nearly as low. In addition, private investment companies will incur selling costs to attract retirement saving, and each company will have to establish a funds collection and distribution system.

Individual retirement accounts have obvious appeal to high-wage workers, especially those with investment expertise. Because an individual retirement account is effectively a defined-contribution pension plan, the establishment of millions of such accounts eliminates the concern about the public sector costs of retirement programs: benefits are determined by workers' contributions and market interest rates, not by government contributions. But if millions of workers suffer low or negative returns on their investments, democratically elected governments may face considerable pressure to compensate them for their losses.

The Saving-Investment Balance

Population aging in industrial societies has heightened concern about the adequacy of future saving and raises questions about the prospect for higher capital costs. Does dissaving within the older

17. Survey evidence in the United States suggests that low-wage workers who are given decisionmaking authority over their pension assets often make extremely risk-averse investment decisions, frequently choosing to place their funds in low-return bank or insurance accounts.

industrial societies imply an increased competition in international markets for capital that would normally be expected to flow to developing countries? In theory, a pattern of aging should first increase private saving rates in the aging population as individuals attempt to amass wealth in anticipation of retirement. The private saving rate should then fall as the proportion of retired workers in the population rises.

The historical record provides only weak support for this theory, however. Empirical studies typically find that life-cycle effects are only a minor determinant of aggregate saving. Moreover, the actual age profile of individual saving is not as extreme as the simple life-cycle model would suggest. For example, most researchers find relatively little evidence of wealth decumulation in old age. The strongest evidence of a link between aging and aggregate saving is based on the experience of Japan. The Japanese private saving rate has declined substantially during the past two decades as a much higher percentage of the population has entered retirement. But variations in U.S. private saving have not been closely related to changes in the age distribution, and the substantial aging that has already occurred within the European economies has not been matched by an equivalent decline in their private saving rates. Finally, there has been a substantial lengthening of the retirement period as workers retire at an earlier age and live longer. To the extent that this pattern was anticipated, it should have induced workers to increase their saving while they were actively employed. Researchers have found little evidence for such an effect in any of the G-5 countries.

Even if population aging eventually reduces the overall saving rate, it is not obvious that this will lead to a "shortage" of aggregate saving. Population aging eventually brings with it a slowing of growth in the working-age population (table 1-1), sharply reducing one of the main sources of demand for domestic capital. With a slowly growing or even shrinking labor force, the industrial economies will have only limited demand for additional private capital. Over the long term, any growth in the stock of capital in excess of that warranted by increases in the labor force and labor-augmenting technical change will continually lower the rate of return to capital. The industrial countries have already felt the effects of a sharp slowing of growth that has since 1973 reduced the rate of investment by more than the rate of saving. Thus in the

G-5 countries, private saving rates actually exceed domestic investment rates, and the size of the surplus has grown. The need for a balancing of growth in the capital stock, technical change, and growth in the labor force suggests that the future decline in required private investment will go a long way toward offsetting any fall in private saving rates. This should be particularly important for Germany and Japan, where the domestic labor force is actually projected to contract by a significant amount. In sum, there are strong internal connections that link the rate of private saving with that of domestic investment, suggesting that aging per se is unlikely to create a shortage of private saving relative to investment needs.

There is a greater reason for concern about the pressure that population aging will place on public budgets and the potential for a large decrease in national saving stemming from public sector dissaving. In view of expanding political opposition to tax increases, it seems probable that future governments will be pressed to maintain the pension and health care programs for the aged by greater reliance on debt finance. We have already shown that the growth of public sector costs will be large—except in the United Kingdom—and they will be accompanied by an equivalent shift in the age distribution of the voting population that will make it difficult to scale the programs back.

Conclusion

The G-5 countries all face major challenges as a result of population aging. The challenges differ somewhat among them because of differences in the rate of change in their population age structures and differences in the national institutions that ensure income support and health protection to their elderly populations.

Most of this overview has focused on the challenge that aging will present to public budgets. The focus is a natural one. All the G-5 countries pay for a large percentage of the current consumption of their elderly citizens through public transfers and publicly financed health insurance. Public spending targeted on the elderly already consumes a large percentage of all public expenditures, and for most of these countries, population aging implies that the percentage will rise sharply unless current laws are changed.

The United Kingdom will face a significantly less serious budgetary challenge than the other G-5 countries. The reason is not that the trend toward aging is slower in Britain—it falls roughly in the middle of the five countries. Nor is it the result of an exceptional employment rate or a pattern of delayed retirement in its work force; in terms of employment and age at retirement, Britain again falls roughly in the middle. Instead, the relatively benign outlook for British public budgets is the result of government policies that tightly restrain the growth of public spending on both health care and first-tier public pensions and that encourage active workers to leave the second-tier public pension scheme. Future retirees are expected to derive much more of their retirement income from privately managed and invested pension accounts rather than from pay-as-you-go public systems.

The United Kingdom will face a smaller increase than the other G-5 countries in public spending on the elderly and will accumulate substantially greater reserves in its (increasingly private) pension system. If its budget deficit is kept low, the growing accumulations in private pension accounts can help boost national saving, which in turn can increase the rate of economic growth. These policies may, however, expose workers to greater risk of low retirement incomes. Workers who invest their retirement funds recklessly or in excessively conservative, low-yield securities may be forced to accept pensions that are low in comparison with their net incomes while at work. And if workers should retire after a lengthy period in which private markets yield low or negative returns, an entire cohort of them may be faced with the prospect of low retirement incomes. The contributions of low-wage workers may also be inadequate to support their retirement because administrative costs absorb a major portion of the return on small retirement accounts. It is tempting to say that a shortfall in retirement income is solely a problem for the unfortunate workers, but it also might be a problem for the public budget if voters demand that public pensions or pension guarantees assure workers of good incomes in retirement.

The United Kingdom, like the other G-5 countries, must support its retired population out of the national income that will be available in the future. Whether retired workers receive most of their income through public pensions, as in Germany, or through private pension funds, as may be the case in the United Kingdom, their consumption will be derived from the output produced with future workers and the future capital stock. If future productivity grows rapidly, the elderly can be generously supported while at the same time active workers continue to enjoy steady increases in their aftertax incomes. If productivity grows slowly, population aging will require future workers to accept lower aftertax incomes or retirees to accept smaller pensions unless workers can be persuaded to delay their retirement. The implications of slow growth will be the same whether retirement incomes are derived from public or private sources. One policy that can increase future growth of the economy is the accumulation of larger pension fund reserves to boost the rate of national saving. This can be accomplished in either a public or a private retirement system. An important question for the G-5 countries is whether greater accumulation is more likely to occur in public or private pension systems.

References

Aaron, Henry J. 1966. "The Social Insurance Paradox." *Canadian Journal of Economics and Political Science* 32 (August): 371–74.

Board of Trustees of the Federal Old-Age and Survivors Insurance and Disability Insurance Trust Fund. 1996. *1996 Annual Report.* Government Printing Office.

Bos, E., and others. 1994. *World Population Projections 1994–1995.* Washington: World Bank.

Franco, Daniele, and Teresa Munzi. 1996. "Public Pension Expenditure Prospects in the European Union: A Survey of National Projections." In *European Economy: Ageing and Pension Expenditures Prospects in the Western World*, reports and studies 3: 1–127. European Commission.

International Monetary Fund. 1996. *World Economic Outlook, March 1996.* Washington.

OECD Health Data File. 1993. Comparative Analysis of Health Systems.

OECD. 1995. *Labor Force Statistics.* Paris.

Roseveare, Deborah, and others. 1996. "Ageing Populations, Pensions Systems and Government Budgets: Simulations for 20 OECD Countries," OECD Economics Department Working Paper 168. Paris.

Samuelson, Paul A. 1958. "An Exact Consumption-Loan Model of Interest with or without the Social Contrivance of Money," *Journal of Political Economy* 66 (December): 467–82.

Sturm, Peter. 1996. *Selected Issues in Population Ageing: Differences and Similarities in OECD Countries. International Symposium on Scenarios to a Vital Aged Society.*

Economics Research Institute, Economic Planning Agency, Government of Japan.

Takayama, Noriyuki. 1996. "Possible Effects of Ageing on the Equilibrium of the Public Pension System in Japan." In *European Economy:Ageing and Pension Expenditures Prospects in the Western World*, reports and studies 3, pp. 155–94. European Commission.

TABLE 1A-1. *Aged Dependency Ratios and Index of Aged Populations Using Common World Bank Demographic Projections, 2000–50*

	1990	2000	2010	2020	2030	2050
Dependency ratio[a] (percent)						
France	20.8	23.6	24.6	32.3	39.1	43.5
Germany	21.7	23.8	30.3	35.4	49.2	51.9
Japan	17.1	24.3	33.0	43.0	44.5	51.6
United Kingdom	24.0	24.4	25.8	31.2	38.7	41.2
United States	19.1	19.0	20.4	27.6	36.8	38.4
Population 65 and older (1990 = 100)						
France	100	118	127	161	187	198
Germany	100	111	134	145	174	159
Japan	100	143	184	220	217	222
United Kingdom	100	104	112	132	155	159
United States	100	110	128	176	228	242
Population aged 15–64 (1990 = 100)						
France	100	104	107	104	99	95
Germany	100	101	96	89	77	66
Japan	100	100	95	87	83	74
United Kingdom	100	102	104	101	96	92
United States	100	110	120	121	118	120

Sources: Bos and others (1994); and World Bank.
a. The dependency ratio is the ratio of the number of persons older than age 64 to the number of persons aged 15–64.

Chapter 2

Population Aging and Retirement Income Provision in the European Union

E. Philip Davis

THIS CHAPTER provides an overview of the main economic and policy issues raised by population aging in the European Union, given the demographic projections for member countries and the differing systems of retirement income provision they employ. The conclusion is that EU countries face broadly similar patterns of population aging, but differ widely in terms of the difficulties likely to be posed by the problem, owing largely to differences in the features of their systems of retirement income provision. In particular, a number of countries may face major difficulties with their generous social security systems, while others that have sizable private pension systems are better placed to face the demographic difficulties of the twenty-first century. Nonetheless, these latter are not without such problems because of the poor returns often obtained on funds that are invested and lack of international diversification, which often results from the effects of portfolio regulations. Policy action is thus warranted in a number of fields.

The individual themes covered here are analyzed extensively

An earlier version of this paper was presented at the conference Economics of Ageing, at the Institut Français des Relations Internationales, Paris, October 1996. The views expressed are those of the author and not necessarily those of the institutions with which he is affiliated. The article draws on the author's book *Pension Funds, Retirement-Income Security and Capital Markets* published in 1995 by Oxford University Press. The author thanks C. Daykin, K. de Ryck, D. Roseveare, D. Franco, and participants in the seminar at the IFRI for their assistance. The errors remain his own responsibility.

elsewhere.[1] But my focus is on the European Union and cross-country comparisons. In taking this approach, I use the main common data sources for the EU, in particular Eurostat. However, it should be noted at the outset that coverage of the fifteen current EU countries is not always complete; in many cases data are only available for a subset of countries.

Demographic Trends

In general, the fifteen EU member countries share a declining birthrate, an increase in life expectancy, and limited migration. These conditions give rise to projections of an aging population, with an increasing burden of dependents relative to the population of working age. In many cases this situation is expected to be accompanied by a decline in the overall population.

The historical developments underlying the aging of the population are illustrated in tables 2-1 to 2-4. Most crucially, there has been a decline in birthrates, with the average fertility rate in the fifteen countries falling from more than 2.5 per woman in 1960 to 1.4 in 1993 (table 2-1). The decline was particularly rapid in the 1970s, but was also marked in all the decades since 1960. Particularly sharp decreases have occurred in Spain, Ireland, the Netherlands and Portugal, each of which had relatively high birthrates in 1960. In contrast, Sweden's birthrate has declined little, having already been barely above replacement in 1960. In 1993 no EU country had a birthrate of more than 2.0 (replacement is about 2.1). There were rates of less than 1.5 in Germany, Greece, Spain and Italy, while 1.8 or more was maintained in Denmark, Ireland, Finland, and the United Kingdom as well as Sweden.

Underlying the falling fertility rates are patterns of later marriage and greater activity of women in the labor market, which has increased the opportunity cost of having children, as well as more general social and attitudinal changes. The highest birthrates in the EU countries today are in Scandinavian countries that provide comprehensive and subsidized child care facilities, thus spreading the burden of child care

1. See, for example, World Bank (1994); Davis (1995); and OECD (1995).

TABLE 2-1. *Fertility Rates, European Union Members,*
Selected Years, 1960–93

Country	1960	1970	1980	1990	1993
Belgium	2.6	2.3	1.7	1.6	1.6
Denmark	2.5	2.0	1.6	1.7	1.8
Germany	2.4	2.0	1.6	1.5	1.3
Greece	2.3	2.4	2.2	1.4	1.3
Spain	2.9	2.9	2.2	1.3	1.3
France	2.7	2.5	2.0	1.8	1.7
Ireland	3.8	3.9	3.3	2.1	1.9
Italy	2.4	2.4	1.6	1.3	1.2
Luxembourg	2.3	2.0	1.5	1.6	1.7
Netherlands	3.1	2.6	1.6	1.6	1.6
Austria	2.7	2.3	1.6	1.5	1.5
Portugal	3.2	3.0	2.2	1.6	1.5
Finland	2.7	1.8	1.6	1.8	1.8
Sweden	2.2	1.9	1.7	2.1	2.0
United Kingdom	2.7	2.5	1.9	1.8	1.8
EU-15	2.7	2.4	1.8	1.5	1.4

Source: Eurostat (1995c).

to the economy as a whole and facilitating high levels of female labor market participation.

Reflecting the decline in fertility, the generation born in the 1970s is 17 percent smaller than that of the 1960s, and the 1980s generation is 25 percent smaller (table 2-2). The main exception to the overall pattern is Ireland, where the generations born in the 1970s and 1980s were larger than those of the 1960s. Otherwise, the 1960s generation was historically large; indeed, it exceeded any born earlier in the twentieth century (obviously the size of generations depends not only on fertility but also on the size of the population). This is the case not only for the European Union as a whole but also for the individual countries.

Greater longevity and generally low levels of immigration are also important features of demographic developments in the fifteen countries. Life expectancy at birth for men has increased from around 67.5 years in 1960 to 73.0 in 1993, while that for women has risen from 72.8 to 79.4 (table 2-3). The increases can be attributed to better health care,

TABLE 2-2. *Size of Generations Born in the Twentieth Century,*
European Union Members, 1900s to 1980s
1900s = 100

Country	1900s	1910s	1920s	1930s	1940s	1950s	1960s	1970s	1980s
Belgium	100	87	108	104	110	133	137	117	110
Denmark	100	103	102	102	141	136	147	130	107
Germany	100	74	90	103	101	113	129	86	84
Greece	100	113	124	153	138	151	170	161	144
Spain	100	112	143	142	154	182	220	212	169
France	100	78	113	109	128	151	154	143	138
Ireland	100	113	107	109	142	183	227	258	251
Italy	100	97	128	131	135	143	172	149	112
Luxembourg	100	86	103	111	123	146	141	110	113
Netherlands	100	109	126	134	182	206	222	175	158
Portugal	100	113	139	143	145	175	209	205	168
United Kingdom	100	97	99	93	114	120	140	109	111
EU-12	100	90	110	113	123	138	157	130	118

Source: Besseling and Zeeuw (1993).

medical advances, and improved living standards. Immigration shows
a low amplitude, particularly in comparison with the United States,
Canada, and Australia. Accordingly, its effect on demographic patterns is limited compared with the effects of low fertility, large generations, and greater life expectancy. Nonetheless, Germany, France,
and the United Kingdom showed net immigration in the 1960s (both
from within and outside the Union), when most other European countries showed outflows (table 2-4). Large inflows in the early 1990s to
Germany, Greece, Austria, and Sweden result from the opening up of
Eastern Europe and consequent flows of workers and refugees.

These patterns provide the basis of demographic projections for the
European Union. Highlights of one of the most recent projections for
EU countries by the World Bank are provided in tables 2-5 to 2-7. The
tables assume that fertility rates converge gradually from current levels
to replacement in 2030, that life expectancy tends gradually toward
peaks of 83.3 years for men and 90.0 for women, and that immigration
remains at current levels, generally zero. Clearly, the fertility assump-

TABLE 2-3. *Life Expectancy at Birth, by Sex, European Union Members, 1960, 1993*

Country	Male		Female	
	1960	1993	1960	1993
Belgium	67.7	73.0	73.5	79.9
Denmark	70.4	72.6	74.4	77.8
Germany	n.a.	72.7	n.a.	79.2
Greece	67.3	75.0	72.4	79.9
Spain	67.4	73.7	72.2	81.0
France	66.9	73.3	73.6	81.5
Ireland	68.1	72.7	71.9	78.2
Italy	67.2	73.4	72.3	80.2
Luxembourg	66.5	72.2	72.2	79.4
Netherlands	71.5	74.0	75.3	80.0
Austria	66.2	72.9	72.7	79.4
Portugal	61.2	70.6	66.8	77.8
Finland	65.5	72.1	72.4	79.5
Sweden	71.2	75.5	74.9	80.8
United Kingdom	67.9	73.6	73.7	79.0
EU-15	67.5	73.0	72.8	79.4

Source: Eurostat (1995c).
n.a. Not available.

tion could be too high. Nevertheless, for at least the next fifty years, such projections can be made with reasonable precision, given that many of the persons concerned are already born and birthrates and life expectancy change slowly. The dominance of the birthrates is shown by the fact that demographic projections are similar for some time in the future whether fertility rates are fixed at 2.5 or 1.7.

The drift to a more aged population will be particularly marked after 2010 (table 2-5). Whereas in 1990 the average EU elderly dependency ratio (defined as the population aged 65 and older as a proportion of those aged 15 to 64) was around 21 percent, it is expected to rise to more than 25 percent in 2010 and 40 percent in 2030. In the Netherlands, Germany, and Italy the ratio will be more than 45 percent in 2030. The smallest increase, 7 percentage points, is expected to be

TABLE 2-4. *Migration in European Union, Selected Years, 1960–93*
Per 1,000 population

Country	1960	1970	1980	1990	1993
Belgium	0.9	−3.4	−0.2	2.0	1.8
Denmark	−0.9	4.3	0.1	1.7	2.2
Germany	2.2	−3.5	3.9	8.3	5.7
Greece	−3.7	−5.3	5.2	7.0	5.4
Spain	−4.6	2.2	3.0	−0.1	0.7
France	3.1	3.6	0.8	1.4	1.2
Ireland	−14.8	−0.9	−0.1	−2.2	−2.5
Italy	−1.6	−2.0	0.1	0.5	3.2
Luxembourg	1.7	3.2	3.7	10.3	10.7
Netherlands	−1.1	2.5	3.6	3.3	2.9
Austria	−0.3	1.4	1.2	16.0	5.0
Portugal	−6.3	−14.0	4.3	−6.1	1.6
Finland	−2.1	−7.9	−0.5	1.7	1.8
Sweden	−0.1	5.8	1.2	4.1	3.7
United Kingdom	2.1	−0.3	−0.6	1.2	1.2
EU-15	0.1	−0.8	1.7	3.0	2.8

Source: Eurostat (1995c).

in Ireland, while the largest, in Germany, is expected to be 27.5 points. There is also expected to be an increasing proportion of very old people, who may need costly health care as well as pensions.

Assuming immigration remains low, aging is expected to be accompanied by decreases in the total population of the European Union between 2010 and 2030, at which point it reverts to the levels of the 1990s (table 2-6). This decrease is expected to be particularly marked in Germany and Italy; in France and the United Kingdom the population is expected to rise until 2030 before stabilizing.

The share of young dependents is expected to remain constant (table 2-7), but they tend to be less costly than the old.[2] And potential savings on education are small, perhaps 0.3 percent of GDP between 2000 and

2. Heller, Hemming, and Kohnert (1986) accordingly estimate that social expenditures will rise in the major industrial countries even if savings in family benefits and the education costs of young dependents are taken into account.

TABLE 2-5. *Projections of Aged Dependency Ratio, European Union Members, 2010, 2030[a]*
Percent

Country	1990	2010	2030
Belgium	22.4	25.6	41.1
Denmark	22.7	24.9	37.7
Germany	21.7	30.3	49.2
Greece	21.2	28.8	40.9
Spain	19.8	25.9	41.0
France	20.8	24.6	39.1
Ireland	18.4	18.0	25.3
Italy	21.6	31.2	48.3
Luxembourg	19.9	25.9	44.2
Netherlands	19.1	24.2	45.1
Austria	22.4	27.7	44.0
Portugal	19.5	22.0	33.5
Finland	19.7	24.3	41.1
Sweden	27.6	29.1	39.4
United Kingdom	24.0	25.8	38.7
EU average	21.4	25.9	40.3

Source: Bos and others (1994).
a. Population aged 65 and older as a percentage of population aged 15–64.

2030.[3] The recovery in this ratio after 2010 is a consequence of the assumption that fertility gradually recovers in the twenty-first century, and thus may not be realized. The total dependency ratio (including those younger than 15 and older than 65 in the numerator) will be more than 70 percent in 2030 in Germany, the Netherlands, Italy, Luxembourg, Austria, Finland, and Sweden.

Patterns of Retirement Income

The pattern of retirement income for existing retirees in the European Union illustrates the dominance of pay-as-you-go pensions as a source of benefits and also as a source of retirement income more generally. Comparable harmonized data for retirement income in EU

3. Leibfritz and others (1996).

TABLE 2-6. *Projections of Total Population, European Union Members, 2010, 2030*
Millions unless otherwise specified

Country	1990	2010	2030	Change 1990–2030 (percent)
Belgium	10.0	10.1	9.8	−2.0
Denmark	5.1	5.3	5.2	2
Germany	79.5	78.9	73.5	−7.5
Greece	10.1	10.7	10.4	3.0
Spain	39.0	39.1	37.8	−3.1
France	56.7	61.0	62.7	10.6
Ireland	3.5	4.0	4.5	28.6
Italy	57.7	56.8	53.2	−7.8
Luxembourg	0.4	0.4	0.4	0
Netherlands	15.0	16.0	15.9	6.0
Austria	7.7	8.2	8.1	5.2
Portugal	9.9	9.9	9.8	−1.0
Finland	5.0	5.3	5.3	6.0
Sweden	8.6	9.1	9.4	9.3
United Kingdom	57.4	59.6	60.6	5.6
EU-15	365.6	374.4	366.6	. . .

Source: Bos and others (1994).

countries are available from Eurostat, but because the data rely on surveys from 1988, their relevance to today's elderly is less than is desirable. Nevertheless some interesting cross-country comparisons, which spring largely from the varying nature of public and private retirement income provision in individual countries, can be made.

In 1988 pay-as-you-go pensions were the dominant source of income for elderly persons in the EU's twelve countries (table 2-8). On average they accounted for 83 percent of benefits, ranging from 50 to 70 percent in Ireland, the Netherlands, and the United Kingdom to more than 95 percent in Spain, Italy, and Luxembourg. If one adds supplementary compulsory pay-as-you-go plans, the average rises to 90 percent in the twelve countries, with this source being important in France, Greece, Denmark, and the United Kingdom. Funded plans accounted for only

TABLE 2-7. *Projections of Total Dependency Ratios, European Union Members, 2010, 2030[a]*
Percent

Country	1990	2010	2030
Belgium	49.2	49.3	68.9
Denmark	47.9	51.3	67.0
Germany	45.3	50.0	75.1
Greece	49.6	51.7	66.3
Spain	49.3	46.9	64.8
France	51.1	51.2	67.9
Ireland	61.4	51.3	54.4
Italy	45.5	51.5	72.7
Luxembourg	44.8	48.7	73.1
Netherlands	44.5	47.5	73.2
Austria	48.2	51.3	71.3
Portugal	50.7	46.7	59.8
Finland	48.5	50.5	70.9
Sweden	55.3	58.5	70.4
United Kingdom	52.9	52.3	68.0
EU average	49.9	50.6	68.3
EU average youth dependency ratio	28.8	24.7	28.0

Source: Bos and others (1994).
a. Population aged 65 and older and 15 and younger as a percentage of population aged 15–64.

4 percent of retirement income, although their importance in the Netherlands, Ireland, and to a lesser extent the United Kingdom is also apparent. German book-reserve-based company plans provided 8 percent of retirement income. Finally, means-tested benefits to alleviate poverty were a key source of retirement income in Ireland (26 percent), albeit much less elsewhere in the European Union. The European Federation for Retirement Provision has attempted to update the table to 1994; its estimates suggest that 89 percent of pensions are still provided by pay-as-you-go, while 8 percent is provided by funded and book-reserve plans and 3 percent by means-tested benefits.[4] In other words, there has been little change in the overall pattern.

4. European Federation for Retirement Provision (1996).

TABLE 2-8. *Sources of Old Age Benefits in European Union Countries, 1988*
Percent

Type of plan	Belgium	Denmark	Germany	Greece	Spain	France	Ireland	Italy	Luxembourg	Netherlands	Portugal	United Kingdom	EU-12
Basic pay-as-you-go	93	84	88	90	98	75	55	95	98	63	91	71	83
Supplementary, compulsory pay-as-you-go	0	11	0	9	0	17	0	1	0	0	0	18	7
Supplementary, compulsory funded	0	1	0	0	0	0	0	0	0	20	0	0	1
Voluntary, funded	0	4	4	0	0	1	17	0	0	6	0	6	3
Voluntary, insured	4	0	0	0	0	0	2	0	0	4	0	0	0
Voluntary, book reserve	0	0	8	0	0	0	0	0	0	0	0	0	2
Voluntary, other	0	0	0	0	0	0	0	0	0	0	0	0	0
Means-tested	3	0	0	1	2	5	26	4	2	7	9	4	3
Total value as percentage of GDP	8.1	10.2	8.5	10.3	6.6	9.9	6.0	10.6	8.6	9.0	5.4	8.4	9.0

Source: Eurostat (1992).

TABLE 2-9. *Sources of Income for the Elderly, European Union Members, 1988*
Percent

Source	Denmark	Germany	Greece	Spain	France	Ireland	Luxembourg	Netherlands	Portugal	United Kingdom
Salary and wages	66	1	3	12	2	3	n.a.	5	45	6
Self-employment	8	7	12	14	4	6	n.a.	0	43	2
Insurance and other social transfers	5	37	0	34	21	52	n.a.	52	5	33
Pension	8	44	56	39	72	25	n.a.	35	8	59
Property and other sources	14	11	29	2	1	14	n.a.	8	0	0
Mean income per person as percentage of national mean	n.a.	102	37	122	94	n.a.	108	115	102	79

Source: Eurostat (1993b).
n.a. Not available.

A set of surveys has been assembled by Eurostat on the overall sources of income for retired persons (table 2-9), but the picture is not always clear. It seems unlikely, for example, that 66 percent of income of Danish retired persons comes from wages and salaries and only 13 percent from pensions and social transfers (it may be that some types of pension have been classified as wages). Nevertheless, some patterns can be discerned. One is the rather high level of property income in Greece, and to a lesser extent Denmark, Germany, and Ireland. Another is that in 1988 in Spain, Luxembourg, and the Netherlands, pensioners already had mean incomes well in excess of the national average. They were just above the national average in Germany and Portugal. In contrast, in France and the United Kingdom incomes of pensioners fell slightly short, while in Greece they were less than half average earnings. These observations underline the fact that age alone is no longer an accurate proxy for poverty in most countries.

Social Security Pension Systems

Social security systems in EU countries tend to offer a compulsory, defined-benefit, public old-age pension.[5] It is generally also pay-as-you-go, usually with wage taxes levied on employees each year sufficient to pay price- or wage-indexed obligations of the system to current pensioners. The backup for the benefit promise is thus the government's power to raise taxes. This backup facilitates the protection of the elderly from risk of longevity and risks arising from the performance of the economy. Two types of systems can be distinguished. *Universal basic systems*, sometimes financed by general taxes, usually offer flat-rate pensions and seek to provide a minimum standard of living for all pensioners. *Insurance-based* systems offer earnings-related pensions intended to provide a standard of living similar to that enjoyed during working life and are invariably financed by earnings-

5. In Sweden defined-contribution elements are being introduced to pay-as-you-go social security, whereby benefits are tailored to precisely match the contribution record of the person concerned. This is intended to minimize distortionary effects of pay-as-you-go financing on labor and financial markets. However, Holzmann (1997) suggests that such schemes may require reserves to be accumulated; that is, they cannot be run on a pay-as-you-go basis from year to year.

based contributions.[6] In practice, pension systems in many EU countries are often hybrids involving both basic and insurance-related elements (table 2-10).

Pension expenditures have grown much faster than GDP in Europe in recent decades. The average ratio of old-age pension expenditures to GDP for the EU-12 countries rose from less than 5 percent in 1960 to 8 percent in 1980 and 10 percent in 1993. A broader definition that includes survivors' and disability benefits now accounts for 14.7 percent compared with 12.2 percent in 1980. Until the first oil shock in 1973–74, in the context of rapid output growth, generous benefits promises and announcements of increases in coverage were often made.[7] If not reversed, these had an increasing impact, notably in insurance-based schemes. In effect, pension expenditures as a proportion of GDP tended to grow at rates well in excess of the elderly dependency ratio. Increases in the ratio to GDP were even more marked in the wake of the first oil shock, reflecting larger numbers of beneficiaries owing to the growing maturity of the plans, more frequent early retirement, slower economic growth, and higher unemployment.[8] Policy-induced increases in coverage were also important, however (including extension to self-employed and part-time workers, and the trend toward equal treatment for women).[9] Growth in pension expenditures was responsible for a quarter of the overall growth of public expenditures in 1960–93, although since 1980 they have grown at a pace similar to that of total spending. Because social security

6. The usual methods of calculating benefits are either the pensionable wage base times an accrual factor or average lifetime earnings revalued to allow for inflation.

7. In 1961–74, growth in the European Union averaged 4.5 percent; in 1975–95 it was only 2.3 percent. Over the same periods unemployment averaged 2.3 percent and 8.0 percent, respectively. World Bank (1994) suggests that a political economy rationale is the best explanation for the (ultimately unsustainable) form benefits have taken. Large benefits could be offered to few initial retirees who had contributed little while the costs were diffused and borne by many in the context of rapid population growth and a low dependency ratio. Distrust of capital markets in the light of historical experience also played a role in countries such as France.

8. In the context of high unemployment, the aim of enabling older workers to retire early was to release jobs for the young or facilitate structural adjustment in declining industries.

9. Elasticities of pension expenditures in relation to GDP from 1965 to 1985 were 1.3 (that is, a 1 percent rise in GDP entailed a 1.3 percent rise in pension expenditure). See Organization for Economic Cooperation and Development (1988).

TABLE 2-10. *Characteristics of Social Security Pension Systems in the European Union*
Percent

Country	Type of old-age system[1]	Form of indexation of benefits	Net social security replacement rate at 1× and 2× average earnings[2]	Social security replacement rate (1992) based on final salary of $20,000 and $50,000[3]	Social security contributions as percentage of GDP	Social security contributions as proportion of earnings (at a salary of $20,000 and $50,000)[4]	Employers' social security contribution rate (at a salary of $20,000 and $50,000)[4]
Belgium	Insurance	Prices	80–62	63–40	18.4	47–47	34–34
Germany	Insurance	Net wages	69–55	70–59	18.9	37–37	18–18
Denmark	Mixed	Wages	77–48	83–33	2.8	3–1[a]	1–1
Greece	Insurance	Wages	114–99	63–39	12.3	47–23	30–14
Spain	Insurance	Prices	98–97	90–60	14.3	38–27	32–22
France	Insurance[b]	Prices	83–73	67–45[c]	21.5	59–59	41–41
Ireland	Basic	Prices (discretionary)	62–35	47–19	5.6	20–14	12–8
Italy	Insurance	Prices	89–94	77–73	15.5	56–54	46–43
Luxembourg	Insurance	Wages	77–65	82–57	12.5	23–23	12–12
Netherlands	Basic	Net wages	67–37	66–26	18.6	32–26	25–16
Austria	Insurance	Net wages	n.a.	70–59	15.8	35–29	19–16
Portugal	Insurance	Prices (discretionary)	98–103	69–68	10.7	36–36	25–25
Finland	Mixed	Prices/net wages	n.a.	71–51	15.4	32–33	25–25
Sweden	Mixed	Prices	n.a.	69–49	14.3	30–30	30–30
United Kingdom	Mixed	Prices	59–39	50–26[d]	6.2	18–16[e]	10–10

Sources: 1. OECD (1988). 2. For married couple, Eurostat (1993a). 3. Wyatt Data Services (1993); for married man; tax treatment of benefits varies across countries. 4. Wyatt Data Services (1993).

a. Contributions to social security are included in state income tax. b. Complemented by mandatory occupational pensions. c. Includes ARRCO. d. Includes state earnings-related pension scheme (SERPS); for those contracted out, the ratios are 35 percent and 14 percent. e. Contributions are 5 percent lower for those contracted out of SERPS.

n.a. Not available.

pensions are usually unfunded, growth has been accompanied by increased revenues from taxes or contributions, with associated distortionary effects on labor markets, and in instances in which revenues are insufficient, by higher public deficits and indebtedness.[10]

Recent data on types of social security pensions in EU countries, indexation, the generosity of the benefits, and the total social security contribution rate are shown in table 2-10. One point to note is that Ireland and the Netherlands have basic pension systems (as defined earlier), and elements of the basic system are present in Denmark, Finland, Sweden, and the United Kingdom. Elsewhere, pensions are provided on the insurance principle. Indexation is based on gross or net wage growth in Austria, Germany, Denmark, Greece, Luxembourg, and the Netherlands. In Finland there is a mixed system of price and net wage indexation. Elsewhere price indexation prevails. This is important because the more generous wage indexation ensures that pensioners' living standards are maintained relative to wage earners (net wage indexation implies that pensioners' incomes will keep pace with workers' precisely; indexation to gross wages implies a wedge, depending on the change in the tax burden on workers). Price indexation implies that pensions will fall behind wages during periods of economic growth unless discretionary increases in excess of inflation are introduced from time to time. The other side of the coin is that wage indexation is costlier to contributors. Although contribution rates must rise in each case broadly in line with the dependency ratio when the population ages, with price indexation rates they may be at a lower level as long as real wages are rising.[11]

Replacement ratios (ratios of pensions to preretirement salaries) are indicated by data from Eurostat for 1993 to have been comparable for those for average incomes in most countries, with the outliers being exceptionally high ratios in Greece, Spain, and Portugal, and relatively low ratios in the United Kingdom and Ireland. Three groups of countries can be distinguished for the benefits they provide upper-middle-

10. Often the original idea was to have partial funding, but this was eroded with increased expenditures. See, for example, Franco and Frasca (1992) on Italy and Schlesinger (1985) on Germany.

11. When there is a switch from wage to price indexation that has not yet produced its full effect on replacement ratios, contribution rates may grow more slowly than the dependency ratio.

income earners (twice average earnings). Replacement ratios for this group are less than 50 percent in Denmark, Ireland, the Netherlands, and the United Kingdom; they are 50 to 75 percent in Belgium, Germany, France, and Luxembourg; and they exceed 90 percent in Greece, Spain, Italy, and Portugal. In considering these data it is important to note that since 1993 reforms have reduced such ratios in many countries.

Complementary estimates by the consultants based on benchmarks of absolute income are also shown in table 2-10. Obviously, the relationship of these benchmarks to average earnings varies among countries, but the overall patterns in the Eurostat data are borne out. Results for Austria, Finland, and Sweden, which were not included in the Eurostat sample, suggest that these countries belong to the same group as France and Germany in terms of benefit generosity. Finally, overall social security contribution rates (for employers and employees) are extremely high in most EU countries. Exceptions are Denmark (where pensions are financed by general taxation), the United Kingdom and Ireland. Total contribution rates of more than 35 percent are payable in Belgium, Germany, France, Italy, and Portugal. It is notable from table 2-10 that such contributions are usually regressive, being proportionately higher for lower-income workers.[12]

The overall burden of these provisions for public finances at present is indicated in table 2-11, which shows pensions as a proportion of GDP and of public expenditure in 1993. Notable features include the high ratio of old-age pension expenditures to GDP for Italy, Sweden, and Denmark, followed by France and the United Kingdom. Old-age pensions took more than 20 percent of government expenditure in 1993 in Austria, Italy, Luxembourg, and the United Kingdom. Similar patterns emerge for a broader definition including survivors' and disability pensions. These figures, however, need to be interpreted in the light of current demographic structures, which show that the United Kingdom and Sweden already have relatively elderly populations (see table 2-5) and long-established public pension schemes. Conversely, the rather low ratios to GDP in Ireland, Spain, and

---

12. This reflects the insurance principle; if benefit replacement ratios are to be higher for lower-income workers, contributions must be too. But such actuarial fairness is often overridden, distorting the labor market.

TABLE 2-11. *Social Security Pension Systems and Public Finance, European Union Members, 1993*
Percent

Country	Ratio of old-age pension expenditure to GDP	Ratio of old-age pension expenditure to government expenditure	Ratio of total pension spending to GDP[a]	Ratio of total pension spending to government expenditure[a]
Belgium	9.1	16.2	14.3	25.4
Germany	9.1	16.0	14.3	28.6
Denmark	11.0	17.7	13.8	22.0
Greece	8.6	18.3	11.8	25.9
Spain	7.1	16.2	11.2	22.7
France	10.7	19.3	14.4	25.9
Ireland	4.5	7.9	7.1	17.2
Italy	12.7	22.3	17.1	30.0
Luxembourg	9.4	21.5	17.1	39.1
Netherlands	10.2	18.1	19.1	33.9
Portugal	5.8	13.4	9.1	21.0
Austria	10.8	20.1	n.a.	n.a.
Finland	10.0	16.2	16.1	26.0
Sweden	12.3	16.9	n.a.	n.a.
United Kingdom	10.7	25.3	14.2	32.8
EU-12	10.0	19.0	14.7	28.0

Sources: Eurostat (1995b); and Franco and Munzi (1996).
a. Includes survivors' and disability pensions.
n.a. Not available.

Portugal are explicable, particularly for the last two, in terms of a relatively young population and immature public schemes.

The Growing Burden of Social Security Pensions

Social security pension systems pose broad problems to public finance and the wider economy, both now and in the future. First, changes in the structure of society, such as increased divorce rates and more single-parent families, are calling into question the assumptions underlying social security (that the nuclear family unit is the building block of society). Also, the incomes pensioners receive from social security, private pensions, and saving are relatively high and have increased significantly, particularly compared with those of families with children.[13] Thus, issues of intergenerational equity are raised (especially because the elderly typically pay no social security contributions, or much lower ones, and in some countries face smaller burdens of income tax than younger age groups). These problems are aggravated by increased individualism, which calls into question intergenerational solidarity more generally.

More crucially, current problems for social security in the European Union arise from factors such as poor economic performance that impinge on the labor market and interact with the distortions that social security induces. For example, growing rates of unemployment have characterized EU economies since the early 1970s (table 2-12). Besides the direct costs of benefits to the unemployed, which raise the costs of social security to the economy, high unemployment raises the contribution rate required to pay for pensions for the part of the labor force still working. In several EU countries, however, overall participation rates have increased to offset the effects of rising unemployment on overall employment, notably as married women entered the labor force. This is partly a corollary of lower fertility but also results from improved education and more available child care. The extent to which such an adjustment in labor force participation can continue is, however, open to doubt.

In this context, there are marked differences in participation rates for adults of prime working age, largely reflecting different rates of women. Participation rates are more than 60 percent in Denmark and the United Kingdom (Sweden and Finland are also considered to belong in this group) and 55 to 60 percent in France, Germany, the Netherlands, and Portugal (table 2-13). But they are below 50 percent in Spain, Italy, and Greece. Depending on unemployment rates, these figures show a marked difference among the countries in the proportion of the population of working age that is paying contributions to finance current pensioners on a pay-as-you-go basis.

13. For example, in the United Kingdom in 1979, 31 percent of the poorest 10 percent of the population were pensioners, while in 1991 just 11 percent were. The mean income of pensioners from all sources rose 52 percent in real terms from 1979 to 1993, while real average earnings grew by 38 percent (Davis (1997).

TABLE 2-12. *Unemployment Rates, European Union Members, Selected Years, 1970–95*
Percent

Country	1970	1980	1990	1995	Labor force participation rate (1993)
Belgium	1.8	7.4	6.7	10.2	50
Denmark	0.6	5.2	7.7	6.9	67
Germany	0.5	2.7	4.8	8.3	58
Greece	4.2	2.7	6 4	8.9	49
Spain	2.6	11.6	16.2	22.5	48
France	2.4	6.2	9.0	11.5	56
Ireland	6.3	8.0	13.4	14.9	53
Italy	5.1	7.1	9.1	11.7	48
Luxembourg	0.0	2.4	1.7	3.8	53
Netherlands	1.0	6.4	6.2	6.7	58
Austria	1.6	1.9	3.2	4.5	n.a.
Portugal	2.6	7.6	4.6	7.2	59
Finland	1.9	5.2	3.4	17.2	n.a.
Sweden	1.5	2.2	1.8	9.1	n.a.
United Kingdom	2.2	5.6	7.0	8.5	62
EU-15	2.3	5.8	7.8	10.7	55[a]

Source: Eurostat (1995a).
n.a. Not available.
a. EU-12.

High contributions combined with high unemployment draw attention to adverse side effects of social security contributions on labor markets and international competitiveness.[14] Clearly, employers' and employees' social security contributions increase the gap between labor costs, which determine labor demand decisions, and net wages, which influence labor supply decisions. This may have various deleterious effects. High nonwage labor costs arising from increased pension contributions, if they affect total labor costs (as is likely in a competitive market), harm the competitiveness of EU economies vis-à-vis countries with a younger population or less generous social

14. Concerns about nonwage labor costs are apparent in countries such as Germany where they are believed to encourage firms to shift production to countries with lower social costs.

TABLE 2-13. *Labor Force Participation Rates and Actual Retirement Age, European Union Members, 1990*
Percent

| Country | Age | | | | | Retirement age | |
	50–54	55–59	60–64	65–69	70 and older	Actual	Statutory
Belgium	53.5	32.5	11.2	2.2	0.5	59.3	65/60
Denmark	85.6	74.4	39.3	17.4	3.0	62.7	67
France	74.5	50.4	14.3	3.8	1.0	59.6	60
Germany	75.7	61.4	22.7	5.6	1.8	61.0	65
Greece	62.0	49.7	32.7	15.1	4.2	63.0	65/60
Ireland	59.3	51.2	34.0	15.3	6.2	63.7	66
Italy	59.5	42.8	21.8	7.9	2.5	61.2	65
Luxembourg	58.7	40.4	16.2	3.5	0.0	60.0	65
Netherlands	61.4	44.8	15.0	5.5	2.7	60.4	65
Portugal	66.8	55.9	38.2	22.3	7.6	63.9	65/62
Spain	57.9	49.0	30.3	5.4	1.0	62.3	65
United Kingdom	78.7	68.0	38.0	10.8	3.0	62.5	65/60
EU-12	69.1	53.4	25.1	7.6	2.2	61.3	65
EU-12 (1993)	71.4	52.3	23.3	6.8	2.1	n.a.	n.a.

Sources: Eurostat (1995a); and Besseling and Zeeuw (1993).
n.a. Not available.

security or both and reduce labor demand, giving an incentive to substitute capital for labor.[15] Industries are moving to countries that require lower contributions, accentuating the existing trend. The implicit rate of return on workers' contributions is falling, thus increasing the disincentive effects of social security on labor supply that arise if schemes are perceived not to be actuarially fair.[16] By reducing hours of work these effects further compound the fiscal difficulties.

A further problem is that early retirement policies promising generous payoffs to employees leaving the labor force are available in various EU countries, notably Belgium, France, Italy, Germany, and the Netherlands.[17] Motivations for such schemes are to enable the long-term unemployed to retire, facilitate adjustment in declining industries, and alleviate youth unemployment. Often the offers are so generous that there are few financial incentives to work beyond the age of 60. This in turn encourages the use of early retirement programs in firms wishing to shed labor during restructuring, who in effect pass the burden on to the economy as a whole. Note that the "backloading" feature of final-salary, defined-benefit privately funded pensions also provides strong motivation to shed older workers, since the cost of their pension accruals increases with age.[18]

The impact of such early retirement provisions is apparent. Less than 20 percent of those older than 60 remain in the labor force (that is, are either employed or unemployed but seeking work) in the Netherlands, France, Belgium, and Luxembourg, and less than 25 percent in Germany and Italy (table 2-13). In contrast, participation rates for those

15. Indeed, there is evidence that the level of wage and nonwage costs together do have a direct link to the level of unemployment; see Balassa (1984). Such effects may be aggravated if dismissal of workers is difficult, as in Germany; Schlesinger (1985).

16. Keyfitz (1985) shows that with current rates of fertility, rates of return to pay-as-you-go plans for the generation born in 2000–05 in the United States will be negative; similar effects are likely in the European Union. Note that in a steady state with a constant demographic structure, the rate of return to pay-as-you-go equals the rate of growth of real wages plus population growth. But it will fall sharply as the age structure changes.

17. Reforms of these policies are currently under way in a number of countries, but it is not yet clear that the reforms have had a major impact on average retirement ages. Moreover, there are social pressures for extension of early retirement, as shown by the success of French lorry drivers in gaining a reduction in their retirement age from 60 to 55 following a strike in November 1996.

18. Davis (1995).

aged 60 to 65 are greater than 30 percent in the United Kingdom, Greece, Ireland, Portugal, and Denmark where early retirement options are absent or less generous. There is also a growing difference between actual and statutory retirement ages. Labor force participation rates in all age groups older than 55 fell between 1990 and 1993 in the European Union as a whole, implying a further decline in actual retirement rates. The decrease in participation rates of older workers is longstanding. In the European Union as a whole, the actual average retirement age has fallen from 64.3 in 1950 to 61.3 in 1990, while life expectancy at retirement age has risen sharply (an indicator of the latter is that life expectancy at birth has risen from 67 to 74).[19]

The maturation of the social security pension systems is posing increasing difficulties, especially where reform has been absent or marginal.[20] Benefits per beneficiary will tend to rise in real terms where they are linked to wages.[21] This is so to some extent even when pension increases are indexed to prices, since the base pension is usually still related to career earnings. Where the average retiree has not yet made a lifetime of contributions to the scheme, and where the ratio of workers to pensioners has not reached the average for the population as a whole, so-called maturation in terms of benefit levels and beneficiary ratios will itself increase the obligations of the systems and the benefits to GDP ratio. The consequences over time of past expansions of eligibility and increases in coverage will compound this problem.

However, the age structure of the population is the primary determinant of likely future strains on EU social security pension systems (as well as impinging on other government expenditures such as those on health care). Populations in EU countries are already aging, and as noted this has had an impact on social security expenditures.[22] But future developments are likely to be yet more dramatic.

19. Besseling and Zeeuw (1993).
20. In several countries reform is inducing a reversed form of maturation, with falling transfers and eligibility ratios.
21. This of course assumes positive real wage growth, which has not been the case recently in some east European countries.
22. The trends toward a growing proportion of elderly are common to all OECD countries, including the United States and Japan, and are beginning to arise in newly industrializing countries, including China.

Indicators of Future Difficulties

In seeking quantitative indicators of future burdens on social security pensions, one may distinguish between projections of future profiles of expenditures and contributions on the one hand and summary measures of future liabilities such as the net present value of accrued and projected benefits on the other. While the former is less easy to summarize, the latter may hide important features of future benefit and contribution patterns. Nevertheless, their message is clear: in a large number of EU countries, pension reform is needed.

A detailed survey of the projections of pension costs made by national authorities or experts has been carried out by Franco and Munzi.[23] In each case, they have sought long-term projections for social security pension costs that are consistent with the most recent reforms. They highlight as a benchmark the most optimistic projections so as to provide a best-case scenario in each country. But they also note the projections with the least favorable assumptions and comment that expenditure projections are usually revised upward. The difference between best and worst cases may be substantial. In 1995–2000, 2000–2010, and 2010–2030, EU average expenditure-to-GDP ratios rise by 0.1 percent, 0.5 percent, and 2.0 percent, respectively, under the most favorable assumptions and 0.4 percent, 1.2 percent, and 2.3 percent, respectively, under the most unfavorable. The results for the most favorable assumptions are summarized in table 2-14. For some countries the indicator highlighted in the national projections is the ratio of expenditures to GDP and for others it is the equilibrium contribution rate needed to maintain a pay-as-you-go system.

The table shows that even under the most optimistic assumptions, increases in the ratio of pension expenditures to GDP are forecast up to 2030 for Belgium, Denmark, and Finland. Spain and Italy are expected to have broadly flat ratios after their most recent reforms, but the projection for Italy excludes civil servants, whose pensions accounted for a further 3.5 percent of GDP in 1995. Meanwhile, increases of 10 percentage points or more in contributions as a proportion of earnings are forecast in Germany and Ireland, and more than 20 percent in France. Portugal and Luxembourg anticipate smaller increases,

---

23. Franco and Munzi (1996).

TABLE 2-14. *Projections of Pension Costs, European Union Members, Selected Years, 1995–2040*

Percent

Country	1995	2000	2010	2020	2030	2040
			Pension expenditure to GDP			
Belgium	10.5	11.6	12.3	14.0	15.7	15.7
Denmark	9.3	9.2	10.9	11.6	12.7	n.a.
Spain	9.1	9.2	9.2	9.3	9.5	n.a.
Italy	8.2	7.8	7.6	7.8	8.3	n.a.
Finland	14.5	13.9	15.2	17.2	17.7	n.a.
			Contribution rate			
Germany	18.6	19.7	21.5	23.1	27	n.a.
France	18.9	20.9	n.a.	28	n.a.	40.8
Ireland	13.6	13.3	13.7	17.1	23.5	n.a.
Luxembourg	22.3	23.9	25.8	n.a.	n.a.	n.a.
Netherlands	11.0	11.0	11.0	12.0	13.0	n.a.
Portugal	25.8	26.9	28.1	31.4	n.a.	n.a.
Sweden	17.0	16.3	16.7	17.5	17.5	n.a.
United Kingdom	n.a.	17.7	17.4	16.8	17.2	n.a.

Source: Franco and Munzi (1996). The principal estimates show the most favorable official scenarios in each case, based on the most recent reforms of the social security pension systems; the authors note that there are significant differences with the least favorable projections, and that expenditure projections are usually revised upward. The pension systems covered in the table are as follows: for Belgium, the Social Security System; for Denmark, the Public Welfare System; for Spain, the Social Security System; for Italy, Private Employees, Self-Employed Artisans and Businessmen; for Finland, the Statutory Pension Scheme; for Germany, the Statutory Pension Insurance Scheme; for France, all basic and supplementary pensions; for Ireland, Social Insurance and Social Assistance Pensions; for Luxembourg, the Private Sector Employees and Self-Employed Scheme; for the Netherlands, the Basic Pension Scheme; for Portugal, the Social Security System; for Sweden, the National Pension System; for the United Kingdom, National Insurance Pensions (including SERPS).

n.a. Not available.

while the Netherlands, Sweden, and the United Kingdom anticipate virtually no increase.

D. Roseveare and colleagues have estimated future pension expenditures for EU countries by constructing detailed simulation models for each country based on known features of the pension plans (retirement age, indexation provisions, and so forth) as well as using demographic projections (see tables 2-5 to 2-7).[24] Estimates cover a broad range of welfare benefits and complementary pension plans as well as basic social security pensions. The projection horizon is 2070. The calculations assume a discount rate of 5 percent and productivity

24. Roseveare and others (1996).

TABLE 2-15. *Projections of Pension Costs, European Union Members, Selected Years, 1995–2040*
Ratio of pension expenditure to GDP

Country	1995	2000	2010	2020	2030	2040
Belgium	10.4	9.7	8.7	10.7	13.9	15.0
Denmark	6.8	6.4	7.6	9.3	10.9	11.6
Spain	10.0	9.8	10.0	11.3	14.1	16.8
Italy	13.3	12.6	13.2	15.3	20.3	21.4
Finland	10.1	9.5	10.7	15.2	17.8	18.0
Germany	11.1	11.5	11.8	12.3	16.5	18.4
France	10.6	9.8	9.7	11.6	13.5	14.3
Ireland	3.6	2.9	2.6	2.7	2.8	2.9
Netherlands	6.0	5.7	6.1	8.4	11.2	12.1
Portugal	7.1	6.9	8.1	9.6	13.0	15.2
Sweden	11.8	11.1	12.4	13.9	15.0	14.9
United Kingdom	4.5	4.5	5.2	5.1	5.5	5.0

Source: Roseveare and others (1996).

growth of 1.5 percent. Naturally, such estimates omit some of the more detailed aspects of national economies and institutional features of social security schemes, but they do have the advantage of a uniform methodology and assumptions.

The estimates suggest that pension expenditures will rise by 7 percent or more of GDP from 1990 to 2040 in Italy, Germany, Finland, and Portugal (table 2-15). With unchanged policies, peak ratios in 2040 would be more than 15 percent of GDP in Belgium, Italy, Germany, Spain, Finland, and Portugal. They would be 5 percent or less in the United Kingdom and Ireland.[25] Assuming unchanged policies on benefits and maintenance of pay-as-you-go financing, contributions would have to increase sharply. With unchanged contribution rates, social security pension contributions would fall far short in most EU countries, implying sizable public sector deficits.[26]

Using the same methods, D. Roseveare and collegues also estimated

25. Details of the United Kingdom reforms that have led to this situation are provided in the appendix to this chapter.
26. Not adjusting contributions would of course be contrary to the principle of pay-as-you-go, according to which contribution rates should be amended regularly to equalize expenditures and revenues.

TABLE 2-16. *Value of Public Pension Liabilities as a Percentage of 1994 GDP,*
European Union Members, 1996

Country	Pension payments	Contributions	Balance
United Kingdom	142	118	−24
Germany	348	286	−62
France	318	216	−102
Italy	401	341	−60
Belgium	300	147	−153
Denmark	234	n.a.	n.a.
Spain	323	214	−109
Finland	384	294	−65
Ireland	107	88	−19
Netherlands	214	161	−53
Portugal	277	168	−109
Sweden	369	219	−132

Source: Roseveare and others (1996). French estimates exclude "fictive contributions," German estimates exclude statutory transfers from the federal government. Finnish estimates exclude assets of 25 percent of GDP. Swedish estimates exclude assets of 30 percent of GDP.
  n.a. Not available.

the current and future discounted liabilities of social security pension systems for most EU countries. These indicate the capitalized value of identified flows up to 2070. Estimates of gross liabilities range from 142 to 401 percent of 1994 GDP, at least three times conventional government debt (table 2-16). In the gross calculation the OECD allows no offset for future contributions in calculating net liabilities, and because (apart from Finland and Sweden) these EU countries do not partially fund social security, there are no financial or real assets to offset gross liabilities, either. Table 2-16 also shows projected contributions and thus net liabilities, assuming current contribution rates are maintained. In general, future contributions are well below present and future obligations, to an extent varying from 19 percent to 153 percent of 1994 GDP. There are net liabilities greater than 100 percent of GDP in France, Belgium, Spain, Portugal, and Sweden. But because the net liabilities are the difference between two large and offsetting numbers, the calculations are sensitive to the choice of discount rate.

Table 2-17 shows the level of pension liabilities for France, Germany, Italy, and the United Kingdom with alternative policy adjustments:

TABLE 2-17. *Effects of Policy Adjustments in OECD Calculations*
Net liabilities as percentage of 1994 GDP

Country	Contribution rates 3 percentage points higher	Replacement rate 10 percentage points lower	Retirement age five years later
United Kingdom	12	32	18
Germany	− 14	9	32
France	− 25	− 12	27
Italy	− 98	− 85	− 46

Source: Organization for Economic Cooperation and Development (1995).

contributions 3 percentage points higher, a replacement ratio 10 percentage points lower, and retirement five years later. For each country except the United Kingdom, the retirement age adjustment has the largest effect. Meanwhile, in the baseline, even on favorable assumptions, projected ratios of public debt to GDP for Germany, France, and Italy on unchanged benefit policies and fixed contribution rates would be more than 100 percent in 2030.[27]

Alternative calculations of gross unfunded liabilities for EU countries have been prepared by J. B. Kuné and collegues of the Dutch public pension fund ABP. The calculations differ from those of the OECD in that the discount rate is assumed to be 4 percent throughout, and no projections for inflation indexation are made. Projected benefits are assumed to remain at current levels, with the difference between the actual interest rate and 4 percent assumed to be available for indexation. The profile of the dependency ratio also differs, because retirement is assumed to be age 65 in all cases, rather than varying between countries. Illustrating the sensitivity of the outturns to the assumptions, the results suggest that gross liabilities for the United Kingdom, Germany, Italy, and France are lower than the OECD predicts (table 2-18). Meanwhile, other EU countries have estimated gross liabilities (including projected as well as accrued benefits) ranging from 117 percent for Denmark to 144 percent for the Netherlands and 219 percent for Luxembourg. Corresponding figures of accrued benefits only are 87 percent, 103 percent, and 156 percent, respectively. Unfortunately, no attempt is made to assess the present value of future con-

27. The OECD simulation includes a decline in Italy's debt ratio to less than 100 percent in the early twenty-first century, after which it rises again.

TABLE 2-18. *Present Value of Gross Unfunded Pension Liabilities as a Percentage of 1990 GDP (ABP Estimates)*
Percent

Country	Accrued rights	Total liabilities
Belgium	75	101
Denmark	87	117
France	83	112
Germany (west)	138	186
Greece	185	245
Ireland	55	78
Italy	157	207
Luxembourg	156	219
Netherlands	103	144
Portugal	93	128
Spain	93	129
United Kingdom	68	92
EU-12	109	147

Sources: Kuné, Petit, and Pinxt (1993); and Hoffman (1993).

tributions, which limits the usefulness of the calculation because net liabilities cannot be calculated.

Further calculations have been prepared by the International Monetary Fund and presented in the *World Economic Outlook* for May 1996. The real interest rate is assumed to be 3.5 percent and productivity growth 1.5 percent. The projection horizon is 2050, and again the demographic projections are those of Bos. The results differ from those of the OECD in that the situation of Sweden is better (table 2-19). The United Kingdom is always in the best position. The IMF also calculates the contribution gap, the difference between the sustainable and actual rate of contributions as a proportion of GDP. In each case the difficulties of the systems in Germany, France, and Italy are greater than those of Sweden and the United Kingdom.

In examining simulations that provide estimates of the discounted present value of future liabilities less future contributions, it is important to be clear what is being shown. D. Franco, for example, argues that it is not legitimate to assimilate the unfunded liabilities to government debt. The calculations, he contends, are subject to great uncertainty; and they have no direct effect on financial markets (for example,

TABLE 2-19. *Present Value of Net Pension Liability, 1995–2050*
Percentage of 1994 GDP

Country	Net pension liability	Contribution gap
United Kingdom	5	0.1
Germany	111	3.4
France	114	3.3
Italy	76	2.5
Sweden	20	0.9

Source: International Monetary Fund (1996). The contribution gap is the difference between the contribution rate needed to reduce the net asset position to zero and the current contribution rate.

the 1992 Italian reform wiped out implicit debt equal to the national debt, but had little effect on markets). In addition, implicit liabilities can be reduced by reforms without default, the effect on consumption and saving differs from conventional debt, a combined figure would give a false reading of the effects of interest payments on total debt (because implicit liabilities fall as interest rates rise), and the calculations would blur international comparisons.[28] Rather, the estimates should be seen as a summary measure of the scale of adjustment that is required of individual countries to ensure that their schemes remain solvent.

Thus the various studies and measures come up with different numerical results as a consequence of differing assumptions, model specifications, and so forth. But all calculations show that EU countries with generous social security pension systems will encounter difficulties. On balance, the budgetary costs of social security pension provisions seem likely to be particularly acute in Belgium, Spain, Greece, France, Italy, Finland, Germany, Luxembourg, Austria, and Portugal. The United Kingdom, Ireland, Denmark, and the Netherlands are in a relatively favorable situation. Sweden is in an intermediate position.

Aging will also probably increase demand for health care and other social services, imposing a further burden on public finances. Oxley and MacFarlan, for example, note that average health spending on people older than age 65 is typically four times that on those younger than 65.[29] Viewed in light of the data shown in table 2-5, it is evident that where health care is publicly provided aging will have a major

28. Franco (1995).
29. Oxley and MacFarlan (1994).

effect on budgets and reform may consequently be warranted in the amount of care provided by governments. Indeed, OECD calculations suggest that health care expenditures in Germany, France, Italy, and the United Kingdom could rise by 1.4 percent, 1.6 percent, 1.7 percent, and 1.2 percent, respectively, as a proportion of GDP from 2000 to 2030.[30]

These budget burdens will be compounded or alleviated by other aspects of public finances, notably the initial state in which these countries enter the period when population aging begins to take its effect. A country with a large deficit and high existing debt would clearly run a much greater risk of a financing crisis than one with a more favorable fiscal position. For example, the OECD has shown that a 1 percent better primary balance from 2000 on would give a reduction in net debt positions of 40 to 55 percent of GDP by 2030.[31] This underlines the importance of early steps to fiscal consolidation, preferably by reducing government outlays. Consolidation also buys time, allowing pension reform to be introduced gradually or with some delay (to allow people to adjust their plans appropriately) and defers the time when adverse debt dynamics emerge. The current fiscal positions of EU countries illustrate particular difficulties for countries with high indebtedness and deficits.[32]

A further note of caution in relation to the estimates that have been presented is that the studies typically do not endogenize the response of the labor force or of private saving to the public pension arrangements and to aging itself, which may affect the results. This brings in a broader issue: the extent to which these burdens will impinge depends also on broader macroeconomic factors that may themselves be influenced by population aging, such as the rate of capital formation, economic growth and associated increases in productivity, labor force participation and, of particular importance, the resolution of structural unemployment.[33] Detailed assessment of this subject is beyond the

30. Leibfritz and others (1996).

31. Organization for Economic Cooperation and Development (1995).

32. For a summary, see European Monetary Institute (1996).

33. Note that an increase in the productivity of the young will have a more rapid effect on the burden of aging if pensions are wage indexed than if they are price indexed and new pensions are related to wage levels. See Auerbach and others (1989); and OECD (1995).

scope of this discussion. However, given the likely effect of these factors on the outcomes for retirement income provision, it is relevant to note some recent estimates of effects of aging on labor markets and saving, with particular emphasis on the European Union.

As regards effects of aging on labor markets, it is often suggested that economic performance may deteriorate as the average age of the labor force increases, owing, among other things, to the inflexibility of older workers with reduced labor mobility and reduced ability to adapt to new techniques. Johnson and Zimmerman have provided a range of papers that address this issue in the context of the European Union.[34] In particular, the authors in their volume consider whether aging may affect economic efficiency via labor costs and productivity, training, skills, and labor mobility. Given the behavior of existing age groups, it is suggested that the aging of the EU labor force will not have much effect on labor market outcomes. Aging is expected to reduce average labor mobility only slightly, and the extent to which such labor force characteristics as productivity, innovation, and career progression vary with the age of workers suggests that aging will have little impact on overall outcomes. The principal note of caution seems to be that if seniority-age profiles are not flexible and older workers are paid higher than their marginal product, as the proportion of these workers increases, firms will be encouraged to push them into early retirement, depending on how much of the pension costs the state bears—as is indeed already happening.

Of course, these results should not be taken to mean that the performance of EU labor markets is in any way optimal. Indeed, the conclusion may be that younger workers are just as inflexible as old. Labor market reform and deregulation would be needed to change this picture. Equally, one should not disregard the possibility that the decrease in the labor supply accompanying aging may affect production and output (which puts an emphasis on increasing participation and raising the effective retirement age). But the results are of interest in suggesting that "the economics literature has been correct to focus on the impact of aging on pension systems and private saving."[35]

Conclusions regarding the likely path for saving as aging proceeds

34. Johnson and Zimmerman (1993).
35. Ermisch (1995).

vary sharply. Roseveare and her colleagues have assessed two scenarios that differ in the size of the assumed negative effect of the dependency ratio on saving and on whether there is Ricardian equivalence.[36] They predict that private saving as a proportion of GDP across all industrial countries will fall 3 to 6 percentage points between 2000 and 2030, depending on the assumptions, and national saving will decline by 8 to 16 percentage points, given unchanged pension policies and assuming a partial response of private saving to government dissaving. In France, Austria, Denmark, and Finland, net national saving is forecast to be negative in 2030 under both sets of assumptions.[37]

Masson and Tryon used the IMFs global econometric model MULTI-MOD to assess the combined effect of aging on private saving, public deficits, and overall production (where production is assumed to link to the labor supply, that is, the size of population of working age times the participation ratio).[38] Their model generated large decreases in national saving in Germany and Japan from 2000 onward, as both private and public sectors reduce their saving, while in France, Italy, and the United Kingdom increased private saving more than compensates for an increase in the fiscal deficit. The difference in private saving links to the differences in demographic profiles. (Note that the model includes endogenous tax rises rather than assuming fixed contribution rates as do the pension simulations in tables 2-14 to 2-19).

A strong effect of demographics on private saving has been found by many studies. Masson and colleagues found the total dependency ratio (table 2-7) to have a significant negative effect on private saving in both advanced and developing countries.[39] Focusing on Europe, Miles and Patel suggest that as long as the baby boom generation remains in the labor force an increase in private saving should be expected in the European Union, building to a maximum of 2.5 percent in 2020, after which saving declines as people retire.[40] The increase in private saving would be more than enough to offset changes in

36. Roseveare and others (1996).
37. Cutler and others (1990) and Heller and Sidgwick (1987) reach similar conclusions.
38. Masson and Tryon (1990).
39. Masson, Bayoumi, and Samiei (1995).
40. Miles and Patel (1996).

government saving.[41] This projection is based on a life-cycle view of saving, whereby assets are accumulated over a working life and used during retirement.[42]

Taking into account different saving propensities of cohorts and population growth, Börsch-Supan comes to a conclusion similar to that of Miles and Patel regarding the profile of private saving for major OECD countries.[43] However, he concludes that increases in governments' demand for funds arising from population aging will outstrip the increase in private saving after 2005.

The effects of aging on balance of payments depend heavily on the conclusions drawn from studies of saving. They may be beneficial as long as national saving is boosted by aging, which seems possible as long as the baby boom generation remains at work.[44] But once people retire and begin to dissave, there could be potential problems as countries with low saving seek to expand their capital stock to compensate for a higher dependency ratio.[45]

It is important to emphasize that the form of a pension arrangement may itself play a crucial role in determining savings' response to population aging, and this factor is difficult to incorporate in the form of simulation set out earlier. In particular, Feldstein presents some evidence for the United States and in international cross-section that unfunded social security pensions reduce aggregate saving and hence

41. The main focus in this section is on implications of aging for saving and labor markets. However, the aging of the population may also have an important effect on financial markets, especially where pensions are largely funded. Although during the transition phase, as the working population ages, there may be excess demand for financial assets as retirement assets are built up, the opposite may be the case when people begin to live on their accumulated assets. This could plausibly entail a situation of excess supply that could depress asset returns significantly compared with those in the earlier period. This of course depends on the extent to which other countries (for example, in the Far East) experience slower demographic aging and thus provide a countervailing factor in the context of globalized financial markets.

42. In a separate paper Miles (1996) notes that cross-sectional evidence of individual households appears to be inconsistent with the life cycle because saving is rarely negative after retirement. But he considers that this is largely a problem of measurement error because the decline in the value of pension assets is rarely allowed for in cross-section data. Thus the predictions based on the life cycle—falls in aggregate saving as the population ages—remain robust.

43. Börsch-Supan (1996).

44. Bikker (1996).

45. Auerbach and others (1989).

capital accumulation and growth.[46] This can be justified theoretically by a life-cycle framework in which people structure their lifetime saving and asset accumulation to maintain steady-state consumption. If social security provides a guarantee of income to maintain consumption after retirement, there is a form of implicit wealth accumulation and the need to save during the working life is lessened.[47] Underlying this approach is a view that workers consider contributions by themselves as a form of saving and not a tax. As the population ages and the size of unfunded liabilities increases, the negative effect on saving could increase sharply (unless it is offset by increasing uncertainty over whether pension promises will be kept).

Feldstein's results have been disputed.[48] And other evidence suggests that the effect, even if negative, may be small, for example because social security induces early retirement, which gives incentives to save more to cover the longer retirement period, or because changes in intrafamily transfers (such as bequests) may offset the increase in public sector transfers, thus leaving the need for old-age saving the same.[49] What is less disputed than Feldstein's results is that if a social security system is structured to provide benefits to a generation in excess of its contributions, there will clearly be a reduction in saving because of the wealth transfer. The more or less free pensions provided to noncontributing first generations in social security systems are examples of this, as long as the public sector did not run an offsetting surplus. This may account for clearer results on the negative effect of social security on saving for certain other countries with generous social security pensions, such as Sweden, Italy, and Japan, than Feldstein obtained for the United States.[50] Moreover, the conditions under which funding will have a positive effect on saving—myopia, limited access to credit, and lack of credibility of the pension scheme—are precisely those whose absence will lead pay-as-you-go plans to reduce

46. Feldstein (1974, 1977, 1995a).

47. A further mechanism inducing lower saving under pay-as-you-go social security is that those who are myopic and would otherwise have continued working until they died are now able to retire.

48. For a review, see Munnell (1987).

49. Barro (1974).

50. Hagemann and Nicoletti (1989).

saving.[51] So switching from pay-as-you-go to funding is likely to increase saving in an economic sense.[52]

Finally, technical progress could help maintain living standards regardless of the effects of aging on saving and investment, depending on the effects of aging on innovation. Wattenburg suggests that aging slows technical progress as innovation becomes less profitable because of a shrinking market for capital goods and the lesser dynamism of an aging population. In contrast, Cutler and colleagues suggest that innovation increases as labor gets scarce.[53]

Reforms of Social Security

The message of the previous section is clear: if policies remain unchanged, social security pension systems will give rise to increasing intergenerational redistribution (not merely transfers), with workers and their employers paying higher contributions for the same pension.[54] Various economic difficulties may arise as a consequence, not least a marked aggravation of the disincentive effects on labor demand and supply. Taking the strain by way of increased public deficits instead of taxation will only postpone the problem until the bonds need to be repaid. In effect the burden is transferred to future generations.[55] In the meantime, real interest rates could increase, together with adverse debt dynamics and the risk of a snowball effect of rising debts and interest payments. Ultimately, governments could face a financing crisis as markets lose confidence in their ability to repay their debts.

EU governments are already seeking to limit social security pension commitments directly. The main policy options within the pay-as-you-go framework are changes in the ratio of beneficiaries to contributors

51 World Bank (1994).

52. In national accounts the capital market returns on funds are counted as savings of households; this must therefore have a positive effect on savings.

53. Wattenburg (1987); and Cutler and others (1990).

54. These problems could be conceptualized as cohort risk in which the advantage goes to members of large cohorts as long as systems remain unchanged. See Frijns and Petersen (1992).

55. A rational private sector, as described by Barro (1974), that perfectly anticipates the future taxes to pay off bonds and immediately adjusts expenditure accordingly would not even differentiate the two cases.

by increasing retirement age, decreasing benefit levels, and increasing revenue.[56] A switch to funding social security and encouraging private pensions are further options that may have a more favorable effect on labor markets and allocation. All of these policies would have far-reaching effects on individuals and thus have often been introduced gradually. In effect, they are an indication of the political risk to which intergenerational contracts such as social security pensions are subject. A summary of the types of recent reforms is shown in table 2-20. Details of programs in the United Kingdom that have gone furthest in reducing social security obligations are provided in the appendix to this chapter.[57]

Cuts in the number of beneficiaries can be achieved by increasing the retirement age. Longer life expectancy gives ample scope for this. Steps in this direction have been taken in a number of EU countries, such as in Italy, which in 1992 raised the statutory retirement age for private sector employees from 60 for men and 55 for women to 65 and 60, respectively, by 2001 (in 1995 a further reform introduced a flexible retirement age range of 57 to 65 with an actuarially discounted pension over a long period). Germany, Greece, Portugal, and the United Kingdom have also raised statutory retirement ages. A higher retirement age has a double benefit of increasing contributions—and possibly GDP itself—and reducing both the number of beneficiaries and the length of time during which they receive pensions.[58] It is particularly necessary in light of the increase in life expectancy since the plans were set up.

But changing the statutory retirement age may not be sufficient. An attack on early retirement provisions is an essential complement to increase actual retirement ages. Ideally this should eliminate any excessive generosity, for example by ensuring a strict relationship of pension to service (Germany, Greece, and Italy) and defined-contribution social security (as planned in Sweden). Such reforms should also reduce the ability of firms to shift the burdens of their

---

56. Related policies could include permitting immigration, promoting fertility, and increasing labor force participation for younger age groups.

57. See also Davis (1997).

58. The possibility of work after retirement should not be disregarded. In Japan this is encouraged by allowing pensions to continue to accrue even after the statutory retirement age.

TABLE 2-20. *Pension Reforms in the European Union, 1984–95*

Country	Change to benefit indexation rules	Increase in retirement age	Cut in replacement ratio	Increased contribution period	Less incentive to early retirement	Fewer credits for higher education	Public employee privileges reduced	Lower eligibility for disabled pension
Belgium (1993)								
Germany (1989)	•	•		•	•	•		
Denmark								
Greece (1990, 1992)	•	•	•	•	•		•	•
Spain (1984, 1985)			•	•				•
France (1993)	•	•	•		•		•	
Italy (1992, 1995)	•		•		•		•	
Netherlands	•		•					•
Austria (1985, 1988, 1993)	•		•			•		
Portugal (1993)		•	•				•	
Finland	•							
Sweden (1994)	•							
United Kingdom (1986, 1995)	•	•	•				•	•

Source: Franco and Munzi (1996).

downsizing to the state. A higher minimum retirement age may also be needed (as planned in Germany and the Netherlands), better retraining for old workers so they are productive longer, and reconsideration of hiring, firing, and automatic age-related pay practices. In the case of private pensions, governments could also promote greater labor participation among those age 60 to 65 by granting tax allowances only to defined-benefit plans covering lifetime earnings rather than to final salaries. This is currently proposed in the Netherlands.

Provisions allowing workers to leave the earnings-related social security plan were extended in the mid-1980s in the United Kingdom. They could thenceforth choose to join a personal pension plan, not just an occupational one (see the appendix). But experience suggests that beyond a certain point the fiscal incentives required to induce a large-scale voluntary switching away from social security may need to be so costly as to outweigh any savings (this seems to have been the case for incentives to take personal pensions in the United Kingdom).[59] Even in the United Kingdom, the basic pension remains universal. A concern is that a marked shift away from universality might undermine political support for social security pensions; it might also lead to adverse selection, because those who consider themselves at a disadvantage in terms of redistribution will leave the social security system.

Aging, together with a stagnant or falling population, will lead to a relatively smaller labor force (see tables 2-5 to 2-7) unless the losses are offset by greater labor force participation.[60] A higher participation ratio for younger age groups could thus be another way to alleviate the burden of pensions, although obviously this policy would be linked to the resolution of the more general problem of unemployment. Higher participation might be achieved by improving both employment incentives and prospects for those of working age who are not currently active. As noted, social security contributions are typically a disincentive to participation even for those to whom jobs are available. Accordingly, countries such as the Netherlands are reducing con-

59. It was estimated by the National Audit Office that between 1988 and 1994, £9.3 billion in National Insurance revenue was forgone, while the gains were estimated at £3.4 billion.

60. In the European Union the size of the group age 25 to 65 will shrink by 5 percent a decade in the twenty-first century, whereas since World War II it has grown by 6 percent a decade.

tribution rates for low-paid workers. Child care facilities (as in Scandinavia) and investment in the human capital of all of the young are also helpful in this regard.[61] The sharp variation in participation shown in table 2-13 shows ample scope for the extension of participation in many EU countries. However, an increase in the effective retirement age may be the best way of increasing participation.

Policies may also seek to redress the demographic balance by increasing fertility and immigration. But experience with trying to increase fertility rates is not encouraging, and immigration would need to be increased on an extremely large scale to make a significant difference to future projections.[62] For example, the immigration needed to offset projected decreases from 2000 to 2050 in the working-age population in Germany and Italy would amount to 13 million to 15 million each.

On the benefit side, and retaining the current structure of social security, there is a choice between reducing income-replacement ratios and curtailing benefit indexation. Changes in replacement ratios need to be announced well in advance of implementation to enable workers to plan ahead. Replacement ratios may be reduced by policies returning plans that are overly generous to actuarial principles, extending the assessment period for pensions to cover lifetime earnings instead of final salaries, extending the number of years of earnings taken into account in assessing pension levels (as in France, Italy, Austria, Portugal, Finland, and the United Kingdom), or reducing the accrual factor (as in France, Austria, Portugal, and the United Kingdom). Such reforms are often easier in immature schemes, as in southern Europe. In Denmark, pensions have been made taxable and rules regarding income received by pensioners tightened. In the Netherlands, income rules were also tightened and eligibility for so-called higher-rate basic pensions limited.

Temporary suspension of indexation (as occurred in the United States in 1984), or a link to prices and not wages (instituted in a number of EU countries) is less politically visible and has major short-term financial effects. However, reduced indexation, if sustained, may hurt

61. The German system of training, whose success is shown by the relatively low level of youth unemployment in Germany, is worthy of attention.

62. Also, experience shows that immigrants gradually adopt the low fertility levels of the home population.

the most vulnerable groups. An alternative adjustment may be to link pensions to net and not gross wages, as was recently done in Germany, Austria, Finland, and the Netherlands, thus sharing the burden of aging among the generations. Attacks have also been made on special privileges such as special pension benefits for public employees (in Finland, Greece, Portugal, and Italy) and "free" credits for years in higher education (in Austria and Germany).

A more radical alternative is to reduce the scope of state pension provision to a universal flat-rate pension, which will ensure the alleviation of poverty but will be insufficient to maintain the standards of living for those earning higher incomes. The pension systems of the United Kingdom, Ireland, the Netherlands, Finland, Sweden, and Denmark are closer to this position than those elsewhere in the European Union (see table 2-10). The United Kingdom has decisively downgraded the State Earnings-Related Pension Scheme (further details of U.K. pension reform are provided in the appendix).[63]

As regards the structure of contributions, a general increase in contribution rates would seem to be undesirable, not least on grounds of adverse incentives, although an increase would be more desirable than running fiscal deficits. There may be a clearer distinction between equity and social welfare components in terms of using contributions relative to depending on general taxation. As in Denmark, there may be switches to general taxation, particularly for the redistributive element of the system, to minimize the adverse labor market effects of redistributive social security financing.[64] Meanwhile, for the insurance element a close link of benefits to contributions is essential to avoid labor market distortion. Contribution periods required for eligibility may be increased (Greece), or more generally a closer link of contributions to pensions may be instituted, rather than a wage basis (Sweden and Italy).[65] Public servants may be obliged to pay standard-rate social security contributions. Introducing social security (pension) con-

63. See Davis (1997).

64. A more radical approach that has been advocated by some analysts is to levy contributions on capital directly rather than on labor, thus compensating for the bias of employment-based contributions toward substitution of capital for labor. However, such an approach could not only lead to misallocation of resources, but also reduce technical progress, competitiveness, and long-term growth. See Schlesinger (1985).

65. Indeed, a form of defined-contribution social security scheme is currently planned in Sweden.

tributions for old-age pensioners' incomes is another possibility. This is attractive because pensioners share the burden of aging and is also appropriate because age is no longer a good indicator of poverty.[66]

Outside the pay-as-you-go framework, a wholesale or partial switch to funding may be an alternative way to alleviate the difficulties of the demographic transition as well as to increase welfare itself. Except in the United Kingdom and to a lesser extent Denmark, no radical shifts in this direction have recently been undertaken in the European Union. Nevertheless, funded sectors are of markedly different size, owing to longer-term trends.

EU countries have thus already started to address the old-age crisis and its effects on social security. Summarizing the effect of the reforms I have outlined, Franco and Munzi (1996) note that in most cases the reforms have succeeded in reducing the future growth of expenditure ratios below that of the dependency ratio, whereas before the reforms expenditures were often set to grow in excess of it.[67] Ireland, France, and Luxembourg are the main exceptions. Nevertheless, the extent to which reforms fall short may be gauged from various projections of the future costs of social security pensions shown earlier. These suggest that potential difficulties remain severe, and further reform is essential.

As shown earlier, demographic problems are expected to become particularly difficult after 2010. but until then there is a window of opportunity for reform. Not that reform should be delayed until then. Delay could be dangerous because vested interests favoring the status quo will strengthen as the proportion of the population approaching or older than retirement age—and thus their weight in the electorate—increases. Rather, the window of opportunity should be seen as facilitating early introduction of decisive but gradual reform that will give people time to adjust their plans and will preempt opposition that would otherwise be likely to form.

66. In 1979 in the United Kingdom, 31 percent of the poorest 10 percent of the population were pensioners; in 1991 it was only 11 percent. For the poorest 20 percent of the population the figures are 38 percent and 24 percent. Again, whereas in 1979 some 46 percent of pensioners were in the lowest 20 percent of the income distribution, in 1991 it was 29 percent. The unemployed, whose increasing numbers have made a major contribution to the increase in general inequality, predominate to a greater extent at the bottom of the income distribution than was the case in the past. See Davis (1997).

67. Franco and Munzi (1996).

Given the historical development of retirement income systems, reform may justifiably take different shapes in different areas of the European Union. For example, where pay-as-you-go plans are not yet fully mature, as in southern Europe, it may be easier to cut back on benefit promises than it would be in France and Germany where pay-as-you-go is a long-established feature. In Scandinavia several countries have established elements of funding of their social security pensions, which provides a base for further expansion of such plans. Finally, with mature privately funded plans, Ireland, the Netherlands, and the United Kingdom may not require such major reforms as those needed elsewhere.

Funding Pensions

Conceptually, funding has a number of advantages. It increases the actuarial fairness of the system, given the tighter link of benefits to contributions than there is in a pay-as-you-go system, and thus contributions are more likely to be seen as saving than paying taxes. Funding is likely to reduce distortions to labor and financial markets and to saving. It may in itself reduce the overall economic impact of aging by boosting labor force participation and potentially raising aggregate saving, thus increasing the stock of fixed capital and the output out of which future pensions are to be paid.[68] Even if saving remains stable, its structure is likely to shift toward longer-term instruments such as equities, which may be favorable to productive investment, aid the development of capital markets, and create more efficient resource allocation.[69] By increasing growth endogenously, such effects could help to provide the resources necessary to cater to the remaining liabilities of a pay-as-you-go system and to those elements of it that for social reasons must be retained.[70]

Funding may also increase overall economic efficiency and flexibility by reducing the conflict between labor and capital because workers do not focus their interest only on high wages and safe employment. This

68. See Feldstein (1977, 1995a).
69. Davis (1996a, 1996c).
70. See Holzmann (1997). Further investigation of these potential endogenous growth effects would be a major contribution to debate, showing that pension reform need not always be a zero-sum game.

may, for example, help moderate wage increases and reduce demand for job security provisions, which would be seen as benefiting future retirement incomes from capital. Funding allows for risk diversification by means of the international investment of accumulated funds, thus reducing the vulnerability of the retired to the overall performance of the domestic economy, which may deteriorate as population aging becomes more severe. And assets accumulated under funding, since they are a form of private property, may be more secure against political developments brought about by population aging than are promises made under pay-as-you-go plans.

In light of an aging population, funding can also be seen as a form of burden transfer and more generally as a buffer against the need to raise contribution rates at a potentially undesirable time of deteriorating economic performance or demographic shocks. The OECD calculates that the maximum rise in contribution ratios required under pay-as-you-go to eliminate unfunded pension liabilities in the EU-4 is 4.4 to 11.9 percent of GDP, whereas for funding it suggests that a sustained increase of 1.1 to 5.3 percent would suffice.[71]

Holzmann notes three particular benefits that funding could offer to the European Union.[72] First, labor mobility between member states would be improved, allowing gains from specialization to be fully realized if there were a coordinated and funded pension plan on a defined-contribution basis (although as noted later, efforts of the European Commission to ensure that such a plan could be introduced have not come to fruition). Second, workers may be more willing to accept the adjustments to labor market conditions required to cope with globalization if they also have a stake in capital market gains at an EU and global level. Third, if the growth effects identified earlier are realized or a significant share of funds is invested internationally, thus allowing risk diversification, partial funding of pensions could help protect the Union against the symmetric demographic shock to which it will be subject.

Despite these arguments, a wholesale switch to funding would be unlikely to be desirable or even feasible, particularly because funding cannot redistribute benefits to retired persons facing poverty in the

71. Organization for Economic Cooperation and Development (1993).
72. Holzmann (1997).

way societies typically prefer.[73] And more generally, funded pensions are often ill suited to low-income workers or those with broken career patterns. Also it may be best to provide both systems to diversify risk. This is because pay-as-you-go and funding are subject to different risks (respectively, the political risk that obligations will be reneged on by governments and market risks of low returns on investments) that are to some extent independent of one another.[74] Finally, a wholesale shift would be extremely costly, given the scope of existing commitments under pay-as-you-go plans that would still have to be honored.

These arguments for a partial shift do not, however, imply a need for comprehensive pay-as-you-go systems that provide high replacement ratios regardless of income and individual preference. Rather, they may justify a basic level of social security to alleviate poverty, allowing pensions above this level to be funded. Such a form of specialization for the two systems, with the unfunded element providing redistribution and the funded element providing annuities, may help reduce the distortions to labor and financial markets induced by the unfunded element.[75]

Taking a "closed economy" view, one objection to funding is that the extra saving generated by a switch to funding may reduce the interest rate, thus reducing the benefit of funding relative to pay-as-you-go, although in practice this seems less likely as long as international investment is permitted.[76] Indeed, there are strong arguments that investment from funding should flow to countries with younger populations, whose investment needs exceed national saving.[77] This would allow a form of burden sharing at a global level, which would

73. Even in Chile, where funding and privatization of retirement income provision have been most prominent, there remains a safety net of social security pension provision.

74. See Davis (1995) for an account of the relative advantages of pay-as-you-go systems as opposed to funded plans.

75. World Bank (1994).

76. In a steady state with a constant demographic structure, the rate of return to pay-as-you-go equals the rate of growth of real wages plus population growth. But it will fall sharply as the age structure changes (Aaron 1966).

77. If international investment is not permitted, and abstracting from increases in saving and beneficial incentive effects, funding and pay-as-you-go are in some ways equivalent because pensions in each case need to be paid from the same national income. Only the source differs: capital income for funding, labor income (through taxation) for pay-as-you-go.

be particularly attractive if, as has recently been the case, these developing countries grow faster than OECD countries.

A more general problem that arises in policy discussion of funding in countries currently depending on pay-as-you-go plans is that there may be major fiscal problems that can inspire political resistance. Funded pensions do not relieve pressure on public finances in the short run because existing pension promises need to be met and, usually, tax relief granted on contribution and asset returns, with little tax revenue from the initially low amounts of funded pension payments to offset these costs. Thus the need for a contractionary fiscal stance and the likelihood of political resistance from the generations in the transition that are forced to "pay twice" for pensions, once for the previous generation through pay-as-you-go and once for their own through funding. These difficulties raise the important policy problem of how a transition is to be financed and the burden distributed among generations. As it stands, a pay-as-you-go system clearly imposes too great a burden on future generations, but how much redistribution of the burden is appropriate?

As Holzmann comments, rather than forcing the current generation to pay twice, an alternative policy would be to recognize the implicit government debt represented by the accumulated benefit obligation of a pay-as-you-go system and convert it immediately to explicit debt. The transition would be financed largely by future generations.[78] In this context Feldstein suggests such bond financing of the transition can help redistribute the burden between generations.[79] So the future generations who will benefit from the efficiency gains of a more flexible labor market and financial market development, as stimulated by funding, will also pay some of the costs.

Given the current accrued obligations under pay-as-you-go, however, which are typically much more than 100 percent of GDP, this would not seem feasible without severe effects on financial markets

78. Holzmann (1997).

79. In this context Feldstein (1995b) shows that the conditions for funding to improve welfare, even abstracting from demographics and distortions to labor markets, are likely to hold. These conditions are that the return on capital exceeds economic growth (so the return to funding exceeds that to pay-as-you-go), that the return on capital exceeds the rate of time preference (the capital intensity of the economy is lower than the welfare-maximizing level), and that the rate of growth of the economy is positive (so there is a gain in extra retirement income that more than offsets the given costs of the transition).

and confidence in the domestic economy. For EU countries, this solution would also seem to be ruled out by the current state of their public finances and the likely threat to the Maastricht ceilings.

Accordingly, EU governments have preferred to focus on scaling back benefit promises to current and future generations, implicitly defaulting on part of their pension obligations. As Holzmann has commented, by reducing the benefit obligation of pay-as-you-go, such a process of reform may facilitate a partial switch to funding, whether financed by borrowing or taxation, at a later stage.[80] It typifies the process undertaken successfully by some Latin American countries, notably Chile, and that is under active consideration in eastern Europe.

Turning to types of funding, one may distinguish partial funding of social security from private funding. Partial funding was adopted at an early stage in Sweden, such that assets valued at around 33 percent of GDP have been accumulated. Similar systems exist in Finland and Denmark. An advantage of a compulsory public system is that the labor mobility problems typical of voluntary occupational systems can be avoided. The difficulties are that, particularly if there is redistribution, contributions to a trust fund may be seen as taxes, thus engendering distortions in labor markets and other welfare losses. Moreover, a social security trust fund may face problems in investment.[81] A large trust fund may induce higher government consumption or even fiscal deficits, thus actually reducing national saving, and its management could be subject to political interference. Investment in government bonds, which is typical of such funds, has ambiguous consequences.[82] It is likely to eliminate any benefit to national saving as a consequence of funding. Even if used to fund investment, finance may be diverted to unprofitable projects for political reasons. Also lack of international investment, which is typical of social security trust funds, leaves them dependent on the performance of the domestic economy. As I discuss later, such problems seem to typify the Swedish system.

80. Holzmann (1997).
81. Thompson (1992).
82. The Swedish ATP fund is an exception, being invested largely in private sector debt instruments. As Bodie and Merton (1992) point out, governments' willingness to repay bonds may not be any more reliable than the promise to pay pensions unless the funds are used for productive capital investment with revenues hypothecated to pay pensions.

Funding through occupational pension funds or individual arrangements avoids some of these difficulties. Benefits to saving from switching out of social security are more likely because workers will perceive contributions as saving invested at market rates of return. Fund managers may focus on maximizing return for a given risk, which will ensure efficient allocation of funds in the capital market.[83] By being better able to invest internationally, they may avoid being constrained by limited investment opportunities in the home economy and may reduce risk.[84] Private pensions, notably defined-contribution plans, are more capable of meeting individual preferences, while defined-benefit plans may provide intergenerational risk sharing similar to pay-as-you-go systems. Private pensions do, however, have some disadvantages, notably cost of regulation, administrative costs, vulnerability to market risks (notably for defined-contribution funds), inability to redistribute and, for defined-benefit funds, obstacles to labor mobility and the need for compulsion at the level of the firm to make them viable.[85] Defined-benefit funds based on final salary may increase incentives of employers to lay off older workers because the rate of their pension accruals increases as retirement age approaches.[86] Also, as noted before, private pensions do not relieve pressure on public finances in the short run.[87]

There are major differences among EU countries in the extent to

83. The impact of institutional investors such as pension funds on the capital market is discussed in Davis (1996c).

84. There are numerous barriers to international investment of private pension funds in the European Union, usually imposed for prudential reasons; see Davis (1995). Lannoo (1996) discusses recent action by the European Union. At present the European Commission is questioning the validity of restrictions under the Capital Movements Directive.

85. In the Netherlands, administrative costs of state pensions are 1 percent of contributions, 7 percent of company pensions, and 24 percent of personal pensions. See Besseling and Zeeuw (1993). Diamond (1993) notes that U.S. social security administrative costs are three to twelve times less than those of private pensions, partly owing to the natural monopoly in the collection of social security contributions.

The future of defined-benefit funds in the United Kingdom, where membership has been made voluntary, will be a test of the hypothesis that labor mobility and the need for compulsion at the level of the firm will prove a problem (Davis 1997).

86. To combat this, the Netherlands is now introducing a reform to make calculations based on average salary standard for defined-benefit funds. With an average-salary base (indexed to inflation), pensions accrue smoothly over the working life of the individual.

87. On related issues, see Franco (1996).

which funding has developed as a complement to the social security systems. In the Netherlands, Denmark, Sweden, and the United Kingdom coverage of the labor force is 75 percent or more; in Spain, France, Italy, and Portugal it is marginal (table 2-21).[88] Germany, Belgium, and Ireland are intermediate. Note that table 2-21 omits the French compulsory unfunded supplementary schemes (ARRCO and AGIRC), which cover 90 percent of the labor force, as well as the funded social security schemes in Sweden and Finland. The table shows that in most EU countries coverage is voluntary (for the employer or the employee), except in Denmark and for the civil servants' scheme (ABP) in the Netherlands. The United Kingdom is exceptional in the size of its personal pension sector. Most EU private pensions are provided on a defined-benefit basis, the main exceptions being Denmark and the United Kingdom (for personal pensions). Funding is typically external to the firm in a diversified portfolio of assets; internal funding on a book-reserve basis is common in Germany, Austria, and to some extent in Sweden.

Table 2-22 shows pension fund assets (excluding funds managed by life insurance companies) in the EU countries for which data are readily available. As in table 2-21, for each measure a contrast is apparent between the role of pension funds in the United Kingdom, Sweden, Ireland, the Netherlands, and Denmark, where they account for a sizable part of personal sector wealth and GDP, and those in Belgium, Germany, Spain, France, Italy, and Portugal. Greece, Austria, and Luxembourg also have vestigial privately funded plans. The low level of external funding in Germany is an inaccurate indicator of the overall size of private pensions because assets equal to about 9 percent of GDP (1994 estimate) are held as reserves on the sponsoring firm's balance sheet.

Various influences could account for the differences in the importance of funded sectors. The most crucial point is that privately funded plans cannot usefully be viewed in isolation; the principal alternative to a private pension fund is the state social security pension system. Not surprisingly, the growth of private plans can be related to the scale

88. For further discussion of issues related to funded schemes in the Netherlands, see Davis (1996b). For further discussion of the United Kingdom see Davis (1997) and the appendix.

TABLE 2-21. *Private Funded Pension Systems in EU Members, 1996*

Country	Coverage of labor force (percent)	Type of benefit	Funding
Belgium	31 (voluntary)	Defined benefit	External
Germany	46 (voluntary)	Defined benefit	Largely internal
Denmark	80 (compulsory)	Defined contribution	External
Greece	5 (voluntary)	Defined benefit	External
Spain	4 for pension funds, 11 for personal pensions (voluntary)	Defined benefit	External
France	Under 10 (voluntary)	Defined benefit	External
Ireland	40 (voluntary)	Defined benefit	External
Italy	5 (voluntary)	Defined benefit	External
Luxembourg	30 (voluntary)	Defined benefit	Internal
Netherlands	85 (voluntary)	Defined benefit	External
Portugal	15 (voluntary)	Defined benefit	External
Sweden	90 (ITP/STP voluntary)	Defined benefit	Partly internal
United Kingdom	50 company, 25 personal (voluntary)	Defined benefit (most occupational), defined contribution (personal)	External

Source: European Federation for Retirement Provision (1996). Includes only independent (private and public sector) funded schemes. In the Netherlands the private schemes are voluntary; the ABP scheme for public employees is compulsory.

of social security pension provision, which imposes limits on private sector plans, particularly if there is generous provision for individuals at higher income levels.

Social security replacement ratios were shown in table 2-10 to be comparable for those on low incomes in most EU countries. It is the share of final earnings replaced that is a crucial determinant of the scope of private funds. If social security provides high replacement ratios to high earners, there will be little incentive to develop private funded plans at all. The replacement ratio declines rapidly with

TABLE 2-22. *Private Pension Financing in EU Members and Others, 1994*

Country	Billions of U.S. dollars	Percent of GDP
United Kingdom	706	68
Germany	111	6
France	50	4
Netherlands	287	82
Italy	23	2
Sweden	51	25
Denmark	28	18
Ireland	21	42
Spain	11	2
Finland	11	10
Belgium	7	3
Portugal	6	8
Austria	1	1
Luxembourg	1	3
United States	4,527	67
Japan (March 1994)	260	6
Canada (1992)	183	34
Australia	139	41

Sources: European Federation for Retirement Provision (1996); and national data.

increases in earnings in Denmark, Ireland, the Netherlands, and the United Kingdom, countries with large funded sectors. Germany, Greece, Spain, France, Italy, and Portugal are notable for comparable replacement ratios to those retiring on higher earnings. Their private funded sectors are much less important.

Where provision is voluntary, tax laws can make it more or less attractive for a firm to offer a pension fund (table 2-23). For example, exemption from taxation of contributions and asset returns will increase funds' attractiveness. But in some countries these factors may be overridden by the imposition of compulsory pension plans on employers. Consistent with this argument, the Netherlands, Ireland, and the United Kingdom offer generous treatment (exemption of contributions and asset returns, while pensions payments are taxed, denoted EET in table 2-23). ''Booking'' is discouraged in these countries by withholding tax privileges from book-reserve funded plans. In

Germany tax incentives to booking of corporate pension liabilities and some tax disadvantages to pension funds have accompanied smaller externally funded plans. Recent imposition of taxes on contributions in Belgium may stunt the growth of private plans, according to some commentators.

Compulsory participation of employers ensures that funds will grow and coverage will remain high regardless of fiscal incentives, although it may have adverse effects on labor supply and raise wage costs for low-income workers. In Denmark membership of funds is now compulsory for blue-collar workers, once collective agreements with unions are concluded.[89] Fiscal treatment is less generous (a tax is imposed on real asset returns to pension funds above a certain level). But even before compulsion was introduced, funds proved attractive in the context of income tax rates of up to 68 percent. The French supplementary plans are also compulsory, but pay-as-you-go financing is enforced.

Funded sectors differ in terms of maturity, which also influences the current and prospective ratio of assets to GDP.[90] In the United Kingdom, Ireland, Sweden, and the Netherlands, defined-benefit plans are largely mature, so the ratio of assets to GDP is near a peak, although personal and defined-contribution funds could spur further growth in the United Kingdom. In Belgium, Denmark, and Germany the immaturity of funded plans suggests further growth is likely.

A simple regression analysis using the broader group of OECD countries in a study by Davis was carried out to test the main influences on the broad ratio of pension assets to GDP.[91] The independent variables were the scope of social security, the tax regime, whether the system is mandatory, and its maturity. Of course, such a regression cannot prove causality. Subject to this caveat, the equation indicated the importance of these factors in discriminating between countries with small and large private funded sectors. It suggests that every 1 percentage point increase in the difference between social security replacement ratios at $20,000 and $50,000 is associated with a

89. More comprehensive compulsory funded plans outside the European Union include those in Australia, Switzerland, Chile, and Singapore.

90. *Terms of maturity* is the extent to which the firms have existed for long enough to have a steady-state distribution of workers and pensioners.

91. Davis (1995).

TABLE 2-23. *Pension Fund Tax Treatment and Asset Regulations in the European Union*[a]

Country	Form of taxation	Portfolio regulations	Regulation of funding[b]
United Kingdom	EET: contributions and asset returns tax free. Benefits taxed, except for tax-free lump sum.	Prudent man concept; 5% self-investment limit, concentration limit for defined-contribution plans.	Maximum 5% overfund of PBO or IBO. Funding only obligatory for contracted-out part of social security.
Germany	TET: Employers' contributions taxed as wages; employees' contributions and asset returns tax-free. Benefits taxed at low rate. (For booked benefits, employers' contributions tax free, benefits taxed at normal rate).	Guidelines; maximum 30% EU equity, 25% EU property, 6% non-EU shares, 6% non-EU bonds, 20% overall foreign assets, 10% self-investment limit.	Funding obligatory up to PBO. Option of book-reserve funding.
Netherlands	EET: Contributions and asset returns tax free. Benefits taxed.	Prudent man concept; 5% self-investment limit.	Funds are expected to cover PBO; maximum 15% overfund of ABO; minimum is ABO itself.
Sweden	ETT: Contributions to ATP tax-free; contributions to ITP/STP subject to social security tax. Tax on asset returns of ITP/STP. Benefits taxed at low rate.	Majority to be in listed bonds, debentures, and retroverse loans to contributors.	For ATP, IBO is funded. Contribution rate adjusted every five years to balance fund.
Denmark	ETT: Contributions tax-free. Tax on real asset returns. Benefits taxed, including 40% of lump sum payments.	Property loans, shares, and investment trust holdings limited to 40%, foreign assets to 20%; 60% to be in domestic debt. No self-investment.	Irrelevant as defined contribution; benefits must be funded externally.

France	E(E)T: Contributions to unfunded ARRCO/AGIRC tax free; separate funded schemes discouraged; insured pension contributions tax free.	Assets of supplementary funds (ARRCO/AGIRC) to be invested 50% in EU government bonds and less than 33% in loans to sponsors. Insured funds maximum 40% property and 15% Treasury deposits.	Funded company schemes discouraged; book-reserve funding subject to tax discrimination.
Italy	EET: Contributions and asset returns tax free; benefits taxed.	No pension law for self-administered plans. Most plans insured, investments may be in state bonds (maximum 90%), bank deposits, property, mortgages, securities, investment funds.	No pension law for self-administered plans; draft law proposes payments equal to 7% of salary. Insured plans must be fully funded on a fifteen-year projection.
Ireland	EET: Contributions and asset returns tax free; benefits taxed.	Plans must diversify prudently; any self-investment to be declared.	Funding of ABO required; deferred rights indexed.
Belgium	EET: Contributions and asset returns tax free; benefits taxed.	15% to be invested in government bonds, no more than 15% in sponsor, 40% limit on real estate, 10% deposits.	Funding obligatory of ABO based on current salary; interest rate 7%.
Spain	TTT: Asset returns taxed, benefits taxed, employee contributions partly tax deductible.	90% in stocks, bonds, mortgages, property, deposits.	Funding obligatory of ABO plus 4% margin; maximum interest rate 6%.
Portugal	EET: Contributions and asset returns tax free; benefits taxed.	Maximum of 50% real estate, 15% self-investment, 40% equities and bonds not listed in Portugal, but limited to large markets.	Funding obligatory of ABO.

Sources: Davis (1995); and European Federation for Retirement Provision (1996).
a. Although the table reflects information available to the author at the time of writing, regulations are not infrequently subject to amendment.
b. ABO refers to the accrued benefit obligation; PBO the projected benefit obligation.

1.2 percent higher ratio of assets to GDP. A deviation from favorable expenditure-tax treatment of pensions is related to 21 percent lower funding. Countries where there is compulsion have a 23 percent higher ratio, all other things being equal, and those with mature systems a 27 percent higher ratio. All variables were significant at the 95 percent level.

Detailed study of national funded sectors suggests that other important factors in the development of occupational pension funds are the ability of employees to leave earnings-related social security for an equivalent private pension (as in the United Kingdom), funding of civil service pensions (Netherlands), and widening of coverage through encouragement of personal pensions (United Kingdom) as well as encouragement of supplementary defined contribution plans, as in the United States.[92] Development can be stopped by simply discouraging company-based externally funded plans, as has historically been the case in France.[93] And funding of social security in Sweden limits growth of private funds.

A striking feature of this analysis of the determinants of private funding is that the development of funding appears to be only tenuously related to the underlying fundamentals. There is little correlation with the future aging of the population in the various countries or the difficulties confronted by social security. These should predispose countries such as France, Italy, and Germany to extend the scope of funding. The costs of allowing tax exemption of contributions (particularly in the context of high current expenditures on pay-as-you-go), difficulties of transition, and a preference for the social solidarity of comprehensive pay-as-you-go plans are among the reasons.

But owing to future demographic difficulties, a major shift to funded schemes is essential.[94] I offered in my 1995 study some illustrative calculations of the potential size of pension funds in EU countries

---

92. Davis (1995).

93. Wyatt Data Services (1993). France is currently introducing measures to encourage funded pensions; see Jack (1997). The reform would enable private sector companies to set up pension funds, providing for all their employees benefits in addition to those provided by social security pensions. Contributions could be made voluntarily by both employers and employees. Exemption from social security charges above a certain level would be the incentive to contribute. The draft bill, however, had not yet completed its parliamentary procedure at the time of writing.

94. See, for example, European Federation for Retirement Provision (1996).

dependent on pay-as-you-go. An update of these figures based on 1994 data shows that, for example, if French pension funds were to reach the size of their U.K. counterparts in terms of shares of personal sector assets, they would total $648 billion. Similar calculations for Germany give $707 billion in assets, which compares with the $965 billion capitalization of the German stock market. In practice, personal sector financial wealth would probably be boosted by a switch from pay-as-you-go to funding, so the increase in value of funds—and consequent stimulus to capital markets—would probably be significantly greater. It is notable that in the United Kingdom, where social security is less comprehensive, the ratio of personal financial wealth to GDP is more than 2, whereas in France and Germany it is less than 1.5. In effect, capital gains have more than offset the lower saving ratio in the United Kingdom. If French financial wealth reached the same level as that of the United Kingdom in relation to GDP and pension funds attained the same share of personal wealth, the stock of pension assets would be greater than $990 billion.

Portfolios and Performance of Pension Funds

How much do portfolio regulations influence asset holdings of pension funds in EU countries, and what is their effect on performance? These regulations are widely held to diminish the efficiency with which funding may provide pensions and reduce the overall attractiveness of funded plans to sponsoring companies and their workers.

Table 2-24 shows the distributions of pension fund portfolios for 1994 in EU and other countries. Equity holdings varied from 4 percent in Spain to 80 percent in the United Kingdom, and foreign assets from 5 percent in France to 37 percent in Ireland. As background, estimates of real total returns and their standard deviations for 1967 90 are shown in table 2-25.

As anticipated, liabilities, asset returns, taxation, and risk reduction are important influences on portfolios.[95] And so are portfolio restrictions (see table 2-23). Such regulations have the ostensible aim of protecting pension fund beneficiaries, or benefit insurers, although motives such as ensuring a steady demand for government bonds may

95. Davis (1995, 1996a).

TABLE 2-24. *Distribution of EU and Other Country Pension Fund Portfolios, 1994*
Percent of assets

Country	Equities	Bonds and loans	Property	Liquidity and deposits	Foreign assets[a]
United Kingdom	80	11	6	3	30
Germany	11	75	11	3	6
France	14	39	7	40	5
Netherlands	23	67	9	2	17
Italy	9	62	23	6	5
Sweden	32	47	8	13	12
Denmark	22	65	9	4	7
Ireland	55	35	6	4	37
Spain	4	82	1	13	5
Finland	5	73	12	10	n.a.
Belgium	36	47	7	10	35
Portugal	10	72	3	15	n.a.
Austria	11	75	2	12	20
Luxembourg	20	70	0	10	n.a.
United States	48	38	0	7	10
Japan (March 1994)	27	61	2	3	7
Canada (1992)	38	49	3	7	9
Australia	48	27	8	17	16

Source: European Federation for Retirement Provision (1996).
a. Foreign assets are included in the categories to the left.
n.a. Not available.

also play a part.[96] Limits are often imposed on holdings of assets with relatively volatile returns, such as equities and property, as well as foreign assets, even if their mean return is high. There are also often limits on self-investment to protect against the associated concentration of risk regarding insolvency of the sponsor.[97] Pension funds are naturally also subject to exchange controls, but all EU countries have abolished theirs.

Apart from the control of self-investment, which is clearly necessary to ensure that funds are not vulnerable to bankruptcy of the sponsor,

96. For example, in France, *caisses de retraite* must invest at least 50 percent of their assets in state bonds.
97. These limits do not, of course, apply to reserve funding systems such as those common in Germany, Austria, and Sweden.

TABLE 2-25. *Returns on Pension Fund Portfolios, 1967–90*

Mean percent (standard deviation) of annual real total returns in local currency

Item	United Kingdom	Germany	Netherlands	Sweden	Denmark	Ireland	France	Italy	Belgium
Estimated portfolio return[a]	5.8 (12.5)	5.1 (4.4)	4.0 (6.0)	0.2 (7.6)	3.6 (12.7)	5.0 (11.9)	n.a. n.a.	n.a. n.a.	n.a. n.a.
Average earnings growth	2.6 (2.5)	4.0 (3.1)	2.4 (3.2)	1.5 (3.5)	2.8 (3.6)	2.0	4.0	3.1 (4.3)	n.a.
Portfolio return less average earnings	3.2	1.1	1.6	-1.3	0.8	3.0	n.a.	n.a.	n.a.
Inflation (CPI)	8.9 (5.3)	3.5 (2.1)	4.9 (3.1)	8.1 (2.7)	7.7 (3.2)	10.0 (6.0)	7.1 (4.1)	11.3 (5.9)	5.5 (3.2)
Returns									
Loans	1.4 (5.0)	5.3 (1.9)	3.8 (3.6)	3.4 (3.1)	6.1 (3.6)	n.a. n.a.	2.6 (3.2)	2.7 (3.7)	n.a. n.a.
Mortgages	2.0 (5.2)	4.7 (1.4)	4.3 (2.6)	2.6 (3.0)	5.8 (3.7)	n.a. n.a.	3.7 (2.6)	n.a. n.a.	n.a. n.a.
Equities	8.1 (20.3)	9.5 (20.3)	7.9 (28.2)	8.4 (23.3)	7.0 (27.5)	8.5 (25.9)	9.4 (26.9)	4.0 (35.9)	6.3 (16.7)
Bonds	-0.5 (13.0)	2.7 (14.9)	1.0 (13.1)	-0.9 (8.5)	3.4 (16.1)	-0.1 (15.3)	1.0 (13.1)	-0.2 (18.3)	1.3 (11.7)
Short-term assets	1.7 (4.9)	3.1 (2.1)	1.6 (4.0)	1.3 (3.5)	1.6 (1.8)	n.a. n.a.	2.4 (3.4)	-2.2 (4.2)	n.a. n.a.
Property	6.7 (11.4)	4.5 (2.9)	4.6 (15.0)	n.a. n.a.	n.a. n.a.	n.a. n.a.	n.a. n.a.	n.a. n.a.	n.a. n.a.
Foreign bonds	-0.1 (15.0)	3.0 (11.2)	-0.7 (11.2)	-0.2 (12.6)	-2.0 (11.6)	-1.4 (11.4)	-0.2 (12.8)	-1.5 (10.7)	0.2 (11.1)
Foreign equities	7.0 (16.2)	10.4 (13.5)	6.6 (14.4)	7.1 (14.0)	5.5 (14.3)	5.9 (14.2)	7.0 (13.5)	6.0 (12.5)	7.5 (13.7)
Portfolio return[b]	6.3 (10.7)	5.5 (3.0)	4.3 (5.5)	2.8 (2.9)	5.8 (3.0)	n.a.	n.a.	n.a.	n.a.

Sources: Davis (1995), using National Flow of Funds Data (for portfolio distributions—see table 2-24) and BIS macroeconomic database (for asset returns).

a. Using holding-period returns on bonds.

b. Using redemption yields on fixed rate instruments.

n.a. Not available.

the extent to which such regulations actually contribute to benefit security is open to doubt, because pension funds, unlike insurance companies, face the risk of increasing liabilities as well as the risk of holding assets, and thus need to trade volatility with return.[98] Moreover, appropriate diversification of assets can eliminate any idiosyncratic risk from holding an individual security (such as an equity), thus minimizing the increase in risk. And if national cycles and markets are imperfectly correlated, international investment will actually reduce otherwise undiversifiable or "systematic" risk. At a macroeconomic level, international investment restrictions limit the possibility of burden sharing between OECD and non-OECD countries.

Such limits may be particularly inappropriate for defined-benefit pensions, given the additional buffer of the guarantee on the part of the company to the worker. Clearly, in such cases portfolio regulations may affect the attractiveness to companies of funding pensions, and the generosity of provision, if they constrain managers in their choice of risk and return, forcing them to hold low-yielding assets and increasing their risks by limiting their possibilities of diversification. They will also restrict the benefits to the capital markets from the development of pension funds. In particular, restrictions that explicitly or implicitly oblige pension funds to invest in government bonds, which must themselves be repaid from taxation, may offer no benefit to capital formation.[99] At a macroeconomic level the funded plans may be equivalent to pay-as-you-go.

Such limits apply in Germany, Sweden, Denmark, France, Portugal, and Belgium. Less severe limits apply in Italy and Spain. The limits are not, however, imposed in all the countries studied. Pension funds in the United Kingdom, Ireland, and the Netherlands are subject to explicit or implicit prudent-man rules as in the United States, which requires managers to carry out sensible portfolio diversification.[100] The

98. In practice, life insurers are more strictly regulated; see Davis (1990).

99. The restrictions may force the funds to invest in government bonds by, for example, closing down all alternative investment strategies such as international diversification.

100. In the United States the precise wording is that fund money must be invested "for the sole benefit of the beneficiaries" and investments must be made with the "care, skill, prudence and diligence under the circumstances then prevailing that a prudent man acting in a like capacity and familiar with such matters would use in the conduct of an enterprise of a like character and with like aims."

only limit on the distributions of portfolio holdings is the limit on self-investment.

Among the influences of such regulations that are apparent in portfolios is that bonds constitute more than two-thirds of pension fund assets in Sweden and Denmark. In Denmark, bonds held by pension funds are subject to a tax on real returns, but equities are exempt. Thus portfolio regulations force funds to hold tax-disadvantaged assets because funds must hold 60 percent of their assets in fixed-interest instruments. Investment of a fifth of the Swedish quasi-public funds' assets in government bonds casts some doubt on their efficacy as a means to protect against future risks to social security, given that the bonds are to be repaid by the taxpayer in the same way as they would to finance future social security burdens through a pay-as-you-go plan. Similar comments can be made about the Dutch civil servants' pension fund, which until 1996 was subject to severe portfolio restrictions, such that at the end of 1994 it held 80 percent of its assets in the form of public sector bonds and loans. Funds in Belgium and France are forced to hold a certain proportion of government bonds, although their actual holdings tend to exceed these ceilings, suggesting that other influences are at work.[101] As regards equities, German funds are limited to a maximum of 36 percent by regulation, but because they held 11 percent in 1994, the ceiling was not binding.[102] Holdings of foreign assets are extremely low in such countries, despite the potential benefit from risk diversification.

As I suggested in 1996, funding rules, accounting standards, the structure of fund management, and the risk aversion of trustees may also induce funds to hold large proportions of domestic debt instruments.[103] A useful means of judging the cost of these regulations and market imperfections, and thus the potential benefit to funds of liberalization, is to assess funds' performance both relative to that in countries without portfolio restrictions and to that of artificial portfolios. The portfolio distributions (see table 2-24) and risks and returns on assets can be used to derive estimates of the returns and risks on

101. Similar restrictions held in Portugal until recently.

102. A nonbinding ceiling need not mean that the limits have no effect; funds may aim for an average holding well below the ceiling to avoid overshooting when asset prices are volatile.

103. Davis (1996a).

portfolios (see table 2-25), and thus the cost to the firm of providing a given level of pension benefits (for a defined-benefit fund) or the return to the member (for a defined-contribution fund).[104]

The most crucial test is ability of a fund to outperform real average earnings. Liabilities of defined-benefit plans are basically indexed to average earnings, and the replacement ratio a defined-contribution fund can offer will depend on asset returns relative to earnings growth.[105] The margin is sizable (more than 3 percent a year) in the United Kingdom and Ireland, and between 1 and 2 percent in Germany and the Netherlands. Except for Germany, these countries have prudent-man rules. The margin remains positive in Denmark, albeit only 0.8 percent. But in Sweden (for the government ATP fund) it is negative, implying that the returns on assets need to be constantly topped up to meet their target. This recurring situation may relate to inefficient asset allocations arising from portfolio restrictions. Taking the results at face value and disregarding demographic issues, a pay-as-you-go plan would have offered a higher rate of return than funding in this manner over this time period in Sweden.

To estimate the trade-off of benefits and contributions in the context of these portfolio choices, table 2-26 shows the results of illustrative calculations on the relation between costs of providing pensions, average earnings, and real returns.[106] This gives an alternative expression of the cost of equity restrictions. The table shows the replacement rate that would be attainable given the real returns attained by funds in each country and the corresponding growth rates of wages shown in table 2-25, assuming indexed pensions, a 10 percent defined-contribution rate, forty years of contributions, and twenty years of retirement. Abstracting from risk, the table illustrates clearly the benefits of a higher return relative to real earnings. Assuming pensions are indexed to prices, U.K. funds can obtain a replacement ratio of 60 percent and Swedish funds only 14 percent. Conversely, to obtain a pen-

---

104. Annual holding-period returns on marketable fixed-rate instruments are used instead of redemption yields. The holding-period returns are the more relevant measure for an ongoing portfolio because they take full account of losses or gains from interest rate changes (although other assumptions regarding holding periods could also be made).

105. It also indicates whether in practice the return to funding (the asset return) exceeds that in pay-as-you-go in a steady state (the growth rate of average earnings).

106. Provided in Vittas (1992).

TABLE 2-26. *Targeted Replacement Rates with Indexed Pensions, 1992*
Percent

Country	Replacement ratio assuming indexation of pensions to prices	Percentage contribution rate for 40 percent replacement rate	Replacement ratio assuming indexation of pensions to wages
United Kingdom	60	6.7	50
Germany	39	10.3	27
Netherlands	44	9.1	37
Sweden	14	28.6	11
Denmark	36	11.1	27
Ireland	60	6.7	50

Sources: Vittas (1992); and estimates of average earnings, inflation, and real returns on pension funds shown in table 2-25. There is assumed a working life of forty years followed by twenty years of retirement.

sion equal to 40 percent of average earnings, U.K. funds need a contribution rate of 6.7 percent and Swedish funds 29 percent.

As a further illustration, table 2-27 shows the returns on hypothetical diversified portfolios holding 50 percent equity and 50 percent bonds between 1967 and 1990, implicitly assuming quantitative portfolio restrictions are replaced by prudent-man rules. Equity holdings for EU pension funds are generally less than 50 percent (see table 2-24); in fact, these portfolios approximate closely those of pension funds in the United States, where a prudent-man rule is in operation. Compared with table 2-24, the results in table 2-27 confirm that returns may be boosted by raising the share of equity, at some cost in terms of risk, although the estimates suggest that risk is mitigated by international diversification.[107] Only for the United Kingdom and Ireland are returns consistently below those actually obtained. Several of the countries that fall below a satisfactory return on assets relative to average earnings (such as Denmark and Sweden) would have found

107. The table only shows international diversification up to 20 percent of the portfolio, holding bonds and equities for the rest of the world in proportion to global portfolio weights in the 1980s. A full global portfolio, in which domestic holdings are reduced to their weight in the global index, would imply more than 95 percent international investment for the small countries and 80 percent even for the United Kingdom and Germany. Similar calculations for such a strategy (not shown in detail), with 50 percent bonds and 50 percent equities, again show lower risk in domestic currency, although the change in return may be in either direction.

TABLE 2-27. *Artificial Diversified Portfolios*
Mean (standard deviation) of real total return in local currency, 1967–90

Country	Domestic[a]	Standard deviation	Domestic minus estimated portfolio return[b]	Domestic and international[c]	Standard deviation	Domestic and international minus estimated portfolio return[b]	Domestic and international minus average earnings
United Kingdom	3.8	(14.8)	-2.0	3.7	(14.1)	-2.1	1.1
Germany	6.1	(15.2)	1.0	6.2	(13.4)	1.1	2.2
Netherlands	4.5	(17.0)	0.5	4.2	(15.2)	0.2	1.6
Sweden	3.8	(13.5)	3.6	3.7	(15.2)	3.5	2.2
Denmark	5.3	(18.9)	1.7	4.6	(13.4)	1.0	1.8
France	5.2	(18.0)	n.a.	4.9	(15.9)	n.a.	0.9
Italy	1.9	(22.1)	n.a.	2.0	(18.7)	n.a.	-1.1
Ireland	3.8	(13.3)	-1.2	3.8	(12.4)	-1.2	1.8
Belgium	4.2	(18.4)	n.a.	3.8	(16.7)	n.a.	n.a.

Source: Davis (1995).
a. 50 percent domestic equity, 50 percent domestic bonds.
b. From table 2-26.
c. 40 percent domestic equity, 40 percent domestic bonds, 10 percent foreign equity, 10 percent foreign bonds.
n.a. Not available.

provision of funded pensions less costly, both of themselves and relative to pay-as-you-go plans, if they had followed such a rule. German funds would also have boosted their headroom considerably.

Broadly speaking, then, this chapter recommends the institution of prudent-man rules to ensure that pension funds reach their optimum trade-off of risk and return.[108] To some extent, depending on liabilities and the investment climate, this arrangement should boost demand for equities. If funded sectors developed in France and Germany on a par with those in the United Kingdom and equity proportions were around 50 percent, similar to the proportions held by U.S. funds, the increase in demand for equities (for 1994) would be $324 billion and $354 billion, respectively.

Policy Action at the EU Level

The discussion of public and private pensions in this chapter has so far focused on national situations and policy initiatives. But action at the level of the Union may also be pertinent. There are no proposals for pan-EU measures to deal with social security, nor are there initiatives to resolve the problem directly. In common with most other details of public finance, these are of purely national responsibility (although limited liberalization of social security pensions permitting cross-border membership in social security systems has been agreed on). Details of national responses to current and future burdens of social security pensions were provided in an earlier section of the chapter. One additional point, however, is that the fiscal convergence criteria of the Maastricht Treaty, which provide for limits on deficits and debts as a precondition for entering the European Monetary Union, have focused much more strongly on public finance issues than hitherto. In particular, attention is being paid to the influence of social security imbalances in contributing to a country's deficits. Equally, it is widely recognized that the need to correct public finance positions before the aging of the population sets in gives a powerful additional justification to adhere to the Maastricht targets.

There has been more activity in the area of private funded pen-

108. See also European Federation for Retirement Provision (1996).

sions.[109] Until mid-1994, the European Union proposed single-market legislation to liberalize funded retirement plans in the form of a Pension Funds Directive. A draft directive addressed, first, the freedom to offer services across borders (in other words, to conduct administration and fund management in another member state), and second, the liberalization of investment throughout the Community (although some commentators noted that this freedom should already exist under the Capital Movements Directive). Freedom to offer services across borders is of course an integral part of the EU Single Market; it has already been introduced for banking, insurance, and investment services.[110] Proposed liberalization of investment restrictions in the directive was intended to eliminate unwarranted limits on certain investments. Governments were not to have privileged access to finance by pension funds through laws mandating that the funds maintain minimum holdings of government bonds. There were to be no requirements to localize assets in individual member states. And there were to be no currency-matching requirements that could not be justified on prudential grounds. The directive also set out principles of investment that would provide the context for these rules. These broad guidelines stressed security (necessitating consistent matching of assets and liabilities, diversification, and limited self-investment), liquidity, and profitability. These are clearly in line with the concept of a prudent-man rule, although they were deliberately not set out in detail. They could nonetheless provide a basis for challenge of limits to domestic equity investment.

Under the draft directive, countries were to be permitted to require matching of domestic liabilities with domestic assets up to a certain percentage, itself a minimum requirement and thus inconsistent with the directive's own principles. This was the matter on which the directive foundered (although there were also concerns about ability to freeze assets managed by a foreign fund manager). The United Kingdom, Ireland, and the Netherlands considered 60 percent (that is, a 40 percent limit on foreign investment) to be a maximum acceptable degree of matching, and preferred no limits at all. Other countries wanted 80 percent, which is the same as in the insurance directives.

109. Lannoo (1996).
110. For banking see Davis (1993).

The Belgian EU presidency's proposal for a compromise on 70 percent was not acceptable.

The current approach of the European Commission seems to be one of applying the Capital Movements Directive to the problem of international investment and attacking the existing regimes in the more restrictive member states for not constituting "reasonable prudential restrictions" as defined in the directive. To this end, it issued a communication in which it sought to clarify the Rome Treaty rules on the free movement of capital, which member states were asked to obey, with a threat of action in the European Court if they did not.[111] These guidelines suggest that imposing both minimums and maximums for asset classes, as well as more than 60 percent currency matching, is contrary to the Maastricht Treaty. France and Spain have challenged this communication as going beyond the rights of the commission. Nevertheless, Commissioner Mario Monti declared in June 1996 that the commission would take further action. He planned to write to member states with restrictions considered unjustifiable on prudential grounds, asking that the restrictions be removed. Failure to act could lead to action in the European Court.

Meanwhile, discussions continue on a third proposal contained in a recent consultative paper to allow pension plans to operate freely across national boundaries on the basis of home state authorization and to allow people to join plans in other member states. This freedom is seen as a very difficult issue, particularly because the countries must agree on funding standards and because of fiscal differences. But it is also the most important obstacle to labor mobility, which is much lower in the European Union than in the United States, and the completion of the single market. A first step is to cover only migrant and frontier workers—those living in one state and working in another—and to provide for mutual recognition of pension funds based in other member states. It is hoped that the existing provision for cross-border membership in social security plans for a limited period will provide the basis for such an agreement.

Finally, in June 1996 Commissioner Monti announced a proposal to widen EC action on pension funds by means of a report on their regulation. The report would address whether they and life insurers

111. Cohen and Tucker (1995).

should not share the same regulation. It would also address the need for optimizing investment opportunities, the need for efficient capital markets, the barriers to cross-border labor mobility, the impact of taxation on pension funds, the need for a global view and coordination at an EU level, and the subject of pension mobility.

Conclusions

The problems demographic trends pose to EU countries are particularly acute. The states are facing the rapid aging of their populations owing to decreasing fertility combined with greater longevity and reduced migration. In many countries these trends are interacting to threaten the generous benefits of national social security pension systems and the early retirement features they offer. Poor economic performance, including high structural unemployment and low growth rates, are generating further difficulties for these systems. Moreover, generous social security provisions, notably when there is no perceived link between contributions and benefits, are likely to induce major distortions to both labor and financial markets.

Social security reforms are already under way in many of the countries. In most cases they have succeeded in reducing the future growth of pension expenditure–GDP ratios below that of the elderly dependency ratio, whereas before the reforms expenditures were often set to grow in excess of it. Nevertheless, projections suggest that difficulties will worsen significantly in the next century unless countries take further action. One indicator is that ratios of expenditures to GDP are still projected to rise sharply; another is that estimates of the discounted present value of future pension expenditures net of contributions are well in excess of conventional government debt for many EU countries. The interaction of aging populations and overall weak economic performance may increase the difficulties for social security systems by reducing saving and decreasing labor market efficiency, although not all observers are agreed on this. Aging will also raise demand for health care and other social services.[112]

Estimates differ, but difficulties arising from the costs of social security pension provisions are likely to be acute in Belgium, Spain,

112. Oxley and MacFarlan (1994).

Greece, France, Italy, Finland, Germany, Luxembourg, Austria, and Portugal. The United Kingdom, Ireland, Denmark, and the Netherlands are in a relatively favorable situation. Sweden is in an intermediate position.

That the aging of the population becomes particularly rapid after 2010 suggests that until then there is a window of opportunity for reform. Not that reform should be delayed until then. Delay could be dangerous because vested interests that favor the status quo will strengthen as the proportion of the population approaching or older than retirement age will increase. Rather, the window should be seen as facilitating the introduction of decisive but gradual reform that would preempt opposition and give people time to adjust their plans.

Experiences with reform in EU countries, as well as the theoretical literature, suggest a wide range of reforms that could help to make the pension systems viable during the demographic shift.

In the context of current pay-as-you-go plans, increases in the retirement age, even encouragement to work beyond retirement age, would seem particularly warranted. Longer life expectancy gives ample scope for raising retirement ages. This needs to be complemented by curtailing early retirement provisions and reducing incentives to retire early. The success of such actions requires eliminating any excessive generosity in an actuarial sense, which might otherwise reward those retiring early. A strict relation of pension to contributions is one way to control such generosity. Private pension plans should also be tailored to avoid providing incentives for firms to lay off workers who are approaching retirement and whose pension accruals are increasing. Adopting a defined-benefit plan based on average salary or a defined-contribution plan rather than a defined-benefit plan based on final salary would be helpful in this respect. A higher minimum retirement age may also be needed, as well as better retraining for older workers so that they can be productive longer and reconsideration of hiring, firing, and automatic age-related pay practices. Policymakers need to avoid the fallacy that it is only by encouraging early retirement that jobs can be made available for the young. Given the relatively high activity rates of people age 55 to 65 in the United Kingdom, Portugal, Denmark, and Ireland, these countries may offer lessons to others regarding policies discouraging early retirement.

Increasing the number of contributors to a retirement system through a higher labor force participation rate for younger age groups could also alleviate the burden of pensions, although obviously this action would depend on resolving the problem of high unemployment. Higher participation might also be achieved by improving both employment incentives and prospects for those of working age who are not currently active in the work force. Labor market deregulation is an important method to pursue. Providing child care facilities (as in Scandinavia) and investing in training the young could also be helpful. It is notable that the Scandinavian countries (and the United Kingdom) show the highest rates of labor force participation in the EU, and relatively high fertility rates.

Among other reforms of social security pensions, price indexation instead of wage indexation of benefits, reductions in replacement ratios and, where feasible, switching from an insurance-based structure to a basic plan offering flat-rate pensions would seem appropriate. Such a switch would take care of the poorest workers, who find that making required contributions is difficult, while inducing the wealthier to save for their retirement. Other options include cutting credits for higher education, reducing privileges for public employees, and tightening controls on eligibility for disability pensions. Taxing the elderly in line with taxing working-age people can also help to spread the burden of an aging population. More generally, the need to correct public finance positions before significant aging sets in gives a powerful justification for fiscal consolidation.

Among overall reforms, funding of private pensions could provide considerable assistance to social security, although given the advantage of pay-as-you-go plans in alleviating poverty and the costs of refinancing the accrued liabilities of social security, private pensions may not entirely supplant the public systems. Funded plans have the advantage of being actuarially fair and thus minimize distortions of incentives in labor and financial markets, which helps increase economic efficiency and growth. Funding also provides the domestic economy with long-term saving; it may raise saving per se and improve long-term growth potential. It offers the possibility of burden sharing on a global scale through international investment by residents of industrialized countries in emerging markets. Funding helps the elderly by diversifying risk and potentially offers greater security in their claims for retirement income (property rights as opposed to the "contract" between the generations). But private plans also have such disadvantages as investment risk in the case of defined-contribution funds and hindrance of labor mobility for defined-benefit funds.[113]

The extent to which private pensions have developed varies considerably among EU countries. Crowding out by social security as well as fiscal and regulatory difficulties stunt their growth in many. It is no coincidence that the countries facing the greatest difficulties with aging populations are those with generous social security plans and few funded plans, while those in a favorable situation, such as the United Kingdom, Ireland, and the Netherlands, have well-developed funded sectors.

Study of the policies adopted in these latter countries is therefore warranted. Curtailing social security promises for higher-income earners, tax deductibility of pension contributions and asset returns, and prudent-man rules to enable asset management to find appropriate trade-offs between risks and returns are among the key policies to pursue. Compulsory provision of private pensions is another option.[114] National experience suggests that funding may also be increased by allowing employees to leave an earnings-related social security plan and join an equivalent private plan, funding civil service pensions, and widening coverage by encouraging people to contribute to personal pensions.

Nevertheless, countries with generous social security benefits must face the difficulties of financing the transition toward greater reliance on funding. One generation may resist paying twice, once for their parents' pay-as-you-go pension and once for their own funded pensions. A reduction in the benefit promises of pay-as-you-go systems,

113. Hindrance of labor mobility is reduced or eliminated when "transfer circuits" are operating or benefits are based on average salaries (indexed appropriately to inflation).

114. Outside the European Union such a policy has been adopted in Australia and Switzerland, and within the EU there is compulsion for some sectors in Denmark and the Netherlands. The policy protects those who would otherwise not save for retirement, takes a greater proportion of employees out of social security than voluntary systems would, and may reduce biases in coverage under voluntary systems, such as a focus on male, white-collar, unionized workers. Less generous tax benefits may be offered, improving the fiscal situation. But there may be labor market distortions, and the unavoidable increase in employers' contributions may affect competitiveness.

a gradual shift to funding, and an equitable imposition of taxation on the elderly (including social security contributions), may be helpful in this respect.

Action at the level of the European Union may also prove helpful to the development of private pensions. Certainly, the objectives of the failed Pension Funds Directive—giving funds the freedom to offer services across borders, liberalizing investment throughout the Union, and allowing workers to join plans in member states that are not their homes—would all have been beneficial. Although the directive failed, the objectives are still being pursued by the European Commission in other forums.

Appendix: Pension Reform in the United Kingdom

The United Kingdom faces few of the difficulties in providing social security that beset other EU countries and has a well-developed private pension sector. This appendix provides further details of the social security reforms that have brought about this situation.[115]

Since the introduction of the compulsory social insurance plan after publication of the Beveridge Report in the 1940s, the United Kingdom has offered a basic pension, intended to provide a means of subsistence and a way of alleviating poverty. Benefits have varied in relation to average earnings. Until 1970 benefits were typically raised in an ad hoc manner and did not always keep pace with inflation. During the 1970s pensions were raised in line with increases in earnings or prices, whichever was greater, thus leading to a marked boost. Since the early 1980s benefits have been indexed only to prices. As a consequence of these policies, between 1948 and 1973 the pension increased twice as fast as prices, and peaked in 1977 at 20 percent of average earnings. By 1994 the ratio was 18 percent.

The basic pension is not adequate to provide income for retirement. Indeed, minimum income levels prescribed for social security purposes typically exceed the basic pension. A third of U.K. pensioners, about 3.1 million people, receive additional means-tested benefits. These benefits discourage saving because there are strict limits on the value of a person's assets before payment can be considered. But given

115. For additional detail see Davis (1997).

the growing inequality among pensioners, means-tested benefits do have the advantage of going only to those who really need them.

This basic system is supplemented by a state earnings-related pension scheme (SERPS) introduced in 1978 as a replacement for the more modest graduated pension introduced in 1961. From the start it was intended as a backup for the minority of the working population not in occupational pension funds. Entitlements are calculated as 1.25 percent of average revalued earnings for each year of membership of SERPS up to twenty years. The best twenty years of earnings are revalued to the retirement date using the annual increase in average earnings. SERPS currently offers a maximum replacement ratio of 25 percent of revalued earnings. Consequently, in combination with the basic pension, a worker on average earnings with full contributions may currently obtain a replacement ratio of just over 40 percent. However, SERPS benefits are due to be cut back.

Contributions to SERPS are payable on income between about 0.2 and 1.3 times average earnings. Employee contributions for those contracted into SERPS (including basic pension entitlements) in 1995 are 2 percent of earnings at the lower earnings limit and rising to a maximum of 10 percent at the upper limit. Employer contributions are 3 percent at the lower limit and 10.2 percent at and above half the upper earnings limit. Those workers below the lower earnings limit are not entitled to SERPS and must rely on the basic pension (which is approximately equal to the lower earnings limit).

Neither the basic pension nor SERPS is funded; both are provided on a pay-as-you-go basis. The Government Actuary periodically assesses whether contribution rates need to be adjusted to keep the schemes solvent.

Concerned with the potential burden on future generations, in the 1986 Social Security Act the government reduced the maximum SERPS benefits from 25 percent to 20 percent of earnings as of April 1999. This was done by reducing the credit for years of contributions from 1.25 percent to 1 percent and changing the wage base from the best twenty years to a lifetime average. This could cut the pension of someone earning 120 percent of average earnings for the best twenty years of his career from 42 percent to 33 percent of final salary.[116] The

116. Atkinson (1991).

changes cast doubt on whether social security, even including SERPS, can provide adequate retirement income for those retiring after 2000 and dependent solely on social security.

Three further developments reinforce this conclusion. First, the replacement ratio may shrink further if the basic pension continues to be indexed to prices. Second, because the SERPS upper earnings limit is indexed to the basic pension, the ratio is falling as a proportion of average earnings. It has already fallen from 140 percent to 120 percent. If the rules are not changed, the upper earnings limit will be only 60 percent of average earnings in 2030, and the maximum SERPS entitlement could be as little as 10 percent of average earnings. Third, the 1995 Pensions Act had the effect of reducing SERPS entitlements further by changing the method of calculating the proportion of earnings on which the pension is paid. As a result of changes in indexation procedures, the amount of earnings from earlier years that count toward SERPS will fall, reducing the amount of the pension.[117] By 2040 this measure may cut the cost of SERPS in half in real terms.

A major element of the social security regulations that has underpinned the growth of occupational pension plans is the ability of employees to choose not to participate in SERPS. This emphasizes the point made earlier that SERPS is a backup for those unable or unwilling to use private pensions. Indeed, the freedom to leave earnings-related social security is one explanation for the high ratio of pension assets to GDP. The only other OECD country with such a system of opting out is Japan.

When employees with company pensions contract out in this way from all but the most basic state plan, there are corresponding reductions in employers' social security contributions equivalent to the estimated cost of providing the liability of the earnings-related pension through funding. This contracted-out contribution rebate was initially 7 percent of the difference in earnings between the upper and lower earnings limits; in 1995 it was 4.8 percent (1.8 percent for the employee and 3 percent for the employer). Not all pension funds take advantage of this system; some occupational funds are contracted in and thus only provide benefits above SERPS benefits, but the majority are contracted out. In 1991 some 9.7 million pension plan members (68 percent

---

117. Disney and Johnson (1995).

of employees) were contracted out and 1 million were contracted in. The latter represented 5 percent of employees; of these, 3 percent have SERPS plus a defined-benefit plan, and 2 percent have SERPS plus a defined-contribution plan. Twelve percent of employees were wholly dependent on SERPS.[118]

Most of those not participating in SERPS still take an occupational defined-benefit plan. This must at the time of writing offer a pension at least as good as the guaranteed minimum pension (GMP).[119] Before retirement the GMP is indexed up to 7.5 percent or average earnings, whichever is the lower, for early leavers; it is indexed after retirement at up to 3 percent. The GMP is roughly equivalent to the difference between the basic state pension and the SERPS earnings-related benefit. Because there is often a shortfall between the 3 percent guaranteed indexation from the employer and actual inflation, to which SERPS is indexed, a pensioner receiving the GMP would usually receive some social security pension to take him up to the SERPS level.[120] A contracted-out fund must also provide a widow's or widower's pension at a rate of half the member's pension. Pensions may not normally commence before age 50 nor after age 75.

Since 1988 there has also been the possibility of choosing an occupational or personal defined-contribution plan. This may involve either contributions at least as large as those required for the GMP or contributions at least equal to the contracted-out contribution rebate (as for defined-benefit funds). For a personal pension a minimum contribution, equal to the contracted-out contribution rebate, is paid by the government, although a person may also make further voluntary contributions to such personal pensions.[121] Social security regulations re-

118. The remaining 15 percent of employees either earned too little to reach the lower earnings limit (12 percent) and had no right to a supplementary pension or they paid the married woman's reduced contribution (3 percent).

119. The 1995 Pensions Act foreshadows abolition of the GMP as of April 1997 and its replacement by a requisite benefits test. The minimum pension will be based on that of a reference scheme accruing 1.25 percent for year of service applied to an earnings definition based on 90 percent of the member's earnings that would qualify for SERPS averaged over the last three years of service.

120. The 1995 Pensions Act proposes to remove this additional layer of protection, so that existing rights to the GMP would only be indexed up to 3 percent.

121. Because people often do not make further contributions, there is a risk of extremely low replacement ratios for a significant proportion of people holding personal pensions.

quire the division of such personal pensions into two parts; first, the national insurance rebate, which is used to buy a so-called protected-rights pension equivalent to SERPS, and the remainder, the so-called personal fund that includes employees' and employers' contributions. Regulations state that the protected-rights element of personal pensions must be taken at the earliest at age 60 and indexed up to a 3 percent inflation rate. The disposition of the remainder is more flexible in terms of timing and type of annuity; 25 percent of the value of the fund at retirement (excluding the protected rights) can be obtained as a tax-free lump sum.

In both defined-benefit and defined-contribution plans there is a safety net; a person who is contracted out may still receive some earnings-related pension if the guaranteed minimum pension payable from a pension fund falls short of the amount of social security to which the employee would have been entitled if not contracted out.[122] Equally, the protected rights element of a personal or defined-contribution fund is guaranteed.

Besides providing the general chance to opt out of SERPS, from 1988 to 1993 the government offered special incentives to workers without a company pension plan who were thus dependent on SERPS to take a personal (defined-contribution) pension instead of an earnings-related state pension. Inducements were rebates of past contributions to the earnings-related plan and an option to reenter, as well as an increase of 2 percent in the rebate. In 1993 the bonus was reduced to 1 percent for workers older than 30 in an attempt to discourage them from contracting back into SERPS.

One may conclude that social security in the United Kingdom has proceeded from modest intentions and been reduced significantly in its scope and ambition in recent years. This may reflect a "political risk" stemming from conflicts over the cost of social security pensions and the burden of the system on successive generations.[123] The result has been that pensioners receive social security benefits that are unrelated to those they were promised when they entered the labor force. In effect, there would appear to be a risk of poverty for those retiring on social security pensions in the future. This risk has provided a

122. Henceforth, the cover will only be for the more modest requisite benefits test.
123. Dilnot and others (1994).

major spur to the development of private pensions and notably in recent years, personal pensions.

References

Aaron, H. J. 1966. "The social insurance paradox." *Canadian Journal of Economic and Political Science* 32: 371–77.

Atkinson, A. B. 1991. "The development of state pensions in the United Kingdom." Discussion paper WPS/58. STICERD, London School of Economics.

Auerbach, A. J., and others. 1989. "The economic dynamics of an aging population: The case of four OECD countries." Department of Economics and Statistics Working Paper 62. Paris: OECD.

Balassa, B. 1984. "The economic consequences of social policies in the industrial countries." *Weltwirtschaftliches Archiv*, 2/84: 213–27.

Barro, R. J. 1974. "Are government bonds net wealth?" *Journal of Political Economy* 82: 1095–1117.

Besseling, P. J., and R. F. Zeeuw. 1993. "The financing of pensions in Europe: Challenges and opportunities." Research memorandum 111. Central Planning Bureau, netherlands.

Bikker, J. A. 1996. "National savings, the current account and aging populations: A pension fund model." *Economic and Financial Modelling* (Summer): 1–20.

Bodie, Z., and R. C. Merton. 1992. "Pension benefit guarantees in the United States: A functional analysis." In R. Schmitt, ed., *The future of pensions in the United States*. University of Pennsylvania Press.

Börsch-Supan, A. 1996. "The impact of population aging on savings, investment and growth in the OECD area." In *Future global capital shortages: Real threat or pure fiction?* Paris: OECD.

Bos, E. 1994. *World population projections 1994–95*. Washington: World Bank.

Cohen, N., and E. Tucker. 1995. "Fund investment rules 'a matter of sovereignty.'" *Financial Times* (May 10).

Cutler, D., and others. 1990. "An aging society: Opportunity or challenge?" *Brookings Papers on Economic Activity* 1.

Davis, E. P. 1990. "International investment of life insurance companies." *European Affairs*, Special Edition on the European Financial Symposium: 240–59.

———. 1993. "Problems of banking regulation: An EC perspective." LSE Financial Markets Group Special Paper.

———. 1995. *Pension Funds, Retirement-income security and capital markets: An international perspective*. Oxford University Press.

———. 1996a. "Pension fund investments." In B. Steil, ed., *The European Equity Markets*. London: Royal Institute of International Affairs.

———. 1996b. "International experience of pension fund reform and its applicability to the Netherlands," Working Paper 96-11. London: Pensions Institute, Birkbeck College.

———. 1996c. "The role of institutional investors in the evolution of financial structure and behaviour." In M. Edey, ed., *The Future of the Financial System: Proceedings of a Conference.* Sydney: Reserve Bank of Australia.

———. 1997. *Private pensions in OECD countries: The United Kingdom.* Labour market and social policy occasional paper 21. Paris: Organization for Economic Cooperation and Development.

Diamond, P. A. 1993. "Privatization of social security: lessons from Chile." Working Paper 4510. National Bureau of Economic Research.

Dilnot, A., and others. 1994. *Pensions policy in the United Kingdom: An economic analysis.* London: Institute for Fiscal Studies.

Disney, R., and P. Johnson. 1995. "The strange death of a pension scheme." *Financial Times* (February 3).

European Federation for Retirement Provision. 1996. *European pension funds: Their impact on capital markets and competitiveness.* Brussels.

European Monetary Institute. 1996. "Progress towards convergence 1996." Frankfurt.

Ermisch, J. 1995. "Demographic developments and European labor markets." *Scottish Journal of Political Economy* 42: 331–46.

Eurostat. 1992. *Digest of statistics on social protection in Europe, vol. 1: Old Age.* Luxembourg.

———. 1993a. *Old age replacement ratios, vol. 1.* Luxembourg

———. 1993b. "Family budgets, comparative tables 1988: Old person or couple." Luxembourg.

———. 1995a. "Labor force survey results 1993." Luxembourg.

———. 1995b. "Social protection expenditure and receipts 1980–93." Luxembourg.

———. 1995c. "Demographic statistics 1995." Luxembourg.

Falkingham, J., and P. Johnson. 1993. "The life cycle distributional consequences of pay-as-you-go and funded pension systems: A microsimulation modelling analysis," paper prepared for World Bank study Income Security for Old Age.

Feldstein, M. 1974. "Social security, induced retirement and aggregate capital formation." *Journal of Political Economy* 82: 905–06.

———. 1977. "Social security and private saving: international evidence in an extended life cycle model." In M. Feldstein and R. Inman, eds., *The Economics of Public Services.* International Economic Association.

———. 1995a. "Social security and saving: new time series evidence." NBER Working Paper 5054.

———. 1995b. "Would privatizing social security raise economic welfare?" NBER Working Paper 5281.

Franco, D. 1995. "Pension liabilities: Their use and misuse in the assessment of fiscal policies." European Commission Economic Paper 110.

————. 1996. "The taxation of funded pension schemes and budgetary policy." European Commission Economic Paper 117.

Franco, D., and F. Frasca. 1992. "Public pensions in an aging society: The case of Italy." In J. Mortensen, ed., *The future of pensions in the European Community*. London: Brassey's for the Centre for European Policy Studies.

Franco, D., and T. Munzi. 1996. "Pension expenditure prospects in the European Union; a survey of national projections." *European Economy* 3: 1–126.

Frijns, J., and C. Petersen. 1992. "Financing, administration and portfolio management; how secure is the pension promise?" In *Private Pensions and Public Policy*. Paris: OECD.

Hagemann, R. P., and G. Nicoletti. 1989. "Aging populations; economic effects and implications for public finance." Department of Economics and Statistics Working paper 61. Paris: OECD.

Heller, P., and E. Sidgwick. 1987. "Aging, savings and the sustainability of the fiscal burden in the G-7 countries."

Heller, P., R. Hemming, and P. W. Kohnert. 1986. "Aging and social expenditures in major industrial countries 1980–2025," Occasional Paper 47. Washington: International Monetary Fund.

Holzmann, R. 1997. "On economic benefits and fiscal requirements of moving from unfunded to funded pensions," Forschungsbericht 9702. University of Saarland.

IMF. 1996. *World economic outlook, May 1996*. Washington: International Monetary Fund.

Jack, A. 1997. "France prepares to top-up its private sector pensions." *Financial Times*, January 6.

Johnson, P., and K. F. Zimmerman. 1993. *Labor markets in an aging Europe*. Cambridge University Press.

Keyfitz, N. 1985. "The demography of unfunded pensions." *European Journal of Population* 1: 5–30.

Kuné, J. B. 1996. "The hidden liabilities: meaning and consequences." Paper presented at the CPB seminar series, November 26, 1996, the Hague.

Lannoo, K. 1996. "The draft Pension Funds Directive and the financing of pensions in the EU." *Geneva Papers* 78: 114–26.

Leibfritz, W., and others. 1996. "Aging populations, pension systems and government budgets—how do they affect saving?" In *Future global capital shortages—real threat or pure fiction?* Paris: OECD.

Masson, P., and R. W. Tryon. 1990. "Macroeconomic effects of projected population aging in industrial countries." IMF Staff Papers 37: 453–85.

Masson, P., T. Bayoumi, and H. Samiei. 1995. "International evidence on the determinants of private saving." IMF Working Paper W95/51.

Miles, D. 1996. "Demographics and saving; can we reconcile the evidence?" Imperial College, London.

Miles, D., and B. Patel. 1996. "Saving and wealth accumulation in Europe, the outlook into the next century." Merrill Lynch Financial Research, June 3.

Munnell, A. H. 1987. "The impact of public and private saving schemes on saving and capital formation." In *Conjugating public and private: the case of pensions*. International Social Security Association, Studies and Research 24: 219–36.

OECD. 1988. *Reforming public pensions*. Paris.

———. 1993. *Pension liabilities in the seven major industrial countries*. Paris.

———. 1995. *Economic Outlook*. Paris.

Oxley, H., and M. MacFarlan. 1994. "Health care reform: controlling spending and increasing efficiency." Economic Department Working Paper 149. Paris: OECD.

Roseveare, D., and others. 1996. "Aging populations, pension systems and government budgets: simulation for 20 OECD countries." Economics Department Working Paper 168. Paris: OECD.

Schlesinger, H. 1985. "Die Finanzierung der sozialen Sicherheitssysteme bei geringerem wirtschaftlichem Wachstum und schrumpfender Bevölkerung." In *Veränderungen in der Arbeitswelt und soziale Sicherung*, Band 28. Wiesbaden: Verlag Chmielorz.

Thompson, L. H. 1992. "Social security surpluses." *New Palgrave dictionary of money and finance*. Macmillan.

Vittas, D. 1992. "The simple(r) algebra of pension plans." Washington: World Bank.

World Bank. 1994. *Averting the old age crisis: policies to protect the old and promote growth*. Washington.

Wattenburg, B. 1987. *The birth dearth*. Pharos Books.

Wyatt Data Services. 1993. *1993 benefits report Europe USA*. Brussels.

Chapter 3

Population Aging and French Economic Performance

Didier Blanchet

F RANCE has a long tradition of concern for demographic problems in general and problems of aging in particular. This concern is usually attributed to the relative anteriority of its demographic transition and explains, for instance, the rather prochild orientation of French family policy.[1] Paradoxically, however, it was not until the beginning of the 1990s that significant public debate emerged about the main consequence of the aging of the population—its implications for pensions.

There are at least three reasons for this tardy recognition. First, after a highly symbolic reform of the pension system occurred in 1983 that lowered the normal retirement age to 60 and was the final outcome of an old claim by labor unions, the time was not ripe for opening a debate about demographics whose apparent conclusion was that the reform had occurred at the wrong time. Second, the publicity occasionally given to demographic problems had generally been suspected to serve particular interests, mainly those of private insurers. Right or wrong, this suspicion weakened the credibility of pension projections. Third, the very activism of the most highly pronatalist circles could by reaction have generated skepticism or even opposition to the idea that population aging was a matter of importance. One episode of this opposition was a heated debate in 1991 concerning the means of projecting demographic trends.[2]

These factors also explain why, when collective contemplation of

1. Chesnais (1986).
2. See Le Bras (1992) for a description of this episode by one of its protagonists.

pensions finally started, it did so in highly unconsensual way: a conflict between those who wished to make the demographic problem seem worse and those who denied any relation of demographic projections with their supposed consequences. This was a conflict between the advocates of a transition toward partially funded plans that relied on private initiative and those who preferred to stick to the public pay-as-you-go pension plans.

Some of these conflicts continue to structure the debate, but the consequences of population aging are now better understood, most notably the long-term links with increases in life expectancy. The necessity of adjusting existing pension systems is no longer denied. In fact, some of these adjustments had to be anticipated, even if it was for reasons that, at the moment, are linked to the poor economic performance of the French economy in recent years.

In this context this chapter presents the main facts and current projections about French population trends and its pension systems. It then discusses the reforms introduced, especially the 1993 reform of the régime général, and finally turns to the debate about the opportunity for creating pension funds on top of existing pay-as-you-go plans and rethinking long-term policy concerning retirement age. Even if the 1993 reform includes some dispositions that should affect, in the long run, the average retirement age, the problem of the transition between activity and retirement remains an acute problem because of the very large disconnection between the beginning of the retirement period and actual exits from the labor force. Finally, the chapter examines the consequences of aging in other domains to consider whether the pension problem is indeed the most important of the problems raised by population aging or whether it is only one part of a more widespread and dramatic socioeconomic challenge.

Demographics and Other Data

The most commonly used demographic projections are those by the Institut National de la Statistique et des Etudes Economique (INSEE). The latest available make three assumptions about future fertility levels, one about life expectancy, and one about migration.[3] These

3. Dinh (1994).

TABLE 3-1. *Demographic Characteristics, Selected Years, 1950–95, and Projected to 2050 (Medium Scenario)*
Thousands unless otherwise specified

Year	Total fertility rate	Life expectancy at birth Male	Life expectancy at birth Female	Population	Age distribution 0–14	Age distribution 15–64	Age distribution 65 and older
1950	2.93	63.40	69.20	41,647	9,380	27,540	4,727
1960	2.73	67.00	73.60	45,465	11,927	28,250	5,288
1970	2.47	68.40	75.90	50,528	12,582	31,472	6,474
1980	1.94	70.20	78.40	53,731	12,088	34,102	7,541
1990	1.78	72.80	81.00	56,577	11,389	37,316	7,872
1995	1.78	73.70	82.00	58,048	11,519	37,863	8,666
2000	1.79	74.60	83.00	59,412	11,420	38,548	9,444
2005	1.80	75.50	83.90	60,642	11,242	39,412	9,988
2010	1.80	76.40	84.80	61,721	11,018	40,314	10,389
2015	1.80	77.20	85.70	62,648	10,795	40,125	11,728
2020	1.80	78.00	86.50	63,453	10,671	39,682	13,100
2025	1.80	78.80	87.20	64,177	10,604	39,188	14,385
2030	1.80	79.50	87.90	64,790	10,515	38,612	15,663
2035	1.80	80.20	88.60	65,212	10,373	38,075	16,764
2040	1.80	80.90	89.20	65,374	10,205	37,469	17,700
2045	1.80	81.60	89.80	65,301	10,059	37,312	17,930
2050	1.80	82.20	90.40	65,098	9,956	36,911	18,231

Source: INSEE.

assumptions can be justified on the following grounds. Between 1950 and 1995 life expectancy in France increased from 63.4 to 73.7 years for men and 69.2 to 81.9 years for women (table 3-1). This evolution is reflected in figure 3-1, which indicates the extrapolations of life expectancy used in various official projections performed since 1954. These extrapolations have usually been conservative, especially during the 1970s when life expectancy was increasing slowly, suggesting a kind of saturation effect. Projections made in 1985 introduced two assumptions: a central trend and a variant with low mortality. The first was used as the basis of most pension projections in the first half of the 1990s (especially the white paper on pensions issued in 1991). But it now seems the low-mortality variant was the closest to actual trends: life expectancy in the past decade has increased by three months a year.

FIGURE 3-1. *Actual Life Expectancy and Various Projections, 1950–2040*

Years

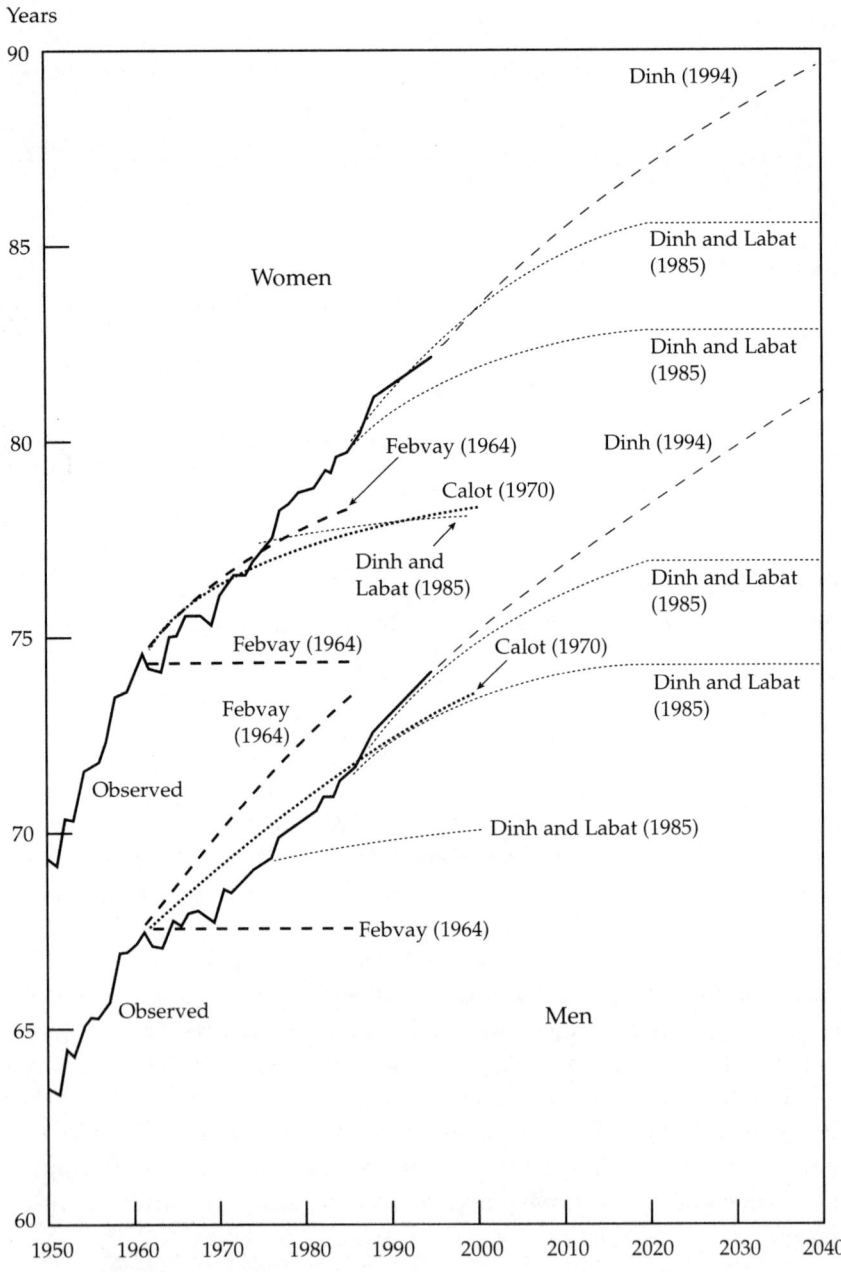

Source: Vallin (1991), updated by the author.

As a consequence, the new projections show a stronger aging of the population: life expectancy is projected to reach 82.2 years for men and 90.4 years for women in 2050. Perhaps these new assumptions are too high (indeed, life expectancy increased by only one month in 1995), but this chapter will use these projections.

The fertility rate reached a second postwar peak in 1965 (2.9 births per woman), then declined to a plateau of about 1.8 from 1975 to 1990, with only a minor temporary increase at the beginning of the 1980s. This plateau has been higher than levels in some neighboring countries such as Germany, and long-term levels of 1.8 and 2.1 were the two assumptions INSEE used for projections in 1979 and 1985. In 1992–94 the rate dropped below 1.7. This led INSEE to add to its fertility scenarios a low variant with a rate declining to 1.5 (table 3-2).

Assumptions concerning immigration also raise problems. Flows reached a peak of 200,000 net entries a year around 1970. Restrictive measures were taken in 1974 that resulted in a steep decline in the registered immigration of workers, partly compensated for by an increase in registered immigration of family members and, very probably, by an increase in illegal immigration, partly converted into official flows, however, by some exceptional measures of regularization (as in 1981). Until 1985 INSEE chose to perform its projections with a conventional assumption of zero net immigration. But this assumption has been relaxed in the latest projections, which now assume an annual net immigration of 50,000 workers (table 3-3).

The main results of these assumptions are presented in tables 3-1 and 3-2. Even with the fertility level of 1.8, which is below the replacement ratio, total population will increase until the middle of the next century because of demographic momentum and immigration. Thus the demographic problem is not basically one of population shrinkage. But all indicators suggest that population aging is unavoidable. This can be observed for the aged dependency ratios (the ratios of those aged 65 or older to those aged 15 to 64) shown in table 3-2. This is also true for the ratios of those older than age 60 to those age 20 to 60 (figure 3-2), which more adequately reflect the current age profile of labor force participation rates shown in table 3-4. Both are expected to double between now and 2050. One difference is, however, that their upturns at the beginning of the next century will not occur at the same time because the upturns correspond to the periods when the first

TABLE 3-2. *Dependency Ratio under Three Fertility Assumptions,*
Selected Years, 1995–2050

Year	Dependency[a]	Fertility					
Actual							
1950	17.16	2.93					
1960	18.72	2.73					
1970	20.57	2.47					
1980	22.11	1.94					
1990	21.10	1.78					

	Medium fertility		Low fertility		High fertility	
	Dependency[a]	Fertility	Dependency[a]	Fertility	Dependency[a]	Fertility
Projected						
1995	22.89	1.78	22.89	1.65	22.89	1.87
2000	24.50	1.79	24.50	1.57	24.50	1.97
2005	25.34	1.80	25.34	1.52	25.34	2.04
2010	25.77	1.80	25.84	1.50	25.72	2.07
2015	29.23	1.80	29.57	1.50	28.97	2.10
2020	33.01	1.80	33.83	1.50	32.39	2.10
2025	36.71	1.80	38.20	1.50	35.55	2.10
2030	40.57	1.80	42.92	1.50	38.72	2.10
2035	44.03	1.80	47.46	1.50	41.35	2.10
2040	47.24	1.80	52.10	1.50	43.52	2.10
2045	48.05	1.80	54.38	1.50	43.33	2.10
2050	49.39	1.80	57.59	1.50	43.46	2.10

Source: INSEE.
a. Ratio of persons 65 and older to those aged 15–64.

baby boom cohorts will move from the denominator to the numerator of the two ratios. This move will occur five years earlier if the limit between the two groups is advanced by five years.

It is interesting to separate more explicitly these numerator and denominator effects and their contribution to the changes of the ratios. Is the increasing ratio to be explained by a decrease of the number of people in working-age groups or by an increase of the number of people older than 60? Figure 3-3 shows the evolution of populations older than 60 and those between ages 20 and 59 rescaled at the same common initial value of 100 in 1995. The number of people between 20 and 60, which is the only cohort to be affected by future fertility trends, contributes little to the overall increase of the ratio. This

TABLE 3-3. *Net Immigration, Selected Years, 1950–95, and Projected to 2050*

Year	Net migration
1950	35,000
1960	140,000
1970	179,900
1980	44,000
1990	80,000
1995	50,000
2000	50,000
2050	50,000

Source: INSEE.

confirms that, unlike the situation in countries with very low fertility levels, France's demographic problem is not basically a shortage in the potential labor force. Most of the problem is due to the increasing number of people older than the retirement age, which is itself explained by the replacement of old pensioners belonging to small or normal cohorts by pensioners belonging to large cohorts, and the fact that people in these larger cohorts will have survived in larger proportions until retirement age and after, this being true even if future mortality decreases were to become more moderate.

The Structure of the Retirement System

The French retirement system is often considered complex, but its structure can be described succinctly. For most of the population (wage earners from the private sector), the pension relies on two pillars: the basic *régime général* and complementary plans. Both pillars are pay-as-you-go.

The general regime offers contributory benefits corresponding to the share of wages below the social security ceiling (about Fr 12,000 a month). Table 3-5 shows numbers of contributors and beneficiaries since the 1960s. I sum up here the rules that applied at the beginning of the 1990s, that is, after the 1983 reform that introduced retirement at age 60 but before the reform introduced in 1993 that will be discussed later. Under these rules the pension was computed on the basis of the number of years during which contributions were made (trun-

FIGURE 3-2. *Aged Dependency Ratio under Three Fertility Assumptions, 1990–2049*

Percent

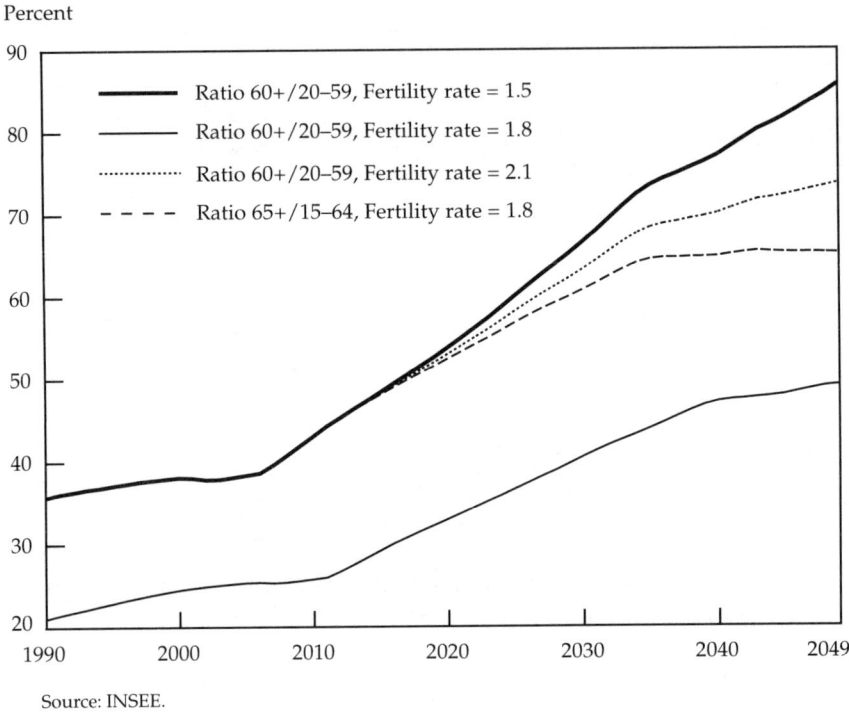

Source: INSEE.

cated to 37.5 years) and to a reference wage that used to be the average wage of the ten best years of a pensioner's working life (past nominal wages being reevaluated at time of liquidation according to retrospective coefficients). The formula was therefore:

$$\text{Pension} = \alpha \times \left[\frac{\text{no. of years (truncated to 37.5)}}{37.5} \right] \times \frac{\text{average wage}}{\text{of 10 best years,}}$$

the proportionality coefficient α being itself modulated. It was maximal when the pensioner left at age 60 with 37.5 years of contributions or more: in that case the value of the proportionality coefficient α was equal to 50 percent and exactly ensured a replacement rate of the reference wage (not necessarily the last wage) equal to 50 percent. The same value of α also applied whatever the number of contributed years

TABLE 3-4. *Labor Force Participation Rates, by Gender and Age Group, Selected Years, 1965–95*
Percent

Year	15–19	20–24	25–29	30–34	35–39	40–44	45–49	50–54	55–59	60–64	65–69	70–74	74+
Men
1965	46.30	83.30	96.30	98.80	98.80	98.50	97.60	93.90	86.30	72.60	41.30	23.80	10.10
1970	36.70	81.50	96.20	98.40	98.80	97.60	96.80	93.60	82.50	65.20	24.90	12.00	5.50
1975	29.90	81.50	95.50	98.70	98.40	97.90	96.50	93.70	82.90	54.50	19.30	8.20	3.60
1980	25.60	80.00	95.00	98.30	98.50	97.80	96.70	93.20	80.90	47.00	11.90	4.80	2.20
1985	20.60	79.40	95.70	98.00	98.50	97.70	96.50	92.50	69.90	30.30	8.40	3.10	1.50
1990	15.00	66.20	95.00	97.80	98.00	97.60	96.90	91.90	71.80	23.20	5.10	1.80	1.30
1995	9.10	56.70	94.00	97.90	97.80	97.40	96.20	92.40	70.90	18.20	3.30	1.40	0.50
Women
1965	35.10	63.40	48.90	38.70	42.20	46.60	46.90	47.90	44.40	35.70	19.40	9.20	3.70
1970	27.30	63.80	54.80	48.20	45.70	48.40	50.00	49.10	45.80	33.70	14.00	7.10	2.40
1975	23.30	65.70	62.90	57.70	55.00	53.80	53.60	51.10	43.20	29.30	10.60	3.70	1.80
1980	18.20	67.20	69.80	65.50	63.20	60.80	57.70	54.30	46.70	27.00	6.00	2.20	1.30
1985	13.00	66.50	73.70	69.90	69.10	68.40	65.70	57.30	43.50	18.90	4.70	1.70	0.80
1990	8.20	59.30	79.10	75.30	72.60	74.90	69.10	63.20	48.00	19.00	3.50	0.80	0.30
1995	4.30	47.50	81.10	79.90	78.10	79.50	77.30	70.50	52.50	16.90	2.90	0.60	0.30

Source: INSEE.

FIGURE 3-3. *Relationships of Populations Aged 60 and Older and 20–59 to the Increase in the Dependency Ratio under Three Fertility Assumptions, 1990–2049*

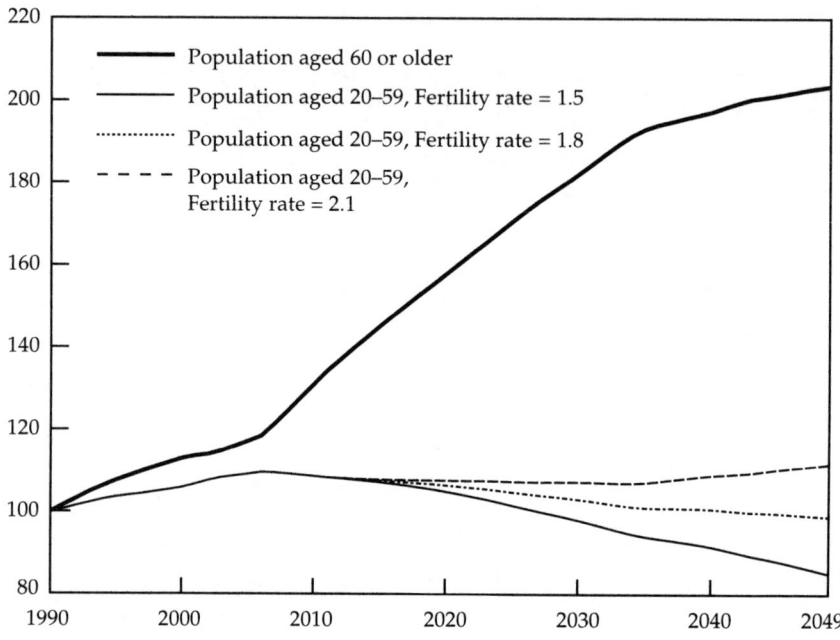

Index (1990 = 100)

Source: INSEE.

when the individual left at age 65 or between 60 and 65 under some special conditions (veterans, handicapped people, and so forth). In all other cases the coefficient is reduced: α declined by 1.25 percentage point for each term missing either to reach the duration of 37.5 years or the age of 65. For instance, somebody leaving at age 60 with twenty-five years of contributions or less would have an α of 25 percent, and this, given the number of years contributed, implied a replacement rate of the reference wage of only 16.66 percent. It is therefore in a limited sense that the system offered retirement at age 60. But because the conditions necessary to benefit from the full rate at the age of 60

TABLE 3-5. *Contributors to and Beneficiaries of the Régime Général,*
Selected Years, 1960–95
Thousands

Year	Contributors	Beneficiaries	Ratio of contributors to beneficiaries
1960	9,700	2,344	24.16
1965	11,500	2,679	23.29
1970	12,610	3,322	26.34
1975	13,016	4,138	31.79
1980	13,354	4,985	37.32
1985	12,944	6,000	46.35
1995	14,056	8,052	55.30

Source: INSEE.

were fulfilled by most people, the system in effect offered uncondi-
tional retirement at age 60.

The complementary pensions, the second pillar, are organized on
a socioprofessional basis. These pensions are offered by a large number of specific plans, but they are federated into two main groups
organizing interregime demographic compensation: AGIRC for *cadres*
(executive workers), covering the fraction of their wages exceeding the
social security ceiling, and ARRCO for other workers and executive's
wages below the ceiling. These plans are almost fully contributive.
Pensions are computed according to a system of points, which are
accumulated during workers' careers in proportion to their contributions. The pension is equal to this cumulated account multiplied by a
coefficient (*valeur du point*) that is one of the parameters that can be
modulated to equilibrate the system.

Besides this two-pillar structure, the major source of complexity of
the French system is the large number of exceptions to these general
rules. The exceptions are the result of two factors. When the general
regime was created in 1945, people who already benefited from more
generous dispositions (for example, people belonging to public or para-
public sectors) refused to join the new system. And some categories
preferred to adopt cheaper systems offering less protection because
they thought that a large part of their retirement needs was likely
to be covered by such other sources as professional capital for the

FIGURE 3-4. *Labor Force Participation Rates for Men Aged 50–75 at Successive Censuses, 1954–90*

Percent

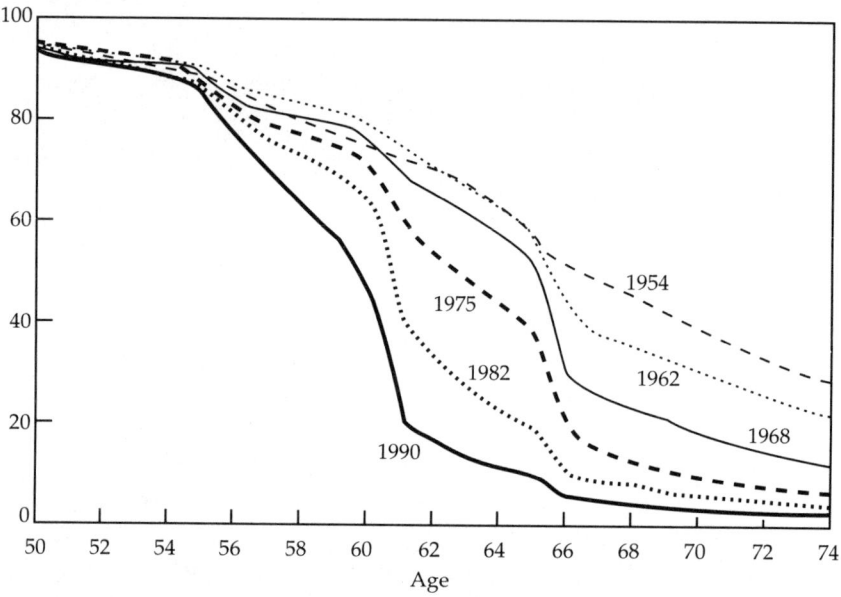

Source: INSEE.

self-employed. There are thus a multiplicity of *régimes spéciaux* and *régimes de non salariés* applying specific rules. In particular, civil servants are not really covered by an autonomous pension system because their pensions are paid directly out of the state budget.

Finally, for all categories of people, there exists a minimum pension (*minimum vieillesse*), which is a means-tested allowance that applies to a shrinking population (due to the increasing coverage by normal pensions). The population benefiting from this allowance is now a little over 1 million, as opposed to 2.55 million in 1959.[4]

The labor force participation of those about age 60 has decreased considerably in the past few decades and is among the lowest in a developed country. Figure 3-4 shows detailed participation rates by single-year age groups at successive censuses. The decline in participation around

4. Commissariat Général du Plan (1995).

age 60 is not only due to the dropping of the normal retirement age in 1983: the process started before and continued after, thanks to the development of early retirement systems.

Preretirement was introduced in France after the first oil shock under the heading *garanties de ressources.* Any person who lost a job after age 60 was assured 60 to 70 percent of his final income until age 65, which was then the normal retirement age. This system was extended in 1983 and covered up to 400,000 people, roughly one-fourth of the population aged 60 to 64. It is in this sense that retirement at age 60 was introduced in 1983. Thus this highly symbolic reform acted as a pure substitution, normal pensioners progressively replacing people benefiting from the *garantie de ressources,* and this explains why the reform did not produce any significant growth of labor force participation.

This does not mean however that the reform was completely neutral. First, it changed considerably the nature and the reversibility of the protection that was offered: there was a shift from a kind of unemployment insurance to a quasi-universal pension. Second, this change created an additional impetus to retire before age 60. The introduction of retirement at 60 was initially expected to eliminate the necessity of any form of preretirement. But, in the face of a still rising rate of unemployment and in a period of rapid industrial reconversion, it quickly became unavoidable to reintroduce some form of special safety net before entry into normal retirement at 60.

This was done in two ways, in proportions that have varied over time and that reflect the fluctuating desire by the state to exert strong control over the process. The first tool was the Fonds National de l'Emploi, a government agency that finances one form of allocation (ASFNE). People who are entitled to such benefits have left their firms under specific conditions resulting from a negotiation between the firm and the state. The second tool, which implies much less control, consists in a specific disposition of the French system of unemployment insurance. Under the common rule, people who become unemployed are entitled to compensation for a limited time. Since 1992 this compensation has decreased with the duration of unemployment. But the rules do not apply to people past a certain age who lose their jobs (age 57 until mid-1993, now age 58). These unemployed can receive full compensation until they are able to qualify for a normal pension at a

TABLE 3-6. *Income Structure for Households with Head Older than 60, 1995*

Income Type	Upper quintile	Percent	Lower quintile	Percent
Household size	1.97	. . .	1.45	. . .
Income (francs)				
Pensions	149,900	58.0	33,600	71.0
Labor income	66,300	25.2	3,200	6.8
Property income	46,800	17.8	1,300	2.7
Minimum old age income	100	0	7,000	14.8
Housing subsidies	0	0	0	4.7
Total	263,100	100.0	47,300	100.0

Source: Hourriez and Legris (1995).

full rate. This system is not officially described as a preretirement system, and there is actually one strong difference between it and a pension system. People cannot enter into it completely freely; they can do so only if they have been laid off by their employers. Yet the extension made by this system raises some strong financial problems, and the question is often asked whether this is actually the best way to deal with employment problems of older workers, especially in the context of population aging.

Sources of Living and Relative Standard of Living of Retired People

The various pension incomes or other public subsidies constitute most of the incomes for low-income households with heads older than age 60 (table 3-6). Labor and property income are greater for the highest quintile, although pensions still provide more than half of their incomes. The result of these various income sources is an average standard of living for retired households that is roughly at parity with the average standard of living of households participating in the labor force (figure 3-5). This contrasts with the situation that still prevailed during the 1970s and that led to a strong policy in favor of pension revalorization.

Some additional observations can be made. First, it is mainly young retirees who benefit from a comfortable standard of living: the mechanical relation between pensions and past wages results in strong cohort effects among the retired population. Second, it is mainly young

FIGURE 3-5. *Standard of Living by Modified Consumption Units and Age of Household Head*

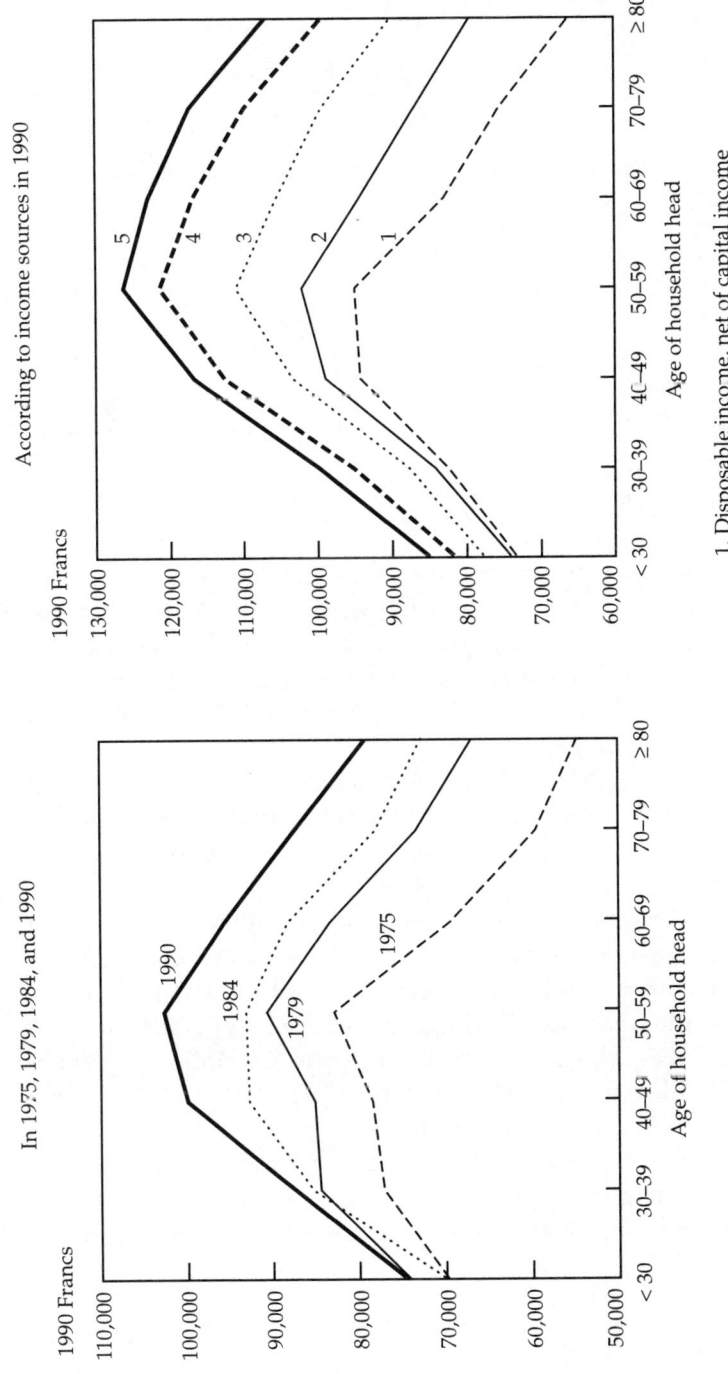

In 1975, 1979, 1984, and 1990

According to income sources in 1990

1. Disposable income, net of capital income
2. Disposable income, according to the survey on fiscal income
3. Noncapital disposable income + adjusted capital income
4. (3) + rental value of housing
5. (4) + reimbursed medical expenditures

Source: Hourriez and Legris (1995).

TABLE 3-7. *Dispersion of Income by Modified Consumption Units, and Age of Household Head, 1995*

Age	Interdecile ratio	Gini coefficient
Total	3.7	0.300
Younger than 30	3.4	0.255
30 to 39	3.3	0.273
40 to 49	3.7	0.303
50 to 59	4.4	0.331
60 to 69	3.5	0.301
70 to 79	3.4	0.287
80 or older	3.6	0.299
Younger than 60	3.7	0.301
60 or older	3.5	0.296

Source: Hourriez and Legris (1995).

workers who appear to be in an unfavorable position because of their specific difficulties in entering the labor market. Third, welfare comparisons between households of different ages appear to be sensitive to the equivalence scales that are used to weight the different members of households. The ones used for figure 3-5 are modified consumption units that assume a uniform weight of 0.35 for all people in the household in excess of the first adult.[5] As compared to the more traditional Oxford scale used in previous studies, it implies a lower weight for the second adult and a deterioration of the relative position of single-person households, including those of widows.[6]

Finally, total resources of older people appear still higher when the rental value of owner-occupied housing and the money equivalent of reimbursed health expenditures is included. But these two elements may be subject to discussion: living in a dwelling that is too big does not have the same welfare effect as a money income equal to its rental value, and health reimbursements are not a net resource but a compensation for a weakened health status.

Income inequality within the retired population is of the same order of magnitude as it is among people in working age groups (table 3-7). Finally, table 3-8 complements the information on standards of living

5. Hourriez and Legris (1995).
6. The Oxford equivalence scale used to consider the second adult as equivalent to 0.7 consumption units, and children as equivalent to 0.5.

TABLE 3-8. *Living Arrangements for People 65 or Older, 1996*
Percent

Arrangement	Men	Women	Total
Living as a couple, with or without children	75.0	38.1	52.7
Living alone	15.5	40.3	30.5
Without spouse in a multiperson household	6.0	14.9	11.3
Not in a household	3.6	6.7	5.5

Source: Desplanques (1996).

by showing the types of living arrangements for people 65 and older. More than 80 percent of people in this age group live either with their spouse or alone. Two-thirds of the rest live in multiperson households, which will generally be the households of their children, and one-third live in institutions.

The Pension Debate

The demographic projections I have presented are the latest available, but their results are not qualitatively different from those that were available in the early 1980s. These earlier projections led during the 1990s to a series of reports that tried to assess their effects on future pension burdens.[7] So most of the diagnosis about pensions was already available. But the influence of the reports often remained limited to academic or administrative circles. When pension problems were raised in public debates, it was generally as an argument for life insurance, that is, in a way that seemed strongly biased in favor of the private interest of insurance companies.

The debate assumed a significant public dimension that motivated the publication in 1992 of a *livre blanc* (white book) on pensions that was widely diffused and was expected to lay the grounds for a socially acceptable reform.[8] The book noted that, after correcting for household size and structure, the standards of living of working and retired households were similar. The conclusion was that there was no more need for the 1970s' and early 1980s' revalorizations of pensions that had been intended to progressively reduce the earnings gap between

7. Malabouche (1987).
8. Commissariat Général du Plan (1992).

workers and retired people. The report also reaffirmed a strong attachment to pay-as-you-go financing and left the field of pension funding or prefinancing to private initiative. Finally, although it did not question directly the retirement age of 60, the white book suggested that the age could be indirectly changed by modifying conditions necessary to get pensions at a full rate at age 60.

No immediate reform was initiated when the report was published. Administrative reflection went on as additional reports that more or less reproduced the basic observations of the white book were published. These diagnoses were also prepared by French insurers, but with different conclusions, of course, concerning the opportunity of voluntarist action in building supplementary prefinanced pensions.[9]

During the summer of 1993 the Balladur government passed a reform that applied to the *régime général* and some assimilated plans. It consisted in the three following points.

—After their liquidation, pensions would be indexed on prices instead of net or gross wages. This measure would reduce the relative standard of living of older pensioners. In fact, it is essentially a confirmation of what had become standard practice during the 1980s. Nevertheless, in case of rapid increases of net wages (high productivity growth), the possibility of some occasional and discretionary reindexation remains.

—Retiring at age 60 remains possible, but to benefit from the full rate, pensioners will need progressively longer working lives to qualify: from 37.5 years under the initial rule to 40 years for people retiring in 2003.

—The reference wage on which the pension depends will be computed on a progressively greater number of years than the ten years used under initial conditions: this duration will increase by one year for each successive annual cohort of retirees until it reaches twenty-five years for those retiring in 2008.

No similar reform has yet been applied to any of the *régimes spéciaux*. For complementary programs, measures have mainly consisted in increasing contribution rates and moderating the *valeur du point*. These programs also suppressed a few noncontributory benefits. The ARRCO agreement that was concluded in February 1993 created a

9. Fédération Française des Sociétés d'Assurance (1991).

gradual increase in the basic contribution rate from 4 percent in 1993 to 6 percent in 1999 and introduced a short-term adjustment of the basic rate of return from 13.8 percent in 1993 to 13.3 percent in 1995.[10] The AGIRC aggreement that was concluded in February 1994 also increased the basic contribution rate (from 12 percent in 1994 to 16 percent in 2003) and introduced a short-term reduction in the rate of return.

Contrary to all expectations, the reform of the general regime, as well as the more punctual adjustments of the complementary plans, did not prompt any large social protest. This suggested that the white book had fulfilled its purpose of preparing public opinion for a major reform. It also created the temporary feeling that the pension problem was solved.

Is this judgment valid? There is no doubt that the reform was an important signal. However, it is also clear that the solutions it brought are only partial. First, it is still not certain that people fully recognize the necessity for the adjustments. One must remember the resistance to the extension of the 1993 reform to special regimes, which was one of the dominant aspects of the conflict that arose after the fall 1995 presentation of the Juppé plan of reform for the whole system of social protection. More recently, a decline in the average age of retirement has reemerged in a sporadic way for specific socioeconomic groups and even for the whole population.

Second, projections showed that the reform would solve problems through the first decade of the 2000s but was inadequate to face the demographic constraints of the period to follow. The development of additional prefinanced pensions remains slow, and the institutional context in which they should be developed remains a matter of controversy, even if it seems that there is convergence toward a final compromise.

10. The rate of return in these regimes is defined as the amount of yearly pension that can be obtained with 1 franc of contribution. A return of 13.8 percent means that 1 franc of contribution, at any point during the working period, entitles the worker to 0.138 franc of additional yearly benefits. In an equilibrium state, this rate of return is equal to the inverse of the average duration of retirement (that is, if retirement lasts for twenty years, the equilibrium rate of return should be 5 percent, rather than the values of 10 to 15 percent that currently prevail and that clearly correspond to non-steady state conditions). This concept is not equivalent to the more standard concept of actuarial rate of return (which in a stationary state is equal to zero).

TABLE 3-9. *Increases in Contribution Rates Necessary to Equilibrate a Stylized Universal System, under Three Assumptions, Selected Years, 1990–2040*
Percent

Year	No reform	1993 reform	Extended reform
1990	18.9	18.9	18.9
2000	22.0	20.9	19.8
2015	32.0	28.0	24.0
2040	48.0	40.8	33.6

Source: Commissariat Général du Plan (1995). Contribution rates are computed as the ratios of total pensions to total crude wages (including income from individual activities).

The question of the effective retirement age remains crucial both because the way in which the Balladur reform will affect retirement behavior remains uncertain and because of the disconnection between normal retirement age and the actual age of exits from the labor force.

The Impact of Recent Reforms

A 1995 updating of the *livre blanc* allows for the impact of the reforms or changes introduced in 1993–94.[11] Two kinds of projections have been made. *National projections* use a fictitious universal plan that generally consists in transposing to the whole population and their full wages the rules that apply in the *régime général* to wages under ceiling.[12] These projections are easy to extrapolate far into the next century. *Detailed projections* for selected plans remain limited to the medium term (up to 2015).

Table 3-9 shows results from the first kind of projection. It shows the increases in contributions needed to equilibrate the fictitious universal system. The demographic scenario is the median one taken from projections by INSEE (fertility level of 1.8). Total factor productivity is expected to grow at 1.5 percent a year. Unemployment is expected to decline from 12.5 percent of the labor force to 8.5 percent by 2005–10. The table gives the results of three simulations: no reform; a scenario including the impact of the 1993 reform but limited to the general

11. Commissariat Général du Plan (1995).
12. Malabouche (1987); Vernière (1990a, 1990b).

regime; and an extended reform that would apply to the whole population and all wages (both below and above the ceiling).

Increases that would have been necessary without reform are impressive, partly because the whole burden of adjustment would be on the shoulders of workers. In that scenario a doubling of the dependency ratio implies a doubling of the contribution rate. A correlation would be that pensioners would receive a large and unjustified increase in their relative standard of living (it also doubles, both because the income of workers is diminished by contributions and because of the end of the system's maturation, which results in higher pension levels, all other things equal). The reform scenarios avoid part but not all of this problem. Even under the extended reform the relative standard of living of pensioners increases by 15.5 percent relative to that of workers. That relative gain results from computing pension benefits on the basis of past gross wages rather than wages net of contributions.

Tables 3-10 and 3-11 show demographic and financial projections for seven pension plans, including the general regime, ARRCO, and AGIRC, whose functioning was described earlier, and a few specialized regimes. Table 3-10 gives the demographic projections of contributors and pensioners, showing the differences in these plans' sizes and ratios of contributors to pensioners but also the simultaneous decreases in the ratios. In fact, it is only in plans with ratios that are already very low that the ratios are not expected to decrease further very much. Plans with higher ratios will see them decrease one-third by 2015, which is roughly consistent with the results of the broader demographic projections presented earlier.

In terms of expenditures, resources, and financial imbalance, the situations of the two groups of plans are again very different (table 3-11). The situation deteriorates most significantly for the special plans. For the *régime général*, ARRCO, and AGIRC, the relative deficit is more limited, thanks to the 1993 reform and the fact that for ARRCO and AGIRC pensions that begin after age 65 are the only ones taken into account, implying that problems of these regimes are delayed by five years and will not fully manifest themselves before 2015. Anyway, these simulations confirm that adjustments realized during the past few years are only a starting point for larger adjustments to come. In particular, the ARRCO-AGIRC agreements of 1993–94 already needed

TABLE 3-10. *Projected Pensioners and Contributors for Selected Pension Plans, Selected Years, 1995–2015*

Millions unless otherwise specified

Plan	1995	2000	2005	2010	2015
Total population					
Pensioners	11.582	12.152	12.611	14.102	15.617
Contributors	25.998	27.055	27.739	27.739	27.481
Contributors ÷ pensioners (percent)	2.24	2.23	2.20	1.97	1.75
Régime général					
Pensioners	8.052	9.207	10.226	11.884	13.590
Contributors	14.056	15.276	16.582	16.854	16.581
Contributors ÷ pensioners (percent)	1.75	1.66	1.62	1.42	1.22
Civil servants					
Pensioners	0.821	0.948	1.118	1.309	1.481
Contributors	2.075	2.075	2.075	2.075	2.075
Contributors ÷ pensioners (percent)	2.53	2.19	1.86	1.59	1.40
CNRACL (agents of local administrations)					
Pensioners	0.426	0.576	0.794	0.984	1.177
Contributors	1.541	1.561	1.560	1.560	1.560
Contributors ÷ pensioners (percent)	3.62	2.71	1.96	1.59	1.40
SNCF (railways)					
Pensioners	0.215	0.201	0.192	0.188	0.186
Contributors	0.183	0.167	0.153	0.139	0.127
Contributors ÷ pensioners (percent)	0.85	0.83	0.79	0.74	0.68
ARRCO					
Pensioners	5.100	8.100	6.530	7.260	8.700
Contributors	13.800	15.010	16.330	16.580	16.330
Contributors ÷ pensioners (percent)	2.71	2.58	2.50	2.28	1.88
AGIRC					
Pensioners	1.063	1.277	1.523	1.930	2.384
Contributors	2.760	3.081	3.427	3.728	4.016
Contributors ÷ pensioners (percent)	2.60	2.41	2.25	1.93	1.68
Cultivators					
Pensioners	2.103	2.007	1.819	1.691	1.588
Contributors	0.911	0.821	0.739	0.666	0.600
Contributors ÷ pensioners (percent)	0.43	0.41	0.41	0.39	0.38

Source: Commissariat Général du Plan (1995).

TABLE 3-11. *Projected Expenditures and Revenues of Selected Pension Plans,*
1995–2015
Billions of francs

	1995	2000	2005	2010	2015
Régime général					
Expenditures	276.2	318.4	363.8	441.8	525.8
Resources	266.7	299.9	346.0	386.4	418.8
Financing needs	9.5	18.4	17.9	55.5	107.0
Civil servants					
Expenditures	104.8	122.7	148.6	182.2	219.6
Resources	101.0	106.2	114.4	126.2	139.4
Financing needs	3.8	16.5	34.2	56.0	80.2
CNRACL (agents of local administrations)					
Expenditures	37.3	50.3	71.2	93.4	119.2
Resources	34.5	36.7	39.8	43.9	48.4
Financing needs	2.8	13.6	31.4	49.5	70.8
SNCF (railways)					
Expenditures	26.4	25.6	25.4	26.0	27.3
Resources	8.3	8.0	7.9	7.9	8.0
Financing needs	0.1	0.2	0.3	0.4	0.7
ARRCO					
Expenditures	119.8	146.1	166.3	189.8	235.3
Resources	117.0	151.8	175.3	195.4	212.4
Financing needs	2.8	−5.7	−9.0	−5.6	22.9
AGIRC					
Expenditures	58.7	72.1	86.0	102.5	129.1
Resources	57.8	68.6	80.3	91.7	103.9
Financing needs	0.9	3.5	5.7	10.8	25.2
Cultivators					
Expenditures	40.5	37.9	33.8	31.0	28.7
Resources	4.7	4.3	4.0	3.7	3.4
Financing needs	35.8	33.6	29.8	27.3	25.3

Source: Commissariat Général du Plan (1995).

some additional amendments in April 1996, which introduced further decreases in expected rates of return by imposing progressive increases in the price at which contributions buy pension points, the underlying mechanism being that the same amount of contributions will generate a lower amount of pension entitlements.

How will these various adjustments affect pensioners' standards of living? Projections offer a partial estimate of how large these adjustments could be. But first a word of caution. If a reform implies a decrease in pensions with respect to the reference scenario, it does not mean a decline of the *absolute* standard of living between successive cohorts of pensioners. The reason is that, as long as one assumes a minimum rate of general economic growth, the reference scenario implies that each cohort is better off than the previous one in absolute terms. The impact of the reform is only to slow the growth of pensions expressed in absolute terms.

The impact of the reform, therefore, is to reduce the standard of living of each successive cohort of pensioners *relative* to the standard of living of workers. This relative reduction will result from two mechanisms. The first is that measures that affect the level of pensions at their first payment correspond to a decline of the relative income status of pensioners, which can also be read as a decrease of the replacement ratio, that is, the ratio of the first pension to the last wage. The associated reduction is then kept constant over the retirement period. The second is that measures that affect indexation rules do not have any impact on short-term replacement ratios, but they generate a progressive decrease of the pension level with respect to the current average wage, so that the relative impact is more pronounced at the end of the retirement period.

Both effects can be computed. The first has been evaluated by the Caisse Nationale d'Assurance Vieillesse to be about 7 percentage points of the replacement rate for men entering retirement in 2015.[13] For women, this drop is compensated by the benefits resulting from longer careers. Concerning the second effect, no simulation is needed to evaluate its importance: if real net wages are supposed to go on increasing at 1 percent a year, and if pensions are only indexed on

13. Gleizes and Plessis (1995).

prices, after twenty years of retirement the relative position of a pensioner with respect to average wage has declined by about 25 percent. The magnitude of this drop doubles if the rate of productivity growth is twice as large, and increases as the pensioner advances further into the retirement period. The loss for older retired people is substantial.

Of course, one cannot completely reject the idea that such a situation would be normal. What is presented by the figures is not an actual loss but the loss of earnings that would have been generated by full indexation. Deciding whether this relative loss is acceptable is partly normative. After all, one may contend that the role of the pension system is only to ensure a relative continuity of *absolute* standards of living during the transition to retirement (the decrease of resources being approximately matched by the increase of leisure time) and to guarantee that this absolute standard of living will be maintained until death but without promising any sharing of the benefits of further general economic growth. But one can argue that the idea of an absolute standard is meaningless over the long run. Even poverty lines are generally defined in relative terms. If such is the case, the mechanical result of deindexation would be to progressively expand the share of older retired people who live below the poverty line. This would undo what was a major achievement of pension policy during the 1970s—the considerable reduction of poverty among the elderly.

There is one more point concerning the effect of deindexation. It may be argued that doing no more than maintaining absolute standards of living among older people is sufficient because consumption declines with age. But although this may be true with respect to general consumption, it is not true with regard to specific needs linked to illness and dependency. Furthermore, the costs of the services required to cover these needs are mainly labor costs, whose price tends to reflect changes in wages rather than changes in the general price index. One consequence of this is that deindexation creates additional need for efficient coverage of dependency costs. Projects to develop a dependency allowance have been repeatedly proposed, and experiments have even been introduced in some regions, but because of their high cost they have not been extended to the whole population.[14]

14. Genier (1996).

The Debate over Funding versus Pay-As-You-Go

For historical reasons, the French system is essentially pay-as-you-go. This choice was made in reaction to the very poor performance of the funded systems that had been established between the two world wars, and it is also linked with the general choice, after World War II, of a rather inflationary monetary policy that was better accommodated by a pay-as-you-go system.

For several decades suggestions to introduce more funding in the system were sporadic and without great influence. But increasing pressure in favor of funding appeared during the 1980s.[15] Part of this pressure was motivated by private interests, and as a result, insurance companies were charged with wanting to expand their role as investors of the national savings and with preparing the dismantling of the welfare state, which would both be to their profit. This suspicion was certainly excessive, but it helped radicalize the debate.

By the early 1990s, advocates of funding insisted on the risks of strong intergenerational inequity that would be generated by the aging of the population, and they pointed to the low level of savings. Some also presented funding as a miracle cure for the pension problem because of its supposed absence of sensitivity to demographic shocks. People responsible for managing the existing pension programs strongly opposed this position, sometimes by minimizing the aging problem itself. More accurately, they contended that funding was not without risk (the Maxwell affair helped strengthen this idea in public opinion) and was not insensitive to demographic changes, especially increasing longevity.

After years of intense controversy, what remains of this debate? It has become less heated and is a bit clearer because of convergence on some basic points. First, the limits of funding are better understood. It is not without costs. More precisely, it even consists in *anticipating* the costs that would inevitably appear if France stayed with a pure pay-as-you-go system. The advantage of this anticipation, therefore, is not to avoid the costs of an aging population. It is at most to lower this cost in the long run, and only if high interest rates are projected to persist. Funded plans are not without risks, both demographic and

---

15. Kessler and Strauss-Kahn (1982).

economic. Funding's beneficial effect on saving and capital accumulation is only potential and far from being strongly attested by empirical evidence.[16] Furthermore, the idea that greater saving is economically beneficial is less in favor today than it was at the end of the 1980s, when there were strong concerns about a worldwide capital shortage.[17] Wrong or right, more recently saving has been suspected of being responsible for France's economic recession and slow recovery. This diagnosis may well be valid in the short run, even if one subscribes to the idea that well-oriented saving may be a good thing in the long run.

The antifunding current of opinion has also lost some of its arguments. Because the mechanics of aging are better understood, it is much less easy to minimize the problem faced by the pay-as-you-go systems on the grounds that demographic projections are too uncertain to justify any fear about the sustainability of their current rules. Furthermore, economic prospects are not favorable and do not suggest any radical economic response to the demographic challenge faced by pension systems.

On the whole, this has resulted in a sort of tacit agreement that funding is neither a radical solution to the pension problem itself nor an indirect solution to the larger problems of capital accumulation and economic slowdown. But funding remains one way to protect against the uncertainties that, because of population aging, affect the pay-as-you-go plans. Indeed, neither the state nor the current managers of pay-as-you-go programs are in a position to commit themselves to maintaining the replacement rates that are now provided: projections have shown that this would require large increases in contribution rates by future generations that cannot be enforced in advance, especially if the next generation's attitude toward mandatory levies is the same as ours. The primary reason to save for retirement, therefore, is simply to anticipate these difficulties. This motive is entirely independent of efficiency arguments such as the macroeconomic value of accumulating more capital or the fact that rates of return on pensions should in the long run be higher than the rate of return on pay-as-you-go contributions.

As a consequence, the debate on the necessity of retirement pre-

16. Caussat (1992).
17. Artus, Bismut, and Plihon (1993).

financing has become a debate concerning the forms it should take. Organizing such funding within current pay-as-you-go programs through the constitution of reserves is not necessarily the best choice. It offers no solution to the problem of resistance to mandatory levies. So the choice is between purely private initiatives, such as buying of life insurance, or a more collective form, such as the creating of pension funds. People have turned to life insurance in greater numbers in the past few years, not necessarily to build pension amounts but rather because the expansion of insurance plans has been boosted by large fiscal incentives: the incentives are not provided to other forms of saving; and because they involve large budget costs, further developments in this direction would seem unlikely. Creating pension funds has been the topic of many proposals by insurance companies, the banking sector, and various members of the parliament, including the current minister of social affairs.[18] But realizing the proposals is still awaited, except for plans for some very specific groups.[19]

Retirement Age and Preretirement

For those irreducibles who still refuse any form of pension prefinancing yet do not wish to face declining replacement ratios when they retire, there is still one possibility to escape from the constraint created by the saturation of contribution rates. It is simply to rely on the "fourth pillar," which is work: in other words, they should anticipate retiring at a later age.

It is probably one important aspect of the evolution of public opinion in the past few years that a gradual increase in the retirement age no longer seems outrageous. In particular, the modification of conditions necessary to reach retirement at full rate, which was introduced in the 1993 Balladur reform, did not confront major opposition. It is true, however, that the transposition of these new rules to special regimes

18. For a deeper examination of these projects see Charpentier (1996). For more international aspects of the debate see Davis (1995).

19. This has been the case for self-employed people (*loi Madelin*). A general framework for the development of pension funds for the rest of the population had been approved by the previous parliament (*loi Thomas*), but its application has been delayed by the new socialist majority; a new project should be submitted to the parliament in a more or less distant future.

faced radical opposition at the end of 1995 within the general protest that arose after the proposal of the Juppé Plan. It is also true that the Balladur reform was presented in a technical form that did not necessarily promote full understanding of its implications because it did not explicitly limit the right to retire at age 60. But workers currently entering the labor force at age 25 know very well that this right will become completely theoretical for them. And this perspective is assumed more or less fatalistically.

This does not mean that there is no problem with this policy, but that the problem lies in labor demand more than labor supply. The decline of labor force participation around age 60 (see figure 3-4) can be attributed to business's employment policies as well as individuals' desire for earlier retirement. And despite general declarations to the contrary, there is no reason to consider that firms' attitudes with respect to older workers are going to change rapidly. This is the major unknown factor for the future.

Population Aging, Economic Activity, and Government Policies

Besides its quasi-mechanical impact on pensions, population aging may have far-reaching implications for many other socioeconomic domains. This view has a long tradition in France, where the precocity of demographic transition has led, since the end of the nineteenth century, to a continuous concern about implications of aging or of a decreasing or stationary population. This is one of the reasons for the introduction before World War II of a pronatalist policy.

I shall not discuss at length the effectiveness of such a policy. Perhaps it does help account for the fact that the French baby boom was somewhat larger than the ones in some other European countries. Perhaps it also accounts for the fact that since 1975 the French fertility rate has remained in the upper average of developed countries.[20] Still, the French baby boom was smaller than the one in the United States,

20. Some attempts have been made to get more precise evaluations of the effects of higher fertility, either through simulation of a simple behavioral model or by direct econometric estimation over a panel of countries. French family policy could account for 0.2 point of the fertility rate, which is not negligible but not that large, either (Blanchet and Ekert, 1993).

where no particular family policy existed. Similarly, the French fertility rate has not been higher than that in the United Kingdom where family policy has no pronatalistic bias. On the whole the evidence for the impact of demographic policy remains scanty, so that I shall assume the aging of the population is unavoidable and rather focus on its consequences. Is it correct to attribute to this aging the large negative consequences that are sometimes predicted?

Aging and Macroeconomic Indicators

Assessing the macroeconomic consequences of an aging population may initially be approached as a simple aggregation problem. The intensity of a given economic parameter is differentiated by age. Given the age structure of the population at a particular time, one can compute the average intensity of this economic variable over the whole population. Population structure, therefore, acts like a series of weighting parameters, and measuring the impact of population aging is equivalent to measuring the impact of a change in this series of weighting parameters, with increasing weights given to older age groups.

But a general statistical result is that a weighted average is not very sensitive to small changes of weighting coefficients, as long as the variable is not too highly concentrated at points where the weighting coefficients change. This simple result applies to the impact of population aging on a large number of economic variables. It can be confirmed either by simple analytical computations of comparative statistics or by simulations. I shall take here the consumption of medical services.

By simulation, it has been repeatedly shown that although health expenditures rapidly increase with age during the second half of life, population aging per se does little to explain the general increase of health expenditures per capita.[21] Most of the increase comes from the simultaneous increase of expenditures at all ages. This is more than the incentive effect of public coverage; it is instead probably supply induced, in particular because of rapid technological changes whose consequences, in the medical field, increase costs.

---

21. The last exercise of this kind for France is Hourriez (1991).

In comparative statics the key parameters in determining the impact of a change in the population growth rate on any variable are the difference between the mean age for the variable considered, here the mean age of consumption of health services (51.45 years), and the mean age for the stationary equivalent of today's French population (41.08 years).[22] The difference is only ten years, which implies that a permanent shift from a stationary population to a population decreasing 1 percent a year (which is a major long-term change) will increase the steady-state value of expenditures, all else equal, by only 10 percent. This response is minor if one considers that a 1 point decline in the population growth rate is something significant (it corresponds to a 0.3 point drop in the total fertility rate), while a long-run change of 10 percent in health expenditures is low when compared with the natural increase of these expenditures in the past decade. The same computation can be redone for pensions, replacing the average age at consumption of health services by the average age of the pensioner (73.08 years). The difference between it and the average age of the entire population is now three times as large, which shows why it was right to be so concerned about the implications for pensions of an aging population.

Equivalent computations can be made for the effects of increased life expectancy. The key parameter here is the relative difference between the average level of health expenditures and the level of health expenditures at ages with lower mortality rates. The numerical result is that, all else equal, and given the current age pattern of expenditures, there is a unit elasticity of expenditures with respect to life expectancy at birth, meaning that a 10 percent increase in life expectancy generates only a 10 percent increase in total expenditures, a relatively minor change that can be reduced still further if one assumes that increasing life expectancy partly results from an increase in life expectancy in good health, with an associated rightward shift of the

---

22. Lee (1980); and Blanchet (1994). If A_x is the mean age for variable x, and A the mean age of the total population, the exact formula is

$$\frac{\Delta \bar{x}}{\bar{x}} = (A_x - A)\Delta n,$$

where n is the population growth rate.

age pattern of expenditures. But here again, the effect of increased life expectancy on pension expenditures is three times as large as it is for health expenditures.

Such computations give useful rules of thumb for rapidly assessing the impact of an aging population on a wide range of economic variables and explain why in many instances the effect remains limited, except for the effect on pensions. This does not mean that aging proves to be innocuous, but it reverses the burden of the proof. If one wants to show large effects of changes in demographic structures, one has to look for other ways to tackle the problem.

Aging and Savings

There would be one first way to do so. The general statistical result according to which weighted averages are not very sensitive to moderate changes of weighting coefficients only applies to variables with positive values. If variables over the life cycle are successively positive or negative, changes of weighting coefficients may generate toppling-over effects, whose relative impact on aggregate balances may be large.

Savings rates by age are one kind of variable for which such an effect may potentially occur. If one accepts a very elementary version of the life-cycle theory of savings in which people save during their working lives and dissave after retirement, one is dealing with a variable that is positive, then negative. In this context, one can intuit that changes in population age structures can have large relative effects because the macroeconomic variable is a residual balance whose relative change can be large even if relative changes of its positive and negative components remain small.

Indeed, one view about the consequences of aging is that it should progressively lead to less savings, less capital accumulation, and, therefore, large final effects on the standard of living. But how far can the effect go?

First, even if one accepts the underlying theory of savings, the macroeconomic consequences may be more complicated than expected. Two possibilities exist. If population aging is due to a declining population growth rate, net savings should decline. But in a standard growth model, capital intensity is negatively affected by increases of the population growth rate (the "capital dilution effect"). On the whole, if it is capital intensity rather than savings that matters, the adverse effects of population declines are not so evident anymore. They are ambiguous and may be positive in a large number of instances.

If aging is due to increased life expectancy, the dissaving period will be longer, assuming no change in the retirement age, but this longer period will require greater savings during working years, so that the result is once again ambiguous. For instance, in a perfectly stationary state, there is a necessary identity between saving by workers and dissaving by older people that implies that net aggregate savings are constantly zero.

Second, the underlying theory of savings can itself be contested. The intensity of dissaving during old age is far from being as large as described by this naïve theory, suggesting that precaution remains high even at later ages or that behavior is also motivated by the desire for intergenerational transmission.

Last, the impact of aging on total savings strongly depends on how the pension system itself will react to the aging population. If it does not fully adapt to the new situation by increasing contributions, more room will be left for pension prefinancing, with an ex ante impact on savings which, at least transitorily, should be positive, until pension funds reach their maturity.

I shall not try to quantify these effects further. But these considerations are sufficient to suggest that, even if the mechanical and ceteris paribus impact of aging on savings may be large, its final impact on economic growth and capital intensity are ambiguous and probably second order.

Other Ways Aging May Matter

What are therefore the remaining possibilities for showing that aging matters? I shall list three on which further research on aging could eventually concentrate. And it is on these three points that I shall conclude.

One way to transform the small ex ante or partial equilibrium effects of aging into large macroeconomic outcomes may be to take into account the endogeneity of technical progress. For instance, an endogenous growth model in which capital accumulation is the engine of growth could explain why small changes in savings rates may result, after some time, in large outcomes, if savings have an impact on economic growth rates, not only on steady-state income levels. This, by the way, would provide a stronger argument in favor of pension funding than the arguments discussed earlier. Amplification could also appear if one assumes that the engine of growth lies within innovation or human capital accumulation and if aging also has adverse effects on these two parameters. But, once again, one must be cautious that ex ante effects on these variables are small, so that significant outcomes can only exist if the amplification mechanism is very large. For instance, even if innovative capacity were concentrated at very young ages, an extreme hypothesis indeed, changes in age structure that are likely to occur would not mechanically result in a very large decline of the average propensity to innovate within the labor force.

Another concern is the adverse consequences of population aging on the equilibrium of political power. More elderly people, with their higher rates of participation in political processes or through direct lobbying, could be in a position to redirect in their favor a large part of the resources flowing through public transfer programs. The existence of more elderly people could thus lead to higher rather than lower pensions, more long-term care units, and less investment in schooling. If this were the case, aging could well have far-reaching economic consequences. Yet some qualifications must be applied. First, indirectly measuring the intensity of the phenomenon by simply plotting the median age of the potential voter over time shows that, while significant, the effect is not that large, suggesting there will be no large majority reversals in favor of old age groups. Second, the years when social transfers toward older people increased most were years where the median age tended to decrease, so that no simple relation can be drawn between age structure and the direction of transfers. Finally, one should avoid excessively simple representation of collective choices, which do not result from simple majority rules and do not necessarily stick to the self-interest of the most influential groups. Cooperative behavior can also have its place in intergenerational relations, whatever its motives (strategic or really altruistic).

The last problem concerns internal labor markets.[23] If companies

---

23. Blanchet (1993).

motivate their workers by paying them less than their productivity would warrant when they are young and more than their productivity would warrant when old, aging generates ex ante disequilibrium.[24] For the firm the worst adjustment to this disequilibrium would be to lay off its older workers. This of course is exactly the opposite of what the pension problem would require. The other possibility would be to solve the problem by questioning seniority rules and narrowing wage and productivity profiles, but with negative effects on workers' motivation. This points to the difficulty of adapting labor force management to the new demographic context. Adaptation of individual life cycles to individual aging is not only a matter of adapting the division of this life cycle between labor and the nonlabor period constituted by retirement and the associated income transfers, which is the pension problem. It is also a problem of adapting careers themselves. This challenge is difficult to solve in a world of growing uncertainty where the management of long-term labor contracts between firms and workers becomes every day more problematic.

References

Artus, P., Cl. Bismut, and D. Plihon. 1993. *L'épargne*. PUF.

Blanchet, D. 1993. "Does an aging labor force call for large adjustments in training or wage policies?" In P. Johnson and K. F. Zimmermann, eds., *Labour markets in an aging Europe*. Cambridge University Press.

———. 1994. "Les structures par âge importent-elles?" Working Paper INSEE-D3E, G9401. Paris: INSEE.

Blanchet, D., and O. Ekert. 1994. "The demographic impact of family benefits: evidence from a micro model and from macro data." In J. Ermisch and N. Ogawa, eds., *The family, the market and the state in aging societies*. Oxford University Press.

Blanchet, D., and J.-A. Monfort. 1995. "Pensions and generational histories in a simple demo-economic model." IUSSP Seminar on Intergenerational economic relations and demographic change, Honolulu.

———. 1996. "L'âge et la durée de la retraite depuis 50 ans." *Insee Première* 448.

Caussat, L. 1992. "Retraite et épargne: historique d'un débat dans la littérature américaine." *Revue d'économie financière* 23: 159–82.

---

24. Lazear (1993).

Charpentier, F. 1996. *Retraites et fonds de pension: l'état de la question en France et à l'étranger.* Paris: Economica.

Chesnais, J. C. 1986. *La transition demographique: étapes, formes, implications,* Travaux et Documents 113. Paris: INED.

Commissariat Général du Plan. 1991. *Livre blanc sur les retraites: garantir dans l'équité les retraites de demain.* La Documentation Française.

————. 1995. *Perspectives à long terme des retraites.* La Documentation Française.

Cornilleau, G., and H. Sterdyniak. 1995. "Les retraites: des réformes sans plan d'ensemble." *Observations et Diagnostics Economiques* 126: 1–6.

Davis, E. P. 1995. *Pension funds, retirement-income security and capital markets: an international perspective.* Oxford University Press.

Desplanques, G. 1996. "La situation familiale des personnes âgées." In *La Société Française, Données Sociales 1996.* INSEE.

Dinh, Q. C. 1994. "La population de la France à l'horizon 2050." *Economie et Statistique* 274: 7–32.

Fédération Française des Sociétés d'Assurance. 1991. "Contributions aux réflexions en cours sur l'avenir des retraites." *Risques,* spécial ed. May.

Feldstein, M. 1974. "Social security, induced retirement and aggregate capital accumulation." *Journal of Political Economy* 82: 905–26.

Genier, P. 1996. "La gestion du risque dépendance: le rôle de la famille, de l'etat et du secteur privé." *Economie et Statistique* 291-292: 103– 17.

Gleizes, M., and C. Plessis. 1995. "Quelles retraites pour les salarés du secteur privé d'ici à 2015? L'etude de six carrieres de reference." *Retraite et societe,* no 9: 25–43.

Hourriez, J. M., and B. Legris. 1995. "Le niveau de vie relatif des personnes âgées." *Economie et Statistique* 283-284: 137–58.

————. 1991. "La consommation medicale a l'horizon 2010." *Economie et Statistique* 265: 17–30.

Kessler, D., and D. Strauss-Kahn, D. 1982. *L'épargne et la retraite: l'avenir des retraites préfinancés.* Paris: Economica.

Lazear, E. P. 1990. "Adjusting to an aging labor force." In D. A. Wise, ed., *Issues in the economics of aging.* NBER/University of Chicago Press.

Le Bras, H. 1992. *Marianne et les lapins: l'obsession démographique.* Paris: Hachette/Pluriel.

Lee, R. 1980. "Age structure, intergenerational transfers and economic growth: an overview." *Revue Economique* 31: 1129–56.

Leibfritz, W., and others. 1995. "Aging populations, pension systems and government budgets: Do they affect saving?" Economic Department Working Paper 156. Paris: OECD.

Malabouche, G. 1987. "L'évolution à long terme du système de retraites: une nouvelle méthode de projection." *Population* 1: 9–38.

Ruellan, R. 1993. "Retraites: l'impossible réforme est-elle achevée?" *Droit Social* 2: 911–29.

Vallin, J. 1991. "Quelles hypothèses peut-on faire sur l'évolution future de la mortalité?" In G. Tapinos, ed., *La France dans deux générations*. Fayard.

Verniere, L. 1990a. "Les retraites pourront-elles être payées après l'an 2000." *Economie et Statistique* 233: 19–27.

Vernière, L. 1990b. "Retraites: l'urgence d'une réforme." *Economie et Statistique* 233: 29–38.

Chapter 4

Population Aging and German Economic Performance

Nicola Düll

THE TOTAL German population, especially of German nationals and to a greater extent in the former East Germany
than in West Germany, has been aging since 1950. The peak years
were 1950 to 1970. Since then, the share of elderly has declined but
still remains above the level of 1950 (table 4-1). Moreover, the youth
dependency rate has decreased, especially in West Germany, since the
1970s. The aging of the population is expected to speed up in the first
half of the next century.

In the former West Germany the fertility rate has declined markedly,
falling from 2.1 to 1.4 births per woman between 1950 and 1991. In East
Germany the fertility rate slowed down more smoothly initially, but
birthrates of eastern German women since German unification have
fallen sharply (table 4-2). In addition, between 1950 and 1991 life expectancy increased by nearly eight years for men and ten for women
in West Germany, six for men and more than eight for women in East
Germany. Since the 1970s more deaths than births have been registered in western Germany.

The most decisive factor for the development of total population in
West Germany has been immigration. While the former East Germany
has experienced net outmigration (mostly in the direction of West
Germany), West Germany has experienced net immigration (table
4-2). Three phases of net immigration to West Germany can be distinguished. From 1945 until the beginning of the 1970s it experienced net
immigration flows (before the closing of the frontier in 1961, the flow
was mainly from East Germany). Between 1950 and 1959 net migration
was 2.8 million persons. Between 1960 and 1970 it increased to

TABLE 4-1. *Aged and Youth Dependency Rates, by Sex, Selected Years, 1950–91*[a]
Percent

	West Germany				East Germany			
Year	*Share of men 60+*	*Share of women 60+*	*Aged dependency rate*	*Youth dependency rate*	*Share of men 60+*	*Share of women 60+*	*Aged dependency rate*	*Youth dependency rate*
1950	13.3	14.6	26	59	15.5	16.7	31	60
1960	14.4	18.3	30	55	18.1	22.2	41	60
1970	16.1	22.3	39	63	18.5	25.1	49	71
1980	14.8	23.6	37	53	14.3	23.4	38	58
1991	16.2	24.9	36	39	14.3	23.6	35	47

Source: Höhn (1994, pp. 36, 38, 209, 213).
a. Aged dependency is ratio of people older than 60 years to those aged 20–59. Youth dependency is ratio of those aged 0–19 to those aged 20–60.

TABLE 4-2. *Fertility Rates (Births per Woman), Life Expectancy at Birth, and Net Migration, Selected Years, 1950–93*

| | Fertility rate | | Life expectancy | | | | Migration | | |
| | | | West Germany[a] | | East Germany[b] | | | | |
Year	West Germany	East Germany	Male	Female	Male	Female	Net migration to West Germany (nonnationals)	East Germany to West Germany	Net migration to East Germany
1950	2.10	2.37	64.56	68.48	63.9	67.96	n.a.	n.a.	n.a.
1960	2.37	2.33	66.86	72.39	67.07	72.02	243,800[c]	n.a.	n.a.
1964	2.54	2.51	n.a.	n.a.	n.a.	n.a.	254,100	24,000[f]	−16,100[f]
1970	2.02	2.19	67.41	73.83	68.52	73.61	541,600	18,600	−13,100
1975	1.45	1.54	n.a.	n.a.	n.a.	n.a.	−233,300	18,900	−11,000
1980	1.44	1.94	70.18	76.85	68.96	74.83	245,600	14,000[e]	−7,700
1984	1.29	1.73	n.a.	n.a.	n.a.	n.a.	−213,900	40,600	−48,500
1989	1.39	1.56	72.21	78.68	70.13	76.38	332,500	383,000	−244,100
1991–93	1.42[f]	0.91[f]	73.11	79.48	69.68	77.18	n.a.	471,145[g]	n.a.

Sources: Höhn (1994, pp. 197, 199, 204, 205); Statistisches Bundesamt, *Statistisches Jahrbuch* (1995).
a. Years/time periods: 1949/51; 1960/62; 1970/72; 1980/82; 1986/88.
b. Years: 1952; 1961; 1971; 1981; 1989.
c. 1962.
d. 1965.
e. 1979.
f. Estimated.
g. 1993 net migration to unified Germany.
n.a. Not available.

FIGURE 4-1. *Total Population, Selected Years, 1960–93*

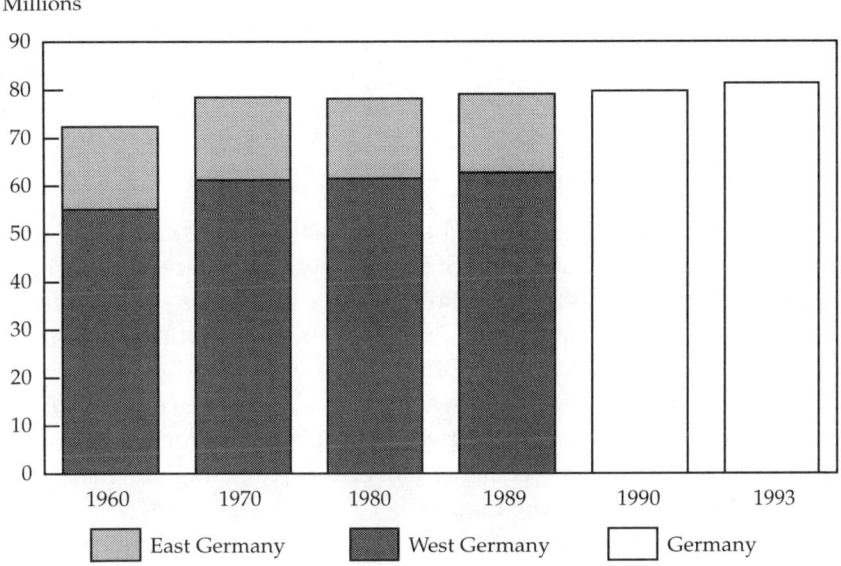

Millions

Source: Höhn (1994, p. 203); and Statistisches Bundesamt.

3.3 million. In this period immigrants were mainly nonnationals who were attracted by West German policies to cure a labor shortage. In the 1970s and 1980s migration flows became less important as the West German government stopped trying to attract foreign workers. But beginning with the fall of the Berlin Wall in 1989 and the opening of eastern European frontiers, major flows of ethnic Germans and persons seeking political asylum swelled the tide. Between 1989 and 1994 net immigration was 3.6 million persons.[1]

Because of the net migration to West Germany, the total population grew, while the population in East Germany decreased slightly (figure 4-1). The sum of net migration to West Germany between 1955 and 1989 was about 8.2 million, and total population growth was 8.92 million. Since the fertility rate of nonnationals was higher than that of nationals, the importance of migration for West Germany's population

1. Höhn (1994, p. 203); DIW (1995); and Statistisches Bundesamt, *Statistisches Jahrbuch* (1995).

is even more evident. Up to now immigrants helped to reduce the share of elderly in the total population. However, the initial effect of former immigration on age structure will diminish in the coming years.

Population Projections

In Germany, population projections are carried out by different institutions, so a brief overview of their main results is necessary. All of the projections are important for the policy discussions in Germany. The most important have been presented by the Statitisches Bundesamt—the Federal Statistical Office (the seventh and eighth coordinated population projections)—and by two research centers, DIW and Prognos AG. Prognos AG carried out its projection for the pension institutions Verband Deutscher Rentenversicherungsträger. The main results of the Eurostat population projection are also of interest.

On life expectancy the basic assumptions are similar. The projections of the Federal Statistical Office assume life expectancy will increase in western Germany about 1.5 years by the turn of the century and will remain constant; eastern German figures will converge with the western figures by 2010 (according to the seventh projection) or 2030 (according to the eighth). According to the DIW projection, life expectancy in western Germany will increase by one and one-half years by 2015. The increases in life expectancy in eastern Germany are projected to be slightly higher and to converge with the western German level by 2040. According to Prognos AG, life expectancy will increase slightly for all age groups.

The seventh and eighth coordinated projections assume a constant birthrate in western Germany during the next two decades. The DIW expects a slightly decreasing fertility rate of the new cohorts. Prognos AG assumes slightly increasing birthrates for national women in western Germany during the next two decades. Generally, it is expected that two kinds of assimilation processes will occur: the eastern German fertility rate, which has seriously decreased since unification, will increase to the western German level (differences will exist then only in regard to the length of the assimilation period), and the fertility rate

TABLE 4-3. *Projected Annual Net Migration, Selected Periods, 1990–2040*

Projection	1990–2000	2001–40	2001–09	2010–40
7th projection	308,000	50,000–60,000[a]	n.a.	n.a.
8th projection (1)	decreasing to 100,000	100,000	n.a.	n.a.
8th projection (2)	decreasing to 200,000[b]	200,000	n.a.	n.a.
8th projection (3)	decreasing to 300,000[b]	300,000	n.a.	n.a.
DIW	340,000	160,000–70,000	190,000	150,000–60,000
Prognos low var.	250,000[c]	70,000	65,000	74,000[d]
Prognos high var.	290,000[c]	280,000	260,000[f]	300,000[g]

Sources: Statistisches Bundesamt; DIW (1995); and Prognos (1995).
a. 2001–30.
b. 1992–2000.
c. 1995–2000.
d. 2010–40.
n.a. Not available.
e. 1993–2000.
f. 2000–20.
g. 2020–40.

of nonnationals will decrease, depending on the level and structure of immigration (the countries of origin and the length of stay of non-national families).

There are major differences among immigration forecasts (table 4-3). The seventh projection of the Federal Statistics Office assumes low figures (300,000 a year between 1990 and 2000 and then 50,000 or 60,000 a year until 2030). Three have been calculated for the eighth projection, allowing for markedly higher figures. All three project that the flows of ethnic Germans from eastern Europe (*Aussiedler*) will decrease sharply after 2000 and will be insignificant by 2010. Net immigration flows of non-Germans will decrease by 2000 and stay at an annual level of 100,000 a year in the first variant, 200,000 in the second, and 300,000 in the third (all variants assume that expansion of the European Union will induce more migration, but migration policy will be more restrictive than it is today).

The DIW expects that 1.4 million eastern European ethnic Germans will move to Germany. Among them the percentage of children will be relatively high and that of the elderly low. All in all, an annual net immigration of 150,000 to 180,000 is assumed.

According to Prognos AG, only another 1 million eastern European

TABLE 4-4. *Projected Total Population, Selected Years, 1989–2040*
Millions

Projection	1989–93	2000	2010	2020	2025	2030	2040
7th projection	79.1[a]	81.1	78.9	75	72.6	69.9	n.a.
8th projection var. 1	81.0[b]	83.3	82	78.6	n.a.	73.7	67.6
8th projection var. 2	81.0	83.7	83.4	81.2	n.a.	77.4	72.4
8th projection var. 3	81.0	84.1	84.9	83.7	n.a.	81.1	77.1
DIW	81.3[c]	83	82.5	80.2	78.2	75.7	69.4
Prognos low var.	81.0[b]	82	80	76.8	n.a.	72.3	66.8
Prognos high var.	81.0	82.3	82.3	81.8	n.a.	80.1	77.6
Eurostat low var.	79.1	80.3	77.6	73.5	n.a.	n.a.	n.a.
Eurostat high var.	n.a.	84.2	87.3	90.3	n.a.	n.a.	n.a.

Sources: See table 4-3.
a. 1989.
b. 1992.
c. 1993.
n.a. Not available.

ethnic Germans will migrate to Germany. The migration from the European Union will be low, about 17,000 in 1993. In contrast to the other projections, which do not take into account economic interdependencies, Prognos AG assumes controlled immigration policy (*gesteuerte Einwanderungspolitik*), depending on economic circumstances. For the high variant, GDP is assumed to grow at a yearly rate of 2.6 percent until 2010, then slow to an average 1.8 percent between 2010 and 2040. The low variant sets the growth rate at 2.1 percent by 2010 and 0.7 percent between then and 2040. In the high variant the average growth rate over the whole projection period is 2.1 percent compared with an average of 2.2 percent for the OECD Europe; the low variant projects 1.2 percent in Germany and 1.6 percent in OECD Europe. It is assumed that international trade will grow at an annual rate of 3.4 percent or 4.1 percent. In the high variant immigration will decline to 150,000 persons annually by 2000 and then increase to 300,000 by 2040. In the low variant immigration in 2000 is 35,000 and increases to 74,000.

Given the variations in assumptions about net immigration, the projections of total population and age structure differ significantly (tables 4-3, 4-4, and 4-5). With the exception of Eurostat's high variant, they estimate that total population will decrease in the first half of the

TABLE 4-5. *Projected Share of Population Aged 60 and Older and Aged 80 and Older of Total Population, Selected Years, 2000–40*
Percent

	Aged 60 and older						Aged 80 and older					
Projection	Base year	2000	2010	2020	2030	2040	Base year	2000	2010	2020	2030	2040
7th projection	n.a.	23.6	25.8	29.4	34.9	n.a.	n.a.	3.6	4.7	6.2	6.2	n.a.
8th projection var. 1	20.4	23.2	25.2	28.9	34.6	35.0	n.a.	n.a.	n.a.	n.a.	n.a.	n.a.
8th projection var. 2	20.4	23.1	24.9	28.2	33.6	33.9	n.a.	n.a.	n.a.	n.a.	n.a.	n.a.
8th projection var. 3	20.4	23.0	24.6	27.7	32.7	33.0	n.a.	n.a.	n.a.	n.a.	n.a.	n.a.
Prognos low var.	20.4	23.3	25.8	29.3	34.3	33.7	3.2	2.8	3.7	4.8	4.6	5.3
Prognos high var.	20.4	23.2	25.2	28.1	32.5	31.7	3.2	2.8	3.7	4.8	4.8	5.5

Sources: See table 4-3.
n.a. Not available.

next century. According to the FSO seventh projection, population will fall by more than 9 million between 1989 and 2030; according to the first variant of the eigthth projection, the DIW projection, and the low variant of Prognos AG it will fall between 11 and 14 million from the beginning of the 1990s to 2040. The high variant of Prognos AG and the high variant of the eighth projection forecast a decrease of 3.4 and 3.9 million, respectively, over the whole period.

Only projections proposed by international organizations such as Eurostat and the United Nations see a growing population—93.6 million in the high variant of the UN's population projection of 1992, and 90.3 million for Eurostat's high variant. (The basic assumptions of Eurostat's high variant are high immigration figures and increasing fertility rates and life expectancies.) Implicitly, current German forecasts assume a politically acceptable level of long-term net immigration because they often do not include overall economic circumstances. Thus, more detailed interdependencies between the development of the labor market on the demand side and total population (on the supply side of the labor market) are usually not taken into consideration, and the question of whether an aging and shrinking population impedes economic growth is not addressed (except for Prognos AG, because it assumes an immigration policy linked to economic circumstances and projects growth rates of the economy). The projections do not tackle the problem of labor or skill shortages. In the face of today's

TABLE 4-6. *Projected Youth Dependency Rate and Aged Dependency Rate, Selected Years, 2000–40*
Percent

	Youth dependency rate						Aged dependency rate					
Projection	Base year	2000	2010	2020	2030	2040	Base year	2000	2010	2020	2030	2040
7th projection	n.a.	38.8	34.1	32.4	35.8	n.a.	n.a.	42.8	46.6	55.1	73.5	n.a.
8th projection var. 1	37.0	38.1	32.9	31.4	34.3	32.4	35.0	41.6	44.9	53.3	71.1	71.2
8th projection var. 2	37.0	38.1	32.9	31.4	33.9	32.2	35.0	41.4	44.1	51.7	67.8	67.8
8th projection var. 3	37.0	38.0	32.9	31.3	33.5	31.8	35.0	41.2	43.3	50.2	65.0	65.0
DIW	37.0	n.a.	32.9	31.5	34.5	33.1	35.0	42.2	46.5	57.4	79.3	83.2

Sources: See table 4-3. For definitions see table 4-1.
n.a. Not available.

high unemployment rates, the immigration figures should decrease in the near term and increase if the work force in Germany shrinks too much. There are good reasons for the migration policy to depend, as in the past, not only on crises abroad but also on the domestic labor market.

To keep the number of persons age 15 to 65 at the current level, annual net immigration would have to be 640,000 (in 2020), 910,000 (in 2029), and 570,000 (in 2040). The total population would amount to 83 million in 2030, according to calculations of the DIW. But even then the problem of an aging population would only be alleviated, not overcome. Even in Prognos's high variant or in the high variant (third variant) of the FSO's eighth projection, the share of the population age 60 and older increases from 20.4 percent in 1992 to 31.7 or 33 percent, respectively, in 2040 (table 4-5). Even in the high variant of the UN's projection of growing population, the share of elderly would be at a higher level in 2025 (25.6 percent) than in 1992. Moreover, in all projections the share of the very old (age 80 and older) will increase from 3.2 percent in 1992 to 5 percent or even more than 6 percent during the projection periods (table 4-5).

Although the youth dependency rate is now at a slightly higher level than the aged dependency rate, defined as the ratio of persons 65 and older to persons 20 to 64, this will change in the next century (table 4-6). In all projections the number of people younger than 20 is expected to shrink more than the population between 20 and 60 years old. The increasing share of elderly is reflected in a growing aged dependency rate, which in the worst projections could double by 2030 or 2040. Even in variations with higher net migration the rate will grow markedly. It is very likely that this development will affect policies to increase labor participation rates, primarily of women and elderly workers, to spread the burden of pension support among a larger number of workers.

The aged dependency rate has not been specified in most projections. According to DIW, the rate defined this way increases from 24 percent in 1993 to 51 percent in 2030 and 60 percent in 2040 in the first variant and 54 percent in 2030 and 62 percent in 2040 in the second.[2]

The Supply Side of the Labor Market

The number of economically active persons in West Germany remained nearly constant between 1960 and the mid-1980s (a bit under 27 million) but has increased markedly since then (29.3 million in 1990 and 36.4 million in the unified Germany of 1993.[3] The share of women among all economically active persons (employees and self-employed) increased from 37 percent in 1962 to 41 percent in 1992.[4] The potential for women to be labor force participants is even more important: their share of all unemployed was 34 percent in 1960, 52 percent in 1980, and 45 percent in 1992.

The activity rate of persons aged 55 and older has declined considerably. In particular, the rate of men aged 60 to 64 decreased and in 1990 was nearly half what it had been in 1975. The activity rate of men aged 65 to 70 decreased from 16.9 percent in 1975 to 7.7 percent in 1990 and that of women decreased from 6.5 percent to 3.3 percent.[5]

The following labor force projections are derived from the population forecasts. They show the main results of recent work carried out by the Ifo Institute for Eurostat on the basis of Eurostat's population projection, by Prognos, and by the Centre for Labor Market Research of the Federal Labor Office (IAB), based approximately on the FSO

2. DIW (1995).
3. Statistisches Bundesamt, *Statistisches Jahrbuch 1995* (1996).
4. Klauder (1993a).
5. Hofmann (1995).

seventh population projection. Some findings of the DIW are also discussed.

The projections for the labor supply not only depend on the assumed development of total population and its age structure, but also on estimates of future labor force participation rates. The Ifo Institute's projection for Eurostat has made various assumptions about these rates. Under the assumption that the rates will remain as they are now, according to Eurostat's population low variant, the work force will decrease by 1.8 percent from 1990 to 2000 and by 12.5 percent between 1990 and 2020 (to 33.5 million). In the high variant a maximum rate will be reached in 1995. The work force will then shrink until 2005, and it will increase again with a new peak of 39.1 million achieved in 2015.

But participation rates may vary (table 4-6). For the low scenario the basic assumption for the development of total population is Eurostat's low variant. In regard to activity rates, continuity is assumed. Thus the trend of the past ten years is extrapolated to 2020, although with diminishing intensity. The difference between the participation rates of men and women will decrease only slightly. For the high variant, which is based on the high variant of Eurostat's population projection, it is assumed that the activity rates of all age groups will increase, and the difference between men and women will be narrowed. The trend toward early retirement will be stopped. The assumptions are shaped as an integration scenario, which assumes a convergence to the highest EU labor market participation rates for each age group (see table 4-7). However, some of the results have to be used with caution. For example, it is unlikely that a large proportion of people aged 15 to 20 will combine education and part-time work. Still, the potential for a lengthening of working life might be underestimated.

The difference between the two Ifo variants shows, besides the enormous migration effect, the potential for activating endogenous potential. The share of women in the labor force will grow from 40.4 percent in 1990 to 48 percent in the high scenario and to 43.1 percent in the low scenario.

The Prognos 1995 projections assume that the activity rate of young men will decrease because the qualification level of the work force will grow. For men age 35 to 54 a slightly lower rate will continue because the participation of women will increase markedly. This increase will

TABLE 4-7. *Projected Ifo Labor Force Activity Rates, by Age Groups and Sex, 2020*[a]
Percent

Age group	Men			Women		
		2020			2020	
	1990	Scenario 1	Scenario 2	1990	Scenario 1	Scenario 2
15–20	42.2	30.6	60.2	36.3	25.6	59.0
20–25	76.6	68.1	84.0	73.2	68.0	83.4
25–30	86.6	82.8	94.9	69.1	73.9	90.6
30–35	95.0	92.5	97.0	63.8	73.1	92.8
35–40	97.0	95.4	97.0	65.6	74.7	93.0
40–45	96.9	95.2	97.0	67.9	76.2	93.1
45–50	95.9	93.8	96.1	64.3	70.9	90.9
50–55	92.9	89.2	92.6	56.1	62.8	86.1
55–60	79.9	72.0	80.7	42.1	48.5	73.6
60–65	34.6	23.5	41.9	11.6	12.1	37.3
65 and older	4.7	2.7	6.9	1.8	1.3	5.3

Source: Hofmann (1994, 1995).
a. The activity rate is the share of the labor force (employees, self-employed, and unemployed) in the total population in the age group.

be small for young women because of their increased participation in higher education and training. For women aged 25 to 35 there will also be a slight increase (childbearing will still be important). The rate of women older than 35 is expected to grow more quickly. Older men and women will increase their activity. Owing to the long-term financial problems of the public pension systems, the government will take appropriate measures to raise retirement age.

The projection from the Centre for Labor Market Research of the Federal Labor Office (IAB), 1991 and 1995, is derived from its population projection, based mainly on the assumptions of the seventh projection, the base year being 1990. The main assumptions are that the fertility rate remains constant at the level of 1987 and net migration by 2010 amounts to 4.2 million persons. Net migration after 2010 is not taken into account. Total population will be 71 million in 2030. The projection takes into account that the potential labor force participation rate depends on labor market indicators. The rate varies among age groups and gender and also between nationals and nonnationals.

TABLE 4-8. *Projections of Potential Total Labor Force, 2000–40*
Millions

Projection	Base year	2000	2010	2020	2030	2040
Ifo low var.	38.3 (1990)	37.49	36.1	33.16	n.a.	n.a.
Ifo high var.		41.1	45.7	48.16	n.a.	n.a.
Prognos low var.	41.1 (1992)	n.a.	39.2	n.a.	n.a.	29.2
Prognos high var.		n.a.	40.6	n.a.	n.a.	34.8
IAB var. 1	41.1 (1990)	41.0	40.2	36.9	31.8	n.a.
IAB var. 2		40.5[a]–40.8[b]	41.4	38.2	32.9	n.a.
IAB var. 3		41.0[a]–41.4[b]	42.4	39.1	33.6	n.a.

Sources: Hofmann (1994, 1995); Prognos (1995); and IAB. IAB variant 1: constant activity rates; IAB variant 2: varying activity rates low; IAB variant 3: varying activity rates high.
a. Convergence of eastern German activity rates to the western German average up to 2000.
b. Convergence of eastern German activity rates to the western German average up to 2010.
n.a. Not available.

Three scenarios have been elaborated with differing potential labor market activity rates (table 4-8).

The total labor force projections vary considerably because of important differences between the population projections and the varying assumptions of activity rates. All forecasts of the labor supply based on projections with a shrinking population result in a more or less shrinking labor force. This indicates that none of the projections assumes that the effect of a shrinking population will be offset by increasing activity rates.

The share of elderly workers will increase. According to the Ifo projection, persons 45 to 65 in a work force of 25- to 65-year-olds will increase from 40 percent in 1990 to more than 47 percent in 2020. The share of persons 50 to 65 will expand from 21 percent in 1990 to nearly 30 percent in 2020. The share of persons 50 and older of the total potential labor force will be larger than of those younger than 30.

Current projections are basically derived from population forecasts. But labor supply also depends on the long-term growth rate of the economy. In particular, there are interdependencies between immigration policy and labor market development. The retirement age is also correlated with the unemployment rate, or, conversely, with the labor shortage. Only the Prognos projection attempts to take these interdependencies into account. The starting point for Prognos lies in assumptions about the growth rate of the economy and labor productivity. Its projection does not directly address the question of the future distribution of labor (the extent of part-time work). But it does make assumptions about the growth rate of the future total of hours worked: from 1992 to 2040 an average annual variation rate of -0.9 percent is expected.

According to estimates put forward by the DIW, the current high unemployment rate will be difficult to lower, at least by 2010, even assuming a favorable economic climate. By assuming continuity in the development of output and productivity, a nominal labor-market equilibrium will be achieved in 2020. Prognos also gives estimates about future unemployment rates derived from aggregate demand and increased productivity. However, the impact of labor market mismatch on unemployment rates will still be important.

Income Sources of the Elderly

The incomes of households headed by retired persons improved during the 1970s from 65 percent of the average of all households to 77 percent and worsened slightly during the 1980s to 73 percent.[6] Taking into account that the average size of households headed by the elderly is smaller, per capita income is approximately the same as for the average of all households, although there are differences when consumer units are considered. The average per capita income was higher for the elderly than for blue-collar households and slightly below that in a white-collar household. It was nearly half of per capita income of households headed by self-employed persons (except farmers).[7] There is a major difference among retired persons between beneficiaries of public pensions and former civil servants. In 1994 the income of households headed by a person receiving a public pension was about 86 percent of the averge received by all households, measured in consumer units, while households headed by a former civil servant had a relative income position of 120 percent.[8]

Pensioner households are concentrated in the DM 1,000–DM 2,000 monthly net income group, where they represent half of all households (table 4-9). The 42 percent share of pensioner households in all

6. Wirtschaft und Statistik (1992); and author's calculations.
7. Wirtschaft und Statistik (1992).
8. DIW (1995); and author's calculations.

TABLE 4-9. *Distribution of Household Earnings within Net Income Groups, by Age of Household Head, 1988*
Percent unless otherwise specified

Monthly net income (deutsche marks)	All households	Households with head 65 or older	Households with head younger than 65
0–1,000	3.7	5.6	3.0
1,000–2,000	21.6	38.8	15.0
2,000–3,000	21.9	27.8	19.6
3,000–4,000	17.5	13.1	19.1
4,000–5,000	13.3	6.8	15.8
5,000–10,000	20.1	7.1	25.2
10,000–25,000	1.9	0.7	2.4

Sources: Statistisches Bundesamt, *Einkommens- und Verbraucherstichproben* (1988); and author's calculations.

households receiving less than DM 1,000 is also very high. Pensioner households are still overrepresented within the DM 2,000–DM 3,000 income group (36 percent in this income group, the share of pensioner households to all households in all income groups being 28 percent). When one interprets these figures, it must be remembered that the average size of pensioner households is smaller and a larger share of households are single people. Poverty is relatively widespread among elderly women. Taken together with the findings that the average income per member of pensioner-headed households is more or less the same as for all households, it can be assumed that income among the elderly is less equally distributed than for all households.

Today's elderly have accumulated significant amounts of both real estate and monetary assets (tables 4-10 and 4-11). More than 63 percent of households headed by persons age 55 to 66 have real estate. The fact that only 50 percent of households headed by persons 65 and older have real estate is partly due to transfers to younger people. According to DIW calculations, real estate has become slightly more equally distributed over time.[9]

Transfers between generations (bequests and donations) accounted for 20 to 25 percent (depending on the age groups considered) of all real estate transactions in 1993.[10] The figures indicate that there is still

9. DIW (1996).
10. Wirtschaft und Statistik (1995b).

TABLE 4-10. *Real Estate of Households, by Age Group of Household Head, 1993*
Percent of age group

Age groups	Western Germany	Eastern Germany
25 and younger	(6.8)	n.a.
25–30	17.3	15.3
30–35	35.0	26.6
35–40	51.0	31.6
40–45	60.0	34.7
45–55	61.1	34.9
55–65	63.3	34.4
65 and older	49.8	20.4

Source: Wirtschaft und Statistik (1995).
n.a. Not available.

a huge potential for future bequests. The value of bequests of financial assets is expected to grow sharply during the 1990s and to double between 2000 and 2030.[11] This development is likely to increase the inequalities in the distribution of private wealth of future elderly.

In western Germany private insurance assets as a share of all financial assets of households whose head is reaching retirement age (55 to 65 years) is important. Figures for households headed by persons 65 or older indicate that dissaving occurs mainly through spending insurance assets; the average financial assets of these households are still important and are comparable to those of households headed by 35- to 40-year-olds. But net financial assets (excluding loans) are between 85 percent and 94 percent of gross financial assets for people 40 or younger, while older households have nearly no borrowed funds. To evaluate correctly the relative wealth of the elderly, various types of transfers such as price reductions for a wide range of goods and services, including public transport, should also be taken into consideration.

In households headed by persons 65 and older, earnings as a share of gross income have diminished since the 1970s (table 4-12). Public pensions as a share of gross income held steady around 70 percent in the 1970s and 1980s. The share represented by income from assets can be expected to increase in the future.

11. Lang (1996).

TABLE 4-11. *Gross Financial Assets (Including Borrowings) of Private Households, 1993*
Deutsche marks

Age group of head of household	Western Germany		Eastern Germany	
	Average of households' gross financial assets	*Average of households' private insurance assets*	*Average of households' gross financial assets*	*Average of households' private insurance assets*
30 and younger	25,100	3,700	11,200	900
30–35	39,100	9,800	19,900	1,800
35–40	52,600	17,400	24,300	2,500
40–45	67,000	29,100	25,900	3,100
45–55	90,400	41,500	30,000	3,200
55–65	89,400	39,100	27,000	2,500
65 and older	55,600	6,500	19,200	1,400

Source: Wirtschaft und Statistik (1995).

TABLE 4-12. *Distribution of Income Sources and Saving Rates of the Elderly,*
West Germany, Selected Years, 1973–88
Percent of gross income unless otherwise specified

Income sources	1973	1978	1983	1988
Earnings	17	12	9	9
Assets	12	11	15	14
Life insurance	0.7	1.1	0.6	1.3
Public pension	67	70	69	69
Employer-based pension	n.a.	n.a.	3.3	3.3
Saving rate 65 and older	14.5	11.3	10.6	7.4
Saving rate 65–70	n.a.	10.7	10.3	7.5
Saving rate 70 and older	n.a.	11.6	10.7	7.3
Saving rate all households	17.6	n.a.	n.a.	12.1
Net income of household head 65 and older/net income all household heads	65.9	n.a.	n.a.	71.2

Source: Statistisches Bundesamt, *Einkommens- und Verbraucherstichproben* (1973, 1978, 1983, 1988); and author's calculations (the data of the sample of 1993 are not yet available).
n.a. Not available.

Family support has to be taken into consideration. Family values are enshrined in the German constitution, which means that in some areas the subsidiarity principle applies: if a family is to receive means-tested social assistance, its income, including that of near relatives, is decisive. The amount of interfamily support is, however, difficult to estimate. It is even more difficult to estimate the value of family networks and help. The share of elderly living with their near relatives is, however, small—less than 10 percent. Most (57 percent) can afford to live on their own or with a spouse only (32.5 percent).[12]

In 1988, dissaving accounted for about 17 percent of disposable income in households headed by persons 55–65. It accounted for 19 percent in households with a 65- to 70-year-old head and 15 percent for households headed by someone older than 70 (the average dissaving rate for all households was about 14 percent).[13] Annuities from life insurance are statistically part of dissaving. The annuities' share of disposable income in 1988 ranged from 1.4 percent for households whose head was 55 to 65, to 2.6 percent for households whose head

12. Heuwinkel, Kujath, and Bergmann (1996, p. 708).
13. Statitstisches Bundesamt, *Einkommens- und Verbraucherstichproben.*

was 65 to 70, to 0.6 percent for households whose head was older than 70.

The saving rate in west Germany declined between the mid-1970s and the mid-1980s but has increased since then, reaching 14.6 percent of income in 1991.[14] Although the life-cycle hypothesis suggests that the elderly spend their savings, data from Germany show that the oldest of the old generally save more (or dissave less). With increasing life expectancy the incentive to save more during active middle age may increase, so that a possible decapitalizing would follow a slower and less dramatic path. Moreover, expectations that future public pension reforms will lower benefits, combined with risk aversion, may be an incentive for people to save more. However, as the share of households with no children increases, saving to provide an inheritance becomes less common. This and a modified lifestyle and the already high level of accumulated private wealth (the effect of bequests) may induce a lower saving rate in the future.

The Pension Programs

Public pension programs in Germany include the statutory public pension plan (Gesetzliche Rentenversicherung, or GRV); public pensions for civil servants; and the supplementary pension program for public sector employees. Private pensions include employer-based programs, life insurance annuities, and so forth.

For retired persons today or in the near future public pensions are more important than employer-based pensions. Ninety percent of all men 55 or older receive or expect to receive income from the public pension program (table 4-13). In the 1980s, employer-based pensions accounted for only 3 percent of gross income of the elderly; public pensions accounted for nearly 70 percent. Pensioners who have made contributions over a period of forty-five years and earned the economywide average wage get nearly 70 percent of the average net wage from the public pension plan. The level of pensions usually varies by gender and occupational status: white-collar workers get a higher income than blue-collar and women on average receive much less than men. The wage differences and differences in the labor market activity

14. Deutsche Bundesbank, *Monatsbericht* (April 1992).

TABLE 4-13. *Share of People Receiving or Expecting Income from Pension Plans, by Sex, 1994*
Percent

Type of plan	Women 55 years or older	Men 55 years or older
Public pension scheme (GRV)	66.6	90.3
Public pensions for civil servants	1.0	12.2
Supplementary public pensions for public service employees	6.1	10.3
Employer-based pensions	4.8	24.0
No income or no expected income from pension scheme	31.9	0

Source: Enquete-Kommission (1994).

rates during working years are thus reflected during retirement. Although nearly a third of all women 55 and older either receive or will receive no income from pensions of their own, all men do. The income of elderly women relative to that of men will increase in the long term as their labor market participation rates increase.

Because public pension benefits are high, income from employer-based pensions, participation in which is voluntary, has a far less important function. Employer-based pension programs have been regulated in general terms by law since 1974. However, specific arrangements are subject to collective bargaining and codetermination. The programs are basically financed by the employers. They are in effect in 35 percent of western German firms and cover 47 percent of all employees, mainly in large manufacturing firms (table 4-14). In 1976 two-thirds of employees were covered by firm-specific pension programs.[15] It can be expected that the importance of these pensions will decline, at least as long as there is no labor shortage. Moreover, it is likely that contributions to the public pension plan will increase, so that nonwage labor costs will rise. In the face of international competition, employers will seek to cut at least voluntary nonwage labor costs.

For the statutory public pension scheme, the "normal" retirement age is fixed at 65. There are special rules for some occupational groups (pilots, for example, must retire earlier). Half of all women that retire

15. Beyer (1994).

TABLE 4-14. *Share of Employees Covered by Employer-Based Pensions, by Firm Size, 1990*[a]

Firm size (employees)	5,000 +	2,000–4,999	500–1,999	100–499	50–99	10–49	Less than 10
Percent of employees covered	86	75	62	43	29	22	13

Source: Beyer (1994).
a. Excludes public service providers.

are 65 years old, whereas the share for men is about 20 percent.[16] Eligibility for preretirement at age 63 (*flexible Altersgrenze*) requires thirty-five years of contributions (there are special provisions for early retirement on the grounds of disability and invalidity). Eligibility for preretirement at age 60 is available to women who have contributed at least fifteen years, ten of them after reaching age 40, and to elderly long-term unemployed (at least one year unemployed just before turning 60 years old and having contributed for at least fifteen years, eight during the last ten). This program applies to 14 percent of all retiring men.

The incentives for early retirement were created to reduce unemployment, but since the end of the 1980s the government has been trying to lengthen working life. From 1984 to 1988 an early retirement act (*Vorruhestandsgesetz*) allowed employees to retire at age 58 (much of the loss of income was made up by employers, who were partly reimbursed by the Labor Office under special circumstances). As of age 60, employees were mostly eligible for the public pension early retirement plan.

The Pension Reform Act of 1992 aimed gradually to abolish the programs for preretirement by 2006 or 2012 and in effect reinstall 65 as the normal retirement age. In 1996 the government decided to accelerate these reforms. The possibilities for preretirement will be limited as of 2000 and the transition period will be shortened to 2001 for men and 2005 for women. Eligibility for early retirement on the grounds of unemployment increased from age 60 to age 63 as of 1997. The pension level will be reduced for pensioners younger than 63.[17]

16. Deutsches Zentrum für Altersfragen (1993).
17. *Süddeutsche Zeitung* 6 (July 7, 1996).

In cases of disability, eligibility for public pensions can be established after a year of unemployment. Persons 50 and older do not even have to fulfil this condition because it is assumed that they have no chance of finding a new job. In 1990 more than one-third of men and 17 percent of women taking retirement were beneficiaries of this special early retirement plan (blue-collar workers, especially, are beneficiaries of this program). The federal government now intends to abolish disability pensions awarded because of labor market conditions.

The statutory public pension insurance is now partly financing unemployment. Despite the possibility of continuing work without pension cuts after age 65, only 0.2 percent of retired men and 0.1 percent of retired women continue working. Although gradual retirement is possible in Germany, it is somewhat rare. The Pension Reform Act of 1992 aimed at reinforcing gradual retirement and partial pension programs. However, the success of the provisions will depend on the labor market, the distribution of labor among generations, and changes in personnel policies.

The younger generations' burden of financing public pensions will increase dramatically in the next century. The *social dependency rate*, the ratio of elderly to economically active persons (employees, civil servants, and self-employed), increased in West Germany between 1960 and 1970 and has since remained around 45 percent (figure 4-2). Thus, lowering the average retirement age in the past was possible without creating an additional burden for younger workers. According to the FSO's seventh population projection, the ratio will increase to 80 percent in 2030 (table 4-15).

Not all economically active persons contribute to the public pension scheme, just employees paying contributions on a compulsory base. The share of all economically active persons who were employees in 1993 was about 83 percent.[18] The social dependency rate of people aged 60 and older was about 55.7 percent in 1992. According to Prognos, in 2040 this rate will be 88 percent in its high-population variant and 101 percent in its low variant (table 4-15). These estimates suggest an enormous potential for future intergenerational conflicts.

This public pension plan works on a pay-as-you-go basis. It is mainly financed by contributions that depend on gross wages and are

18. Statistisches Bundesamt, *Statistisches Jahrbuch* (1996).

FIGURE 4-2. *Social Dependency Rate, Selected Years, 1960–90, and Projected to 2030*[a]

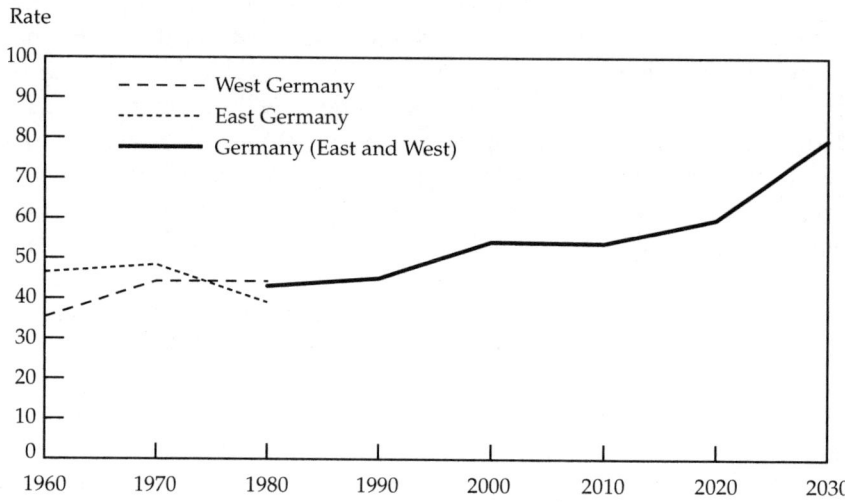

Source: Höhn (1994).
a. Population aged 60 and older in relation to 100 economically active persons.

shared equally by employees and employers. In 1992 contributions for employees accounted for 75.5 percent of all revenues. In total all contributions (including unemployed) were 80.8 percent, and the Bundeszuschuß (the tax-based transfer of the federal government to the statutory public pension institution) 17.6 percent. The contributions to the GRV are compulsory for all blue- and white-collar employees with gross monthly earnings more than a minimum (DM 610 in western Germany in 1997). The contributions are imposed up to a ceiling (*Beitragsbemessungsgrenze*). For 1994 this was DM 7,600 in western Germany and DM 5,900 in eastern Germany. The ceiling is intended to promote private pension programs because those earning more have incentives to make additional private retirement provisions.

The size of the pensions is mainly based on the years of contribution (with a current minimum participation of five years), the relative income of the beneficiary during the working period, the development

TABLE 4-15. *Projected Aged Dependency Rate (DR) on Economically Active Persons (EAP) and Social Dependency Rate (SDR) on All Employees, Selected Years, 2000–40*

Item	1990	2000	2010	2020	2030
DR 60+ on EAP	45	54	54	60	80
DR 65+ on EAP	33	38	42	45	61
	1992		2010	2030	2040
SDR high variant	55.7		67.4	89.5	88.4
SDR low variant	55.7		69.2	98.5	101.1

Sources: Höhn (1994, p. 52); and Prognos (1995).

of average net wages of all contributors, and a potentially fixed-weight factor (for retirement pensions the factor is 1, for disability 0.66). The Public Pension Reform Act introduced a special factor that reduced pensions for beneficiaries younger than 65 and increased them for workers who retire after 65. In addition, a partial pension system allowing for gradual retirement was introduced (on the basis of a third, half, or two-thirds of the eligible pension level). Given partial pensions and part-time earnings together, a retired person can nearly reach his or her former earnings. The new rules will have an impact only at the beginning of the next century, when the average retirement age will be slowly increased.

Pensions are linked to the development of net wages and are readjusted yearly. Consequently, an increase in contribution rates or income taxes lowers the level of public pensions. Before 1992 they were based on the development of gross wages (net wages being defined as gross wages minus social security contributions and income taxes). The indexing of pensions at gross earnings instead of net earnings led to an increase in the ratio of the net pension level to average net earnings.

In 1995, expenditures exceeded the revenues of the public pension system by DM 6,245 million.[19] German unification and high unemployment are contributing to the financing problems. To have a balanced or even positive financing balance in the future, the contribution rates will, as in the past, have to rise (figure 4-3). The basic assumption for the projections carried out by Prognos is that in the future, pen-

19. Bernstein and Blossfeld (1995).

FIGURE 4-3. *Projected Contribution Rates to the Public Pension Program under Two Scenarios, Selected Years, 2010–40*

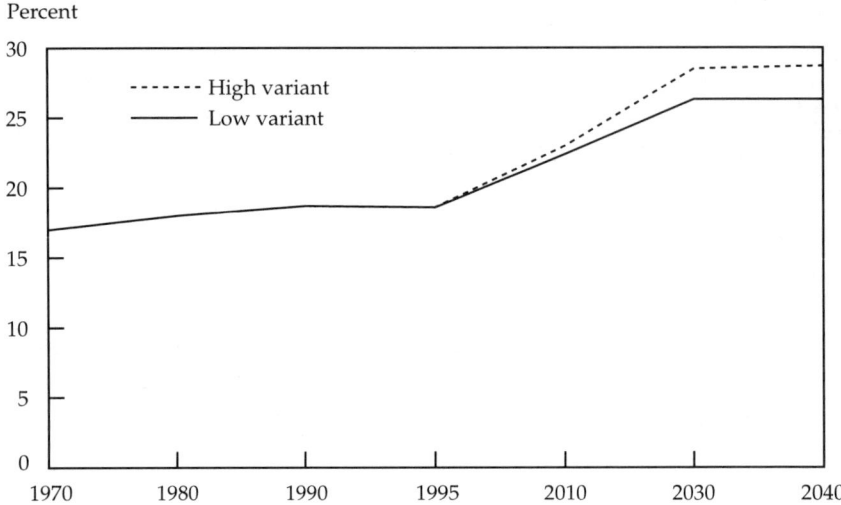

Sources: 1970–95: Lampert (1994); and Rentenversicherungsbericht (1995). Projection: Prognos (1995).

sions will be linked, as they are today, to the net wage development. According to Prognos's projection, federal payments to the public system (*Bundeszuschuß*) will first decrease in the high-population variant and then rise to 18.1 percent in 2040, which would be only slightly above the level of 1992. In the low variant the share of the Bundeszuschuß of all revenues would increase, especially after 2020, to 21.4 percent in 2040. This larger share as compared to the high variant is due to the fact that the Bundeszuschuß is linked to variations of gross income and contribution rates.

Implications for the Fiscal Balance

Besides its effect on the public pension system, the aging of the population will have a major impact on the expenditures of the public health care system (statutory health care insurance and statutory long-term care insurance). Private health insurance plans are of minor importance in Germany. Their outlays for health care accounted only for 5 percent of total health care expenditures in 1992, as in 1970.[20]

Statutory health insurance (GKV) is mandatory for employees earning up to a certain ceiling (DM 5,700 in 1994 in western Germany) and for retired beneficiaries of public pensions and others such as students and unemployed persons. Among the beneficiaries, 18.1 percent were insured on a voluntary basis (1993).[21] In 1992 some 90 percent of the population was covered by the GKV. Among the contributors, 17.7 percent were pensioners in 1993.

Contributions finance 95 percent of the GKV. The contributions for employees are equally shared between employers and employees. Family members with no income or very little (29 percent of all beneficiaries in 1993) are insured free. About 20 percent of the contributors are either retired or unemployed. Half of the contributions for retired elderly are paid by the statutory public pension system; the contributions for unemployed are paid by the statutory unemployment insurance, or in some cases by the federal government. A variation in the contribution rates to the GKV directly affects the level of public pensions, which are based on net wages. Moreover, the outlays of the public pension program are affected by a change in contribution rates.

The growth rates of medical care expenditures were particularly high until 1978, but since then they have fallen. Per capita expenditures are much higher for elderly people than for the young, and the difference is expected to widen (table 4-16). According to the projections of Prognos, the average growth rate of outlays per head will be higher in eastern than in western Germany. In the high-population variant the rate will amount to 3 percent (2.2 percent in western Germany) for the forecasting period, and in the low variant 2.6 percent (1.9 percent in western Germany), starting from an average lower level (DM 2,016 in 1992). Together with an increasing share of elderly, and among them of those 80 and older, and a higher level of medical care, the expenditure for health care could easily explode.

Basically, Prognos is assuming that in the future the outlays of the GKV will still mainly depend on contributions. Contributions will only

20. Statistisches Bundesamt, *Statistisches Jahrbuch* (1996).
21. Statistisches Bundesamt, *Statistisches Jahrbuch* (1996).

TABLE 4-16. Expenditures of the GKV (without Administrative Costs), by Age Group, 1992 and Real Annual Growth Rates and Prospects, Western Germany
Real annual growth rate (percent)

Age group	Deutsche marks per capita	Index, average = 100	High variant			Low variant	
			1974/1992	2010/1992	2040/2010	2010/1992	2040/2010
0–19	1,138	44	0.8	1.2	1.1	1.1	0.7
20–59	2,165	84	2.7	1.4	1.4	1.3	0.7
60–69	3,932	152	3.8	2.0	1.5	1.9	0.8
70–79	5,690	220	4.8	2.3	2.3	2.2	1.7
80 and older	7,890	305	4.9	2.1	2.6	2.1	1.9
Total	2,588	100	3.4	2.1	2.3	2.1	1.8

Source: Prognos (1995).

rise within an "accepted" margin. However, the study does not specify the implications for the quality of health care. Instead of lowering the quality, it is possible that the costs will be lowered through weakening the medical sector lobby, allowing for more competition. The contribution rates to the public health care system increased from 8.2 percent in 1970 to 12.7 percent in 1992, and Prognos expects them to rise to 15 percent by 2030 and 16 percent by 2040.[22]

Since 1995 a new public statutory long-term care insurance has been in effect. Before 1995 most people in need of long-term care were dependent on means-tested social assistance (*Sozialhilfe*), and DM 12.7 billion was spent in this way (one-third of social assistance expenditures).[23] The new insurance is compulsory for 83 percent of the population. The system is based on a pay-as-you-go plan and is financed by assessments (currently 1 percent) on gross earnings (up to a ceiling), equally shared between employees and employers. As in the statutory health care insurance, family members without income or with very low incomes are insured free. To alleviate these new indirect labor costs for employers, one public holiday has been abolished.

The Long-Term Care Insurance Act favors care at home rather than in a nursing home. Frail persons getting domiciliary care can choose between transfers in cash, which allow them to compensate family members or friends for their help (the transfers currently range from DM 400 a month to DM 2,800, according to three categories of care needs), or in kind (which means receiving help from professionals). Combinations are permitted. If a transfer to a nursing home is considered necessary, the expenses are refunded up to a certain limit (which normally covers the share of care expenditures, but not accommodation and food).

Forecasts based on the FSO's seventh population projection assume that the number of frail persons living in private households who are beneficiaries of the plan will increase from 1.12 million to 1.5 million by 2030 (2.1 percent of all persons living in private households).[24] The share of care provided by nursing homes is expected to increase from

22. Lampert (1994, p. 230); and Prognos (1995).
23. Schmähl (1995).
24. Höhn (1994, p. 273).

27 percent in 1991 to 30 percent in 2030, so that the total number of persons benefiting will reach 2 million by 2030.[25]

According to Prognos estimates in the high-population variant, the number of all persons needing care will increase from 1.65 million in 1994 to 2.32 million in 2040 in the high variant and to 2.14 million in the low variant. Thus contribution rates are expected to increase from 1.0 percent in 1995 to 2.3 percent (low variant) or 2.6 percent (high variant) by 2040.[26]

Social spending, including spending by the public social insurance system and additional employer-based programs and indirect transfers such as tax exemptions or special rules such as spouse splitting, increased from 26.5 percent of GNP to 32.5 percent during the 1970s, decreased slightly during the 1980s, and has increased again since 1990. In 1994 the social budget accounted for a third of GNP.[27] The increase of more than 4 percentage points between 1990 and 1994 can be explained by additional social costs caused by German unification and increasing unemployment in recent years. Within the social budget, the public pension system accounted for one-third of total outlays in 1994, statutory health insurance accounted for a fifth, the expenditures of the Labor Office for 11 percent, means-tested social assistance for 5 percent, and employer-based pensions for 2 percent.[28]

The sum of public social transfers in cash and the transfer in kind from the GKV and the public long- term care insurance accounted for 23 percent of GNP in 1992 (*Sozialleistungsquote*). According to Prognos's estimates, by 2020 this share will contract slightly in the high-population variant and then will rise to 24 percent in 2040. In the low variant the share is higher in 2020 and will reach 28.5 percent in 2040.

Contribution rates for employers and employees to the public social security system (in percent of the gross wage paid to the employee) include contributions to the public pension system, public health insurance, long-term care insurance, and unemployment insurance. Additionally, employers must pay contribution rates to statutory accident insurance and in the public sector contribute to an additional pension plan. According to Prognos, employees' contribution rates will in-

25. Schmähl (1995).
26. Prognos (1995).
27. Achenbach and Haneberg (1995, p. 9).
28. Statistisches Bundesamt, *Statistisches Jahrbuch* (1996).

TABLE 4-17. *Projected Employer and Employee Contribution Rates to Social Security System and Income Taxes, 2000–40*
Percent

Item	1992	2000	2010	2020	2030	2040
High variant						
Employer rate	18.5	20.4	21.1	21.7	23.0	23.2
Employee rate	15.0	17.1	18.1	18.5	19.6	20.3
Income tax	17.3	17.2	17.0	17.5	20.0	21.7
Low variant						
Employer rate	18.5	19.9	21.4	22.4	24.2	24.8
Employee rate	15.0	17.1	18.5	19.3	20.8	22.0
Income tax	17.8	17.2	17.3	18.3	21.5	23.6

Source: Prognos (1995).

crease from 15 percent to 20.3 percent by 2040. In the high variant the contribution rates of employers will rise from 18.5 to 23.2 percent, and the average income tax will amount to 21.7 percent (table 4-17). In the low variant the increases are more important: employers' contribution rates will be nearly 25 percent in 2040, employees' contribution rates 22 percent, and income taxes 23.6 percent.

Net wages (gross wages less social security contributions and income taxes) share of gross wages will decrease in the high variant from 65 percent in 2010, to 60.4 percent in 2030, and to 58 percent in 2040. In the low variant the ratio will be 64 percent in 2010, 58 percent in 2030, and 55 percent in 2040. Prognos assumes in its high-variant projections that the net wage per employee in 1991 prices will increase annually by 1.8 percent between 1992 and 2010 and by 1.6 percent afterward; in the low variant it will increase by 1.5 percent until 2010 and then by 1.0 percent.

It is questionable whether younger workers will accept such a declining percentage of their gross wages. Considering that employers' higher contribution rates are very likely to be (at least partially) compensated by less growth in the rates of gross wages than would otherwise be the case, the burden for the working population could be even heavier.

In regard to other public expenditures in the long term, Prognos assumes a slight decrease in public sector employment (table 4-18) due to fewer teachers in the public education system (the demographic effect being more important than a growing education level and life-long learning). However, this assumption is questionable because over-all investments in human capital are not likely to decrease, even if a decline of population is assumed. The projections also assume fewer persons will be employed in general public administration due to shrinking population and employment increases in long-term care. In health care two contradictory developments are taking place (shrinking population but poor age structure).

In general, growing public investments in environmental protection, public transport, research, and worker retraining can be assumed. This is partly due to the aging of the population, since an aging work force will induce more retraining expenditures and elderly people's increasing demand for mobility but decreased capacity to drive cars will place more demands on public transport. Despite the shrinking of the population, the number of people older than age 60 will increase in absolute terms. This will trigger additional needs for investments in nursing homes and other age-related things.

Prognos also estimates that public investments as a share of GDP will increase slightly in the low variant and decrease slightly in the high variant. The estimates assume a greater need for public investments in eastern Germany and smaller investments in schools and universities (table 4-19).

Even assuming public expenditures' share of GDP will shrink, the share of total public spending, including spending for the public social security system, is expected to increase from about 50 percent in the early 1990s to 49 percent (high variant) or about 55 percent (low variant) by 2040. Prognos is projecting in both variants that demographic development will not harm the fiscal balance until after 2010. Later on, the low variant predicts a negative effect, while in the high variant the share will not increase by 2040. It is assumed that new net public indebtedness as a percentage of GNP will contract slightly.

Whether the expenditures of the federal, regional, and local authorities (thus not including the social security institutions) will decline as forecast by Prognos is questionable. For example, increased numbers of migrant workers and greater labor force participation can be linked to costs (kindergartens and so forth). The increased public expenditures for the elderly that will be needed just to maintain the current welfare level will probably not be offset by declining expendi-

TABLE 4-18. *Projected Public Spending (without Public Investments and Outlays for Transfer Incomes) and Investment, Selected Years, 2000–40*

Item	1979[a]	1992	2000		2010		2020		2040	
			High variant	*Low variant*	*High variant*	*Low variant*	*High variant*	*Low variant*	*High variant*	*Low variant*
Public sector employment (millions)	2.98	5.77	5.62	5.60	n.a.	n.a.	5.70	5.35	5.12	4.42
Public expenditures (percent of GDP)		19.4	n.a.	n.a.	16.3	17.4	n.a.	n.a.	13.9	16.7
Public investment (percent of GDP)		2.8	n.a.	n.a.	2.8	3.0	n.a.	n.a.	2.4	3.0

Source: Prognos (1995).
a. West Germany only.
n.a. Not available.

TABLE 4-19. *Public Expenditures Including Social Security as Share of GDP under Two Assumptions, 1992 Actual and Projected to 2040*
Percent

Assumption	1992	2010	2030	2040
High variant	49.5	47.5	48.5	49.1
Low variant	49.5	48.9	52.2	54.6

Source: Prognos (1995).

tures for the education system, because a permanent (re)training of the labor force, especially of the older age groups, will be more and more necessary. Cuts in public investment in human capital would decrease the potential for economic growth and thus worsen the financial situation of pension programs. Nevertheless, it has to be taken into consideration that possibly an increase of social activities of "younger old" (*aktives Altern*) related to changes in life style, and the decreasing average household size of the elderly, will take place. This may help to reduce public expenditures for social services. The future level of social welfare for the elderly is related to long-term economic performance and, most importantly, to how the intergenerational distribution conflict will be resolved.

Demographic Change, Distribution Conflict, and Policy Options

The potential intergenerational income distribution conflict is mainly reflected by the potential future financing problems of the public pension programs. But other aspects of public spending and issues related to the labor market will also cause distribution conflicts.

Pension Programs

The policy measures that have been proposed fall into two categories: those that will cause the younger generation to bear the bulk of the burden of an aging population or those that will cause the elderly to bear the burden. As long as pension benefits are linked to increases in wages and no measures are taken to lower the eligible pension levels, it is the younger generation that is mainly affected. This can occur in two ways.

To keep the GDP growth rate at a constant level (in order to avoid a possibly negative effect of a shrinking working population), the government must either boost productivity or increase the number of contributors or, better, do both. Productivity growth raises wages, but the share of this increase that younger workers will have to bear through contributions will be high: first, because a small number of earners must pay for a large number of retired persons, and second, because the design of the pension system lets the beneficiaries participate in the productivity growth as long as the dynamization of pensions is connected to increases in net wages. Wages would be lower if instead of through productivity growth the same GDP would be reached by expanding the working population: then workers would have to distribute the economic potentials among themselves. Even if both models led theoretically to the same net wages, workers' perception of bearing the financial burden for an aging population would be different. If GDP growth is reached solely through productivity increases, higher gross wages and higher contribution rates will be the result. If growth is reached through higher employment but slower productivity growth, gross wages as well as the contribution rates would be lower. The perception of bearing the financial burden differs not only in the employees' view. Current political discussion is focusing more on nonwage labor costs than on unit labor costs.

The current debate on the problem of intergenerational distribution of the public pension scheme focuses on how to augment the number of contributors and spread the burden among the whole population. Under discussion also is what part of the burden the elderly should bear themselves. The distribution conflict will be solved most easily if growth of the working population is combined with labor productivity growth. The prospects for economic growth and the development of labor productivity will be analyzed later in this chapter.

INCREASING THE NUMBER OF CONTRIBUTORS.   One way to increase the number of workers is to adjust immigration policies. Many academics favor increasing immigration in the long term. This is perceived as a means to counter the effects of an otherwise shrinking population.

Additional arguments stress the necessity of selective immigration to rectify labor shortages in some market segments.

But in an economy with high unemployment, policies to encourage immigration are not popular. The opening of eastern Europe and civil war in the former Yugoslavia have led to high immigration. It can be expected that pressure for immigration from central and eastern European countries and regions south of the Mediterranean will persist. It is difficult to predict whether public opinion will change on this point once the labor force has shrunk. As long as structural unemployment persists, xenophobia is unlikely to be fully overcome.

In recent years the immigration of refugees has been far more important in Germany than in other EU member states.[29] The percentage coming from the former Yugoslavia has been particularly large. Therefore, Germany has a pronounced interest in a long-term immigration policy designed in accordance with the policies of other member states. In particular, controlling the regional distribution of gains and losses related to migration within the European Union by introducing a quota system has been suggested.[30] Because such proposals run against the interest of most of the other member states, agreement on a common regulation is uncertain in the foreseeable future. Moreover, the member states are generally worried about a loss of sovereignty.

Most of the political debate in Germany concentrates on how the number of immigrants can be reduced. A more restrictive law covering political asylum was enacted in 1992, allowing persons to ask for asylum only if they did not cross the border of a declared "safe" country. As a result, the number of persons asking for political asylum in Germany fell from 438,000 in 1992 to 127,000 in 1994.[31] According to information provided by the Federal Office for the Recognition of Refugees, the share of these people that have been given the right to stay in Germany was 4.4 percent in 1990, 6.9 percent in 1991, 3.2 percent in 1993, and 7.3 percent in 1994. In addition, a number of refugees have received special permission to stay for a limited time. More than half of all persons asking for political asylum come from the former Yugoslavia, Poland, Romania, and Turkey. The new asylum law has

29. Gimbal (1994, p. 87).
30. Gimbal (1994, p. 70).
31. Statistisches Bundesamt (1995).

been criticized on humanitarian grounds, especially by the Green party and parts of the Social Democratic party. Officially, Germany is not an immigration country, and the federal government stresses this as a basic political principle for the future.

Other political options to expand the pool of workers are also subject to public discussion. A debate has been unleashed on reforming eligibility for German citizenship, which is now guided by the principle of the *jus sangui* instead of the *jus solis* that applies in most other European countries. Arguments in favor of the *jus solis* have been put forward by some Social Democrats with the objective of removing any special treatment of ethnic eastern European Germans (*Aussiedler*) vis-à-vis other immigrant groups. Ethnic Germans, with a long tradition in eastern European countries, have been an important immigration group in the 1990s. More important, some political groups have contended that the *jus solis* would facilitate the integration of immigrants who have lived in Germany for a long time. However, this proposal has not been accepted by most in the political arena.

In contrast to the expressed aims of the federal government, academics and some politicians have supported a selective immigration policy on economic grounds. Under discussion is how to manage a selective policy, on what criteria to set quotas, how flexible the system should be, and what time scale for migration flows should be realized. Of major importance is not only the educational attainment of the immigrants but also their age and sex.

There is a stark contrast between the official statements and the actual immigration policies because Germany is de facto an immigration country. Moreover, especially in the 1960s and 1970s, selective immigration has been the immigration policy, and it is still pursued in some areas, although at a comparatively low level compared with previous periods. It is likely that a selective immigration policy will be pursued ad hoc when labor is scarce.

From the academic point of view, a liberal immigration policy must be supplemented by expanding the labor market participation of women and the elderly. Net immigration will be needed by 2006 to cover the lack of workers in some labor market segments. This does not mean that unemployment will disappear in the first decade of the twenty-first century but only that a shortage of skilled labor in some fields is predicted.

An immigration policy that would be shaped to react only to short-term labor-market developments can cover shortages only of unskilled labor or of workers with very specific qualifications (where the knowledge of the German language and German technical standards is not necessary). Investments in the human capital of migrants is sensible, but this implies a long-term orientation for immigration and integration policy.

Many academics hold that immigration, especially of young persons, can alleviate but not reverse the aging of the population unless numbers higher than a politically acceptable level are permitted. The necessary volume needed to avoid a shrinking population still implies a process of aging.[32]

The benefits of immigration for the financing of the public pension system are estimated to be more important than the benefits for public health care insurance.[33] In general terms, immigration affects the average wage level and the wage structure and thus revenues and expenditures. Two effects of lower wages have to be distinguished. Immigration lowers the average macroeconomic wage bill. And because the pension level is set yearly in accordance with the level of the average wage, an increasing number of low-paid immigrants lowers the amounts of the pensions paid. The second major factor determining a pension is the relative income of the retired person for every year of contribution. Thus, if immigration enhances wage inequality by nationality, which is likely to occur, more German nationals will be eligible for higher pensions as their relative income position improves.[34] However, the educational and skills profiles of immigrants could change with the increasing demand for skilled labor. Among nonnationals the share of unskilled persons working in low-paid sectors will diminish if the sectors become economically less important. This can be expected at least for industry (this trend has already been observed for many years). Most important, however, is the beneficial effect of migration on the age structure of the population and thus on the financing of public pensions on a pay-as-you-go basis. The positive

32. See the calculations carried out by Steinmann (1996) and Lesthaeghe, Page, and Surkyn (1991, p. 292).
33. Schmähl (1995, p. 13).
34. Schmähl (1995, p. 24).

effect on revenues for the public pension system is diminished if there is discrimination by nationality on the labor market because contributions are linked to the individual wage levels.

Immigrants who return to their countries of origin once they reach retirement age are still eligible for German public pensions. Thus they export purchasing power, which weakens the beneficial effect of immigration on the German economy, although this result is modified by the fact that typically the home countries import goods from Germany. The German economy profits somewhat from the higher purchasing power in those countries because of the elderly that receive German pensions.

The current political debate generally concentrates on how to reduce immigration. The more academic oriented debate focuses on how to control immigrant flows to adapt them to economic needs. Thus immigration policy is not only discussed as a means of overcoming labor market shortages but also in the context of a shrinking share of the population contributing to the social security system. A more liberal immigration policy is generally regarded by academics as being inevitable, but it is not perceived as being the only way of responding to demographic change.

Population growth can also be achieved by increasing births, but the fertility rate is less easily influenced than levels of immigration. According to some calculations, increasing the fertility rate in Germany to 1.7 per woman by 2000 (nearly a one-third increase from the present level) and keeping it at this level would have the same effect on the proportion of elderly in the population as the yearly immigration of 150,000 persons.[35] But even that fertility level combined with a yearly immigration of 500,000 could not reverse the projected increased share of elderly in the population or the decreasing share of working people.

Family values are enshrined in the German Constitution. Special tax treatments and transfers (*Familienlastenausgleich*) apply to families with children. Since 1996 parents have been able to choose between a tax exemption for a child or a fixed direct transfer per child. But it seems that the financial incentives have either not been large enough

35. Steinmann (1996, p. 14 ff).

or are not decisive enough to induce more births. Meanwhile, a distributional conflict between families with children and couples or singles without children has arisen.

The Public Pension Reform Act of 1992 has lengthened the possibility for periods free of contributions to the public pension plan to bring up a child. Three years are now taken into account for the individual pension (for children born before 1992 only one year is taken into consideration). The current debate aimed at reducing public pension expenditures is not questioning this achievement. The debate concentrates on whether the regulation should be financed by the public pension plan or through general taxes.

Measures to allow a career and family duties to be carried out simultaneously are tremendously important in maintaining the labor pool. A study carried out at the end of the 1980s indicates that in the past few decades the family policy of the German government failed to increase the fertility rate. However, those Länder (states in the German federation) that have taken additional measures have been somewhat more successful.[36] Financial incentives combined with labor market security for employed women (the possibility of taking three years off work and for low-income families to receive public transfers for two years) were introduced in the 1980s. However, greater labor market flexibility and an increasing frequency of atypical work contracts (for example, fixed-term contracts) have reduced the effectiveness of employment protection laws passed to help young mothers stay employed.

Labor force growth (or lower rates of shrinkage) can also be achieved by increasing the labor market participation rates of women and the elderly. In general, a growing labor market participation rate is predicted for women, but it is questionable whether the potential of the situation will be fully exploited.[37] Not only the federal government's policy, which includes the same measures as for raising the fertility rate, but also business personnel policies are important. A change of personnel policies and values to improve women's career prospects and other determinants of job satisfaction will be necessary. The lack of child care facilities has always represented a major obstacle

36. Schwarz (1990).
37. Munz (1996).

for combining work and family duties. In the coming years a right to a place in nursery school will be gradually implemented. But no reforms are envisaged for the German school system, which has classes only in the morning.

Increasing the labor force participation rate of women would not only increase the number of contributors, but would also allow for a means-tested reduction of pensions for widows and lower means-tested social assistance expenditures. However, it is evident that the total sum of pensions to be paid in the long term will be higher as more women become eligible (this argument also applies to increasing immigration). A higher living standard of elderly couples can then be expected and cuts in pension benefits may then be politically more feasible, although still personally unacceptable.

Raising the activity rates of women cannot be the only measure taken. Even if their participation rate reaches the level of men, the demographic gap in the labor market cannot be closed.[38]

Another means of expanding the number of pension plan contributors is to lengthen everyone's working life. Increasing the labor force participation rates of the elderly would have two beneficial effects on the financial situation of the public pension system: the number of contributors would be increased, and the period of retirement would be shortened, which means that the pension sum to be paid would be reduced. But these effects are modified by the fact that a longer working life increases the pension level an individual is eligible for and that longer life expectancy is lengthening the retirement period.

A major emphasis of recent pension system reforms has been to limit the possibilities for early retirement and to promote gradual retirement from age 55 on. The net wages of older employees who reduce their average weekly working hours by a half will be at least 70 percent of their former net wages. Within the next five years, employers can receive subsidies from the Labor Office if they employ an unemployed person or an apprentice part-time.[39] The part-time retirement scheme will give the same eligibility for early retirement (after two years of part-time work) as long-term unemployment.

The present willingness to accelerate the reforms for lengthening

38. Schmid (1994, p. 113).
39. *Süddeutsche Zeitung* 6 (July 7, 1996).

working life is aimed at reducing the outlays of the public pension scheme, not increasing the number of contributors. The percentage of persons who receive public pensions on the grounds of early retirement due to unemployment has increased markedly since 1993.[40] Currently, the measures will result in higher expenditures from unemployment insurance or a general reduction in social benefits or both. The debate on early retirement is linked to the discussion of financing general economic risks by means other than the public pension scheme.

According to the minister for labor, a one-year increase of the average age of going into retirement would reduce the financial burden of the public pension system by DM 27 billion: DM 10 billion in additional revenues and DM 17 billion in less expenditure. This could represent a lowering of contribution rates by two percentage points.[41] Whether the present labor market situation will permit the expected additional revenues is questionable.

If lengthening working life is effectively to aid in financing the pension system, two conditions have to be fulfilled. First, younger employees should not be replaced by elderly ones because this would just mean shifting public pension expenditures to finance rising unemployment benefits. Second, businesses and employees will have to alter their attitudes toward gradual retirement. Shaping personnel policies to expedite integrating the elderly in internal labor markets will be inevitable. Moreover, appropriate tasks, including new types of activities, will have to be assigned to older employees.[42]

In addition, proposals to lengthen working life by reducing by one year the thirteen years of general education up to university entrance qualification would mean adapting the number of school years in Germany to the European average of twelve. Proposals have also been made to shorten the average stay at a university, which is comparatively long, by increasing the diversity of possible university degrees. The arguments for these proposals are, however, not based on the financial burden of public pensions but on improving Germany's international competitiveness, since the average age for entering the

40. Steffen (1996, p. 223 ff).
41. Blüm (1996).
42. Ritter (1995); and Wenzel and Flöter (1993, p. 47).

labor market is comparatively high in Germany. Moreover, the reforms would reduce expenditures for education.

Policies for boosting labor market participation rates can only be successful if there is sufficient demand for labor. As long as unemployment is high, increasing the supply of labor through immigration, rising birthrates, or greater labor market participation will result in either higher unemployment for some groups (segregation by nationality, gender, and age group) or reduced average working hours (redistribution of total working hours in the economy among all persons offering their labor).

Distributing labor fairly among all age groups while also lengthening working life can only be achieved by reducing the average number of hours worked each year. However, this also means a loss of income for the younger generation. The overall beneficial effect of this scheme for younger people would merely rely on a reduced number of eligible persons and thus lower expenditures on public pensions. For the elderly a system of lengthening working life and reducing yearly working time for the whole working population means a loss of income compared with today because the income lost through reduced working hours affects the level of pensions. The strengthening of gradual retirement is an appropriate measure in this respect. Thus, in the first stage, when unemployment is still at a high level, reduced working hours for the elderly will soften the impact of lengthening the working life on the labor market chances for younger people.

In the past the average number of hours worked yearly decreased considerably due to increased part-time work and more holidays and reduced weekly hours for full-time employed. The number of hours worked yearly has fallen by 25 percent since 1960, 15 percent since 1973, and 9 percent since 1980 (an average of −0.7 percent a year). It is questionable whether this trend can and should be reversed. According to W. Klauder, the trend toward reduced working hours will be stopped as a result of increasing individualization and flexibility of working time, which may sufficiently cover the needs of employees.[43] In any case the outcome of future distributional conflicts with regard to working hours is uncertain.

It is also assumed that immigration causes additional demand on

43. Klauder (1993a, p. 488).

the labor market because of a price effect (lower wages) and an income effect (higher consumption). Immigrants also show more flexibility on the labor market. Furthermore, labor shortages in very specific labor market segments, which exist in Germany despite high unemployment, can be overcome if the immigrants have the desired skills. If a sharp segmentation of the labor market by nationality occurs together with a high proportion of immigrants working within the nontradable goods and services sector, a shift in the relative prices of goods and services would occur. Thus demand for nontradable goods and services might increase, which leads to additional labor demand in the sector. Taking these factors together, decreased unemployment could be expected. Higher employment figures combined with greater population produces additional demand and benefits domestic economic development. According to a macroeconomic simulation carried out by the Ifo Institute, higher immigration in one period has a positive macroeconomic effect over the following decade.[44] The effect is weakened as long as the immigrants are substitutes rather than complementary to the otherwise available labor supply.[45]

If demand for labor remains unchanged over the next decades, labor shortages may occur, but not before about 2020. Using the IAB labor supply projection, W. Klauder has calculated that raising the retirement age to 70 and raising women's labor market participation rate to match that of men would compensate for half of the projected diminished labor supply.[46] However, the likely larger share of part-time work among women and the elderly and thus fewer hours worked has not been taken into account. Moreover, according to the projection, 6 million additional persons offering their labor would still be needed in 2030 to achieve today's labor supply. According to the Ifo simulation, a positive effect of migrant workers on the fiscal balance can be expected, although public expenditures for integration policies would increase at the same time.[47] A mostly positive effect of immigration on employment, economic growth, and the fiscal balance has also been predicted by others.[48]

44. Koll, Ochel, and Vogler-Ludwig (1992).
45. Schmähl (1995).
46. Klauder (1993a).
47. Koll, Ochel, and Vogler-Ludwig (1992, p. 167).
48. For example, Klauder (1993a).

Increasing the size of the population might lead to a different result for aggregate demand and employment than would increasing participation rates, while achieving the same number of hours worked. The difference results from the different income effect. An increase in population implies that output has to be distributed among more people, which lowers per capita income as compared with increased activity rates. Because one can assume the propensity to consume can be negatively correlated with income, an increase in population leads, other things being equal, to greater aggregate demand. However, the difference might not be substantial because additional employment effects of increasing labor market participation (such as outsourcing housework) have to be taken into account.

POLICIES FOR THE FINANCING STRUCTURE.   The financing philosophy and structure of the public pension have been subject to public debate for a long time. Since its introduction, the pay-as-you-go financing has been under attack, but always with little political support. In recent years the increase in financing elements of general social policy through the public pension system has been criticized. The background for the present reform discussion is not only the long-term prospect of demographic change but also the competitive pressure on labor costs.

It has been suggested that benefits that do not reflect the insurance character of the public pension system, such as partially financing unemployment through early retirement programs, be paid by the whole society through taxes and not just by labor through wage-related contributions. These factors include:

—early retirement arrangements to alleviate youth unemployment, including disability pensions based on the labor market situation;

—special provisions for retirees in eastern Germany and for ethnic German immigrants from eastern Europe;

—contribution-free periods for education and training, bringing up a child, or unemployment, that are taken into account for individual pensions;

—enhancing the eligible pension connected to very low income earned in the years before 1992;

—the share of contributions to the statutory health care insurance paid by the public pension system (not clear-cut); and

—pensions for widows (not clear-cut).

Foreign elements for insurance can also be found in the statutory health care system and the statutory unemployment insurance system. They represent between 20 and 25 percent of the benefits of the social security system. The burden for the system is approximately 15 percent, when deducting the federal transfer to the public pension scheme that is tax financed (*Bundeszuschuß*).[49] Foreign elements within the public pension system amount to nearly a third: 60 percent of this share is covered by the federal transfer and the remainder through contributions. Financing these elements by other means would allow for a 1.4 percentage point reduction in contribution rates to the statutory pension insurance.[50]

The main arguments in favor of tax-funded financing of the public pension plan that contradict the idea of equivalency are based on distributional policy and competition policy. The proposals include an increase in income taxes, an increase in value-added taxes, an increase in energy taxes or the introduction of new types of ecological taxes or both, and an increase in property taxes and taxes on bequests.

At first glance income taxes are more encompassing than contributions: they include a wider range of persons and different types of revenue. Income taxes are progressive, while contributions are proportional up to a defined income ceiling and regressive above this ceiling. However, the biggest share of income tax is wage-related and is paid mainly by employees. Thus most of a contribution reduction, shared equally between employers and employees, would be financed by the employees through higher income taxes (the wage-related part of income tax revenues was about 73 percent in 1994).[51] As labor costs are lowered, a higher demand for labor is induced.[52] Consequently, these kinds of reform measures should be taken as long as the unemployment problem persists. However, the net wages would be lower as well. The net medium-term effect would rely on higher employment figures combined with a lower GDP than would otherwise be the case.

49. Vogler-Ludwig and others (1996, p. 9).
50. Vogler-Ludwig and others (1996).
51. Vogler-Ludwig and others (1996).
52. Vogler-Ludwig and others (1996). In regard to wage-related contributions, a labor demand elasticity of −0.3 is assumed.

An increase in value-added taxes has been proposed by the minister for labor. This proposal is controversial within the major political parties. The main argument directed against it refers to the regressive character of direct taxation, although it is doubtful that this effect is significant. Another argument is that because firms cannot pass all of an increase in value-added taxes on to the consumer, a 1 percentage point increase will probably raise prices by 0.7 percent.[53] This will depress demand, reducing consumption expenditures and thus shrinking the tax base. Because net wages would be higher, the shrinkage of the tax base would be overcompensated and GDP growth could reach a higher level.[54] However, due to the price increase, workers might demand higher wages. An increase in net wages would not only increase unemployment but also raise public pension expenditures. With these arguments, the initial beneficial effect of lowering contributions through raising value-added taxes is diminished.

In recent years, popular proposals have been made to institute an ecological tax or increase existing energy taxes to realize ecological objectives and at the same time lower total labor costs by financing social security expenditures with the tax revenues. The revenues of such a tax would be high enough to reduce contribution rates markedly. However, the same criticism applies to ecological taxes as to increasing value-added taxes: an ecological tax is even more regressive than a general value-added tax because the share of energy expenditures of households with low incomes is larger.[55] Moreover, the effect on prices is greater, and with higher prices may come demands for wage increases. Net real wages could stagnate and gross net wages fall. Nevertheless, because of a more important change in relative prices of inputs (energy is becoming more expensive), the employment increases would be greater than with the reform model using higher value-added taxes. However, higher employment would be related to lower GDP growth rates because the shift toward more labor- intensive sectors is related to slower productivity growth in the medium term. In the long term the effects on GDP could be more important, assuming an expanding worldwide market for ecological products. Germany

53. Vogler-Ludwig and others (1996).
54. Vogler-Ludwig and others (1996).
55. Vogler-Ludwig and others (1996).

might then have advantages if its industry is seriously involved in that sector. If the introduction of the new taxation model was successful, the consumption of energy would be reduced. Achieving ecological aims would thus mean a smaller tax base. Consequently, the tax rate would have to be increased to keep revenues from slipping.

Increasing property taxes and taxes on bequests has also been demanded by various groups. The government, however, recently decided to abolish the property tax to boost economic growth. Taxes on bequests are still subject to debate. For a very long time higher taxation on bequests has been demanded on egalitarian grounds. Opponents of this tax argue that savings will decrease and families may be unable to keep family businesses. Greater taxation of bequests is primarily demanded by politicians. Debates focus on the level and kind of tax exemptions and the tax rates.[56] Reforming taxes on bequests is generally discussed in combination with a reform of income taxes.

A pension system based partly on taxes aims not only at reinvigorating the principle of equivalency but also reducing labor costs. In addition to altering the financing structure of public pensions, removing some foreign elements to the pension insurance system has been proposed, which will mean cuts in public pensions. In some cases income losses or contributions will be paid by other social security programs. For example, if restrictions on early retirement lead to higher expenditures for unemployment insurance, contributions during unemployment or illness now normally must be paid by the unemployment or health care insurance (before 1995 these periods were contribution free).[57] Rather than arguing for a fundamental change of the financing system of the public pensions, the proposals for tax-financing some elements of the public pension system or shifting the financial burden to other institutions stress the idea of insurance and equivalency of the system.

Instead of partial tax financing, a more encompassing base for the contributions has been proposed. It has been argued that contributions should not only be related to the input of labor but also capital through linking contributions to the whole value added as a sum of wages, interest rates, and profits. This reform proposal has been de-

56. *Wirtschaftswoche* (March 7, 1996).
57. Vogler-Ludwig and others (1996, p. 12).

bated for decades—most recently before passage of the Public Pension Reform of 1992—but because it goes against the idea of making capital cheaper and attracting investments, it is presently not so prominent. The current reform debate favors the proposal of introducing a labor market rate (*Arbeitsmarktabgabe*) for those economically active persons such as civil servants and the self-employed who do not contribute to the social security system.

A shift from the current pay-as-you-go scheme to a capital-funded system has also been proposed for years. But the proposal is politically impractical because younger workers would have to bear a double burden. And there would be severe macroeconomic transition problems. An immense capital stock would have to be accumulated. According to calculations carried out in 1988 for West Germany, about DM 7 trillion would be necessary to cover current pension claims as well as those future pensions for which contributions have already been paid; the amount equaled more than three times the GDP in 1988. For 1993 the needed capital was estimated at DM 10 trillion, which again represented more than three times GDP.[58] The requested capital would amount to more than two-thirds of the gross tangible assets of the German economy. This would afford high savings for the first generation and dramatically cut consumption. Moreover, as long as the number of beneficiaries grows at a higher rate than the generation of savers, which is the case with an aging and shrinking population, the capital stock will be gradually diminished in the second period. This may cripple macroeconomic performance. It is questionable whether the elasticity of savings in regard to interest rate variation would be great enough to compensate for the decapitalization resulting from an aging and shrinking population. Higher interest rates would thus discourage investments.

Most important is the future growth rate of the economy. A pay-as-you-go plan depends on the development of domestic wages, while a pension fund scheme relies more on the development of the international capital markets. Supporters of the pay-as-you-go system argue that international capital markets can pose a risk to pension funds (especially an exchange rate risk). At the same time, the access to

58. Less recent calculations led to comparable figures; see Müller and Roppel (1990, p. 437).

international capital markets can benefit the system because the risk of economic development is spread and the whole system is less dependent on the national economy.

To alleviate the transition problems, proposals have been made to change the system over a very long period. It has been proposed that the current contribution rate be kept at a constant level and that an additional part of the wages be directed into a private pension fund on a compulsory base.[59]

The Public Pension Reform Act of 1992 is far from installing a capital-funded pension system. Instead, the reform included a new mechanism to create a stronger link between revenues and outlays. This led to a lowering of contribution rates in 1992, 1993, and 1995, instead of creating more important reserves.[60] An increase in unemployment figures, however, leads more or less automatically to an increase in contribution rates. The public pension scheme is now even more strongly related to labor market development, thus emphasizing the fundamental element of a pay-as-you-go system. The revenues of the public pension system are mainly determined by increases in wages and employment. With this automatic mechanism, total labor costs are indirectly pushed up in bad economic circumstances and lowered in periods of economic growth. This aggravates unemployment in periods of bad economic performance.

The reforms currently intended will lead to smaller pensions or smaller pension increases. The Public Pension Reform Act of 1992 already contains this trend through linking the dynamization of wages to the development of net wages rather than gross wages. Because of changing expectations concerning individual pensions, a slow shift to more private pension provisions on a voluntary base is expected. Rather than changing the financing of the current public pension system, the government intends to create more incentives for private savings.

Basically, the debate on reforming the financing structure of public pensions refers to the total and relative costs of production factors. It is argued that lowering nonwage labor costs will boost employment (and thus the number of contributors) and also ameliorate Germany's

59. Dresdner Bank (1995).
60. Steffen, (1996, p. 220).

competitive stance. The effects on the overall economic performance of the different reform proposals, which is crucial for financing public pensions, are, however, not all positive because lowered labor costs might create fewer incentives to substitute capital for labor and thus enhance labor productivity. Moreover, a shift in the financing structure might reduce aggregate demand should disposable income be lowered. On the other hand, it is also argued that promoting savings will increase the supply of capital and thus lower interest rates, which should result in a positive effect on the economic climate.

INCOME DISTRIBUTION POLICIES AND INCOME SOURCES.   The 1992 reform clearly showed that most politicians do not want a fundamental change in the system. Nevertheless, that reform and others that were recently decided or are currently being discussed clearly demonstrate that there is a tendency to diminish the importance of public pensions as a source of income. The data showed that the elderly had a relatively high income, especially if various tax breaks and other advantages were taken into account. Moreover, in regard to the enormous amount of expected bequests, a lowering of the average public pension income should be possible. However, income is less equally distributed among the elderly than among other age groups, and the polarization of income among the elderly is expected to increase.[61] Thus policy should, on the one hand, reduce the average income of the elderly as compared with that of younger people and, on the other hand, reduce income disparities among the elderly.

The reform proposals, which have been mainly put forward by a report of the federal government, the advisory board to the Ministry of Labor, the Council of Economic Advisors, and employer associations include the following aspects.[62]

—Reducing the pension level by abolishing some of the elements that do not reflect the insurance character. One proposal would reduce the contribution-free periods that give eligibility for future pensions. The restrictions would not affect the three contribution-free years to bring up a child. Eventually, the federal government envisages

61. Rürup and Sesselmeier (1993).
62. Deutsche Bundesbank (1995).

reducing from seven to three the number of years of education that are contribution free but are taken into account for the pension.

—Eliminating redistributive elements in the pension system.

—Reducing the ratio of pensions to average net wages according to the amount of contributions in each period (for example, relating pensions to the total wage sum of a period). This reform is intended to alleviate the burden of aging for the younger generation and distribute it among the elderly. The minister of labor has proposed partially linking the pension level to a demographic factor expressing changes in life expectancy. A pensioner who made contributions over a period of forty-five years and earned the economywide average wage would receive a pension amounting to 64 percent of the average net wage in 2030. Today this ratio amounts to nearly 70 percent. With this regulation the contribution rate to the public pension plan would only rise to 22.9 percent by 2030.[63] The burden of aging would thus be shared between the younger generation and the pensioners.

—Abolishing the existing partial tax exemptions for pensions, as proposed by the Ifo Institute and others.[64]

Cutting social benefits by reducing contribution rates by 2 percentage points will lower total labor costs and the inflation rate. Real net wages will be higher than they would otherwise be. However, because of the smaller transfer income of private households, private demand would decrease. According to medium-term projections carried out by the Ifo Institute, employment would be increased by 0.7 percentage points, but GDP growth would be slightly slower.[65]

In addition to lowering public pensions, plans call for encouraging savings.

In this context the federal government decided to abolish the property tax. Proposals have been made by political parties to reform taxes on bequests (broad tax base but low rates). However, the minister of finance proposes widening the tax base for capital income and imposing taxes on annuities from life insurance.

Subsidies to buy real estate through special tax treatment have been in effect for years. Real estate can be regarded as an important (indi-

63. *Der Spiegel* (February 3, 1997).
64. Parsche (1996).
65. Vogler-Ludwig and others (1996, p. 2 ff).

rect) income source for the elderly. The percentage of persons owning property is still small compared with most other western European countries and the United States. In particular, the percentage in eastern Germany is low. An expanding share of property in eastern Germany and western Germany is expected in the coming years.[66]

Criticism of a reduction in social transfers linked to promotion of private savings stresses first that the overall public expenditures for the elderly may not be significantly reduced since a shift from payments for the public pension system to subsidies and public revenue losses occurs. Second, because assets are less equally distributed than labor income, this kind of policy measure will increase income disparities among the elderly. This may induce additional costs to the public sector, for example, outlays for means-tested social assistance. Most important, it has been argued that a reduction in social transfers would lead to lower aggregate demand and slower economic growth. However, cutting advantages for higher-income groups will diminish the negative effect on aggregate demand because the propensity to consume is negatively correlated to income level.[67]

As long as beneficial macroeconomic effects can be expected from this smooth change from a public pay-as-you-go pension system to private-capital funded pensions, the intergenerational distribution problem will be more easily tackled because the transition generation would partly offset their welfare losses from bearing the double burden by greater economic growth induced by their savings. In any case, increasing income disparities are feared. Consequently, some analysts and politicians recommend concentrating on fiscal reforms to distribute property more equally.

A wide range of proposals have been made to broaden property ownership. In the face of high unemployment and high labor costs, proposals aiming at reducing the relative importance of wage income have recently gained attention. In addition to already existing contracts, which promote employee savings as a nonwage benefit (*Arbeitnehmersparzulage*), the federal government has considered linking a part of the wage to an investive function either within or outside the firm (*Investivlohn*). Moreover, models of employee financial participation,

66. Bucher and Gatzweiler (1995).
67. Vogler-Ludwig and others (1996, p. 3).

either directly output oriented or through spreading firm-specific assets among the firm's employees, are under discussion.

To tackle poverty among the elderly, a tax-based flat-rate public pension has been proposed. Thus, a minimum living standard would be guaranteed for all elderly, supplemented by private income provisions. This would result in an important share of private provisions (private pensions, real estate, and other assets) for retirement age. Even though the introduction of a flat-rate pension system was discussed before the 1992 public pension reform and is still being proposed, the idea has not gained much political support.

Basically, two proposals for tax-financed minimum pensions deserve mentioning, either as the only public pension system, as proposed by Kurt Biedenkopf of the Christian Democratic party, or combined with an earnings-related second tier, as envisaged by the Green party. Accordingly, two proposals for a minimum flat-rate contribution have been made: either as the only public pension system, as put forward by neoliberal authors, or integrated as a floor into the earnings-related public pension plan, as proposed by some academics more oriented toward social democratic positions. Most of the proposals are intended to allow the elderly a minimum standard of living without applying for means-tested social assistance. A minimum level of public pensions is also being discussed in the light of the growing frequency of atypical working arrangements (including part-time work).

Proposals for a flat-rate pension as the only public pension also aim at boosting private savings and capital formation and thus stimulating economic growth. In addition, tax-based flat-rate pension systems have been proposed either to reduce labor costs (the neoliberals) or to create a citizen's right to a minimum income (mainly the Green party).

The plan faces a number of problems and criticisms. Distributional problems will arise, especially if means testing is abandoned. Financing through flat-rate contributions would have a regressive effect; in fact, proposals on the grounds of taxes rather than flat-rate contributions have been seriously debated in Germany. A shift toward a flat-rate scheme would also dissociate work and pensions and thus lower incentives to work. Moreover, while the new scheme was being implemented, there would be serious problems for those earning more than a minimum because they would have to contribute during (at least part of) their working life in proportion to their income but would get only a minimum flat-rate pension. Finally, a significant effect on additional savings is doubtful for a large part of the population. It is feared that there will not be enough willingness for people to make additional saving, and thus there would be widespread poverty, defined as receiving only the minimum income, among the elderly in the future.

The present discussion focuses more on a mixed system than a pure flat-rate plan. The debate concentrates on whether low pensions, under certain conditions, should be increased within the pension system or provided by a separate institution, that is, social assistance. Both strategies include means testing and financing additional payments out of the federal budget. And in both strategies the rules for means testing can be less severe than existing social assistance rules, mainly by not including children's income for eligibility.[68]

Up to now the problem of the elderly poor has been a problem of poor women because they often have not worked or have worked for only a few years. Often, they have not asked for social assistance because they do not want their children's income to be tested. It can be expected that the problem of very small pensions will be less pronounced in the future because women's labor market participation rates have increased. The gap between average earnings of men and women has decreased, although it is still considerable. Measures have been taken to lengthen contribution-free periods from one year to three years per child born after 1992, which will increase pensions. Since long-term unemployment can easily lead to poverty, the problem of elderly people in poverty may become a problem not of gender but a general pattern.

It is claimed that a flat-rate pension will overcome the problem of poverty in old age because a minimum standard of living would no longer be linked to a person's working life. As long as most people are not increasing their private savings during their working life, a negative effect on economic performance can be feared. The large share of elderly whose income would be dramatically lowered compared to the current system would induce declining consumer demand. But the reduction in contribution rates or general taxes could increase the disposable income of the young. They will, however, save a greater

68. Schmähl (1992, p. 15).

share of their income not only due to a positive income effect but also with regard to the smallness of the expected pension.

Cuts in public pensions are claimed to a varying extent. Flat-rate pensions are proposed to allow for a minimum standard of living. A smaller public pension is generally proposed to be supplemented by income from private pension provisions. A positive effect can be expected if it is assumed that major cuts in wage costs are necessary for the competitive position of the German economy.

The distributional effects of boosting savings are controversial. On the one hand, property and assets are assumed to be less equally distributed than labor income and are consequently not regarded as being a good substitute for wage-related pensions. On the other hand, in the face of increasing labor market problems, dependency on labor income as the main source of private welfare may cause major problems. Consequently, promoting savings while pursuing policies shaped to distribute assets more equally (for example, through financial-participation models) has gained support.

Reforming Other Areas of Social Policy

A generally accepted goal in Germany is reducing the public debt. To fulfill the Maastricht criteria, a policy of public saving is generally accepted. In the face of long-term economic change, it is argued that limiting public expenditures can best be realized now, before population aging becomes a greater problem. In the face of growing global competition, employers are demanding that the government help reduce their labor costs by lowering the contributions they must make to the social security system.

The appropriate measures to accomplish these tasks are extremely controversial. The intended reductions in a wide range of social benefits, as recently decided by the federal government, have created major political conflicts. The proposed reforms—restrictions of unemployment benefits, means-tested social assistance, limiting eligibility for public pensions (starting work requirements earlier in a person's life and removing the option of early retirement), and measures concerning vague public health care—affect the main areas of social policy.

Besides the public pension system, population aging primarily affects public health care expenditures. The most important reform has been the introduction of a statutory long-term care insurance. This not only removes long-term care from the public health insurance system, but also lowers total costs. Moreover it helps to increase transparency on the risk of old age. Contributions to the insurance are in principle shared equally by employees and employers. To alleviate the burden for employers, one public holiday has been abolished. Except for these arrangements, reforms have not addressed the problem that the increasing share of elderly will dramatically boost health care expenditures. Specifically, the current debate has not confronted the potential conflict of intergenerational distribution of benefits.

Discussions of reforming the health care system have focused on limiting increases in contributions because they affect labor costs. The reforms of 1988 and 1992 and most reform proposals concentrate on the following factors:

—increasing competition among health care providers to hold down costs;

—removing some benefits and services;

—strengthening income-oriented expenditure policies;

—increasing cost-sharing for dental work and prescription drugs and introducing fixed reimbursement prices for prescription drugs;

—strengthening the principle of self-management and especially the principle that health care suppliers manage within sectorally fixed budgets (*Budgetierung*);

—favoring more ambulatory services to keep the growth rate of hospital expenditures low;

—removing benefits that do not reflect the insurance character (especially that family members having no earnings of their own are insured for free, although this would conflict with the goal of raising the fertility rate); and

—introducing more incentives for patients to behave more responsibly. However, even if a more risk-oriented scheme is proposed by some, increasing the financial burden on the elderly is not envisaged. During their working life they paid higher contributions than their personal risk required, so they are eligible for solidarity from the younger generation.

Measures to increase the population have not been explicitly discussed in regard to financing the health care system. Unfortunately, detailed data concerning the effect of migration on the system are not available. But a change in the age structure of the population combined with the fact that health care services are not exportable should constrain costs. However, the positive effect of a flow of young immigrants paying contributions combined with emigration of elderly would be diminished by the fact that elderly are not contributing to the system to the extent they should as representing higher risk. Moreover, the positive effect is smaller if migrants have more children that are insured but do not pay contributions. In this respect a higher fertility rate of nationals would initially also have a negative impact on health care system financing.

The objective of the current and intended reforms is to limit the growth of public health care expenditures. This leads to contradictory effects. Through stabilizing contributions, increases in labor costs can be avoided and beneficial labor market effects induced. At the same time, benefits for health care suppliers are diminished. There may be no further major effects if this represents only a cut in monopoly rents. But there is a danger of hindering the expansion of one of the most important markets for the future. The impact on employment figures within the health sector and a possible further segmentation of this labor market have not been assessed yet. It is questionable whether the substitution of private for public financing of health care services will occur.

Conclusions

Policies directed at restraining the increases in contribution rates for the public pension plan are under debate. High contribution rates hurt Germany's international competitiveness as long as the working population does not accept major cuts in their wages, which would be necessary to keep total labor costs in line with productivity.

Apart from gaining control over health care costs, the reform proposals born of demographic change concentrate on the pension system. At present, proposals range from a fundamental change of the system to a purification of it. Principally, the options include increasing the number of contributors and cutting benefits. Most of the approaches also aim to strengthen private rather than public pension provisions to initiate a slow shift from the prevalent pay-as-you-go system to funded programs. However, it is questionable whether the economic effects of such a change will be positive. The problems of intergenerational distribution can hardly be solved in this way.

Distributional proposals such as increasing or abolishing property taxes are particularly controversial. Those who favor cutting social benefits point to the resulting increase in the competitiveness of German industry. Those who argue against substantially reducing benefits point to the resulting fall in aggregate demand.

Assuming that increases in total labor costs (wages and contributions to the social security system) have to be accompanied by productivity gains for Germany to remain competitive, increasing contributions reduce disposable income and thus reduce savings and consumption. Because savings are positively correlated to the income level, the loss of savings will be relatively more important than the decrease in consumption. A constant contribution rate implies smaller pensions. This leads to savings today since a shift to more private provisions is likely to occur.

A mixture of several policy measures seems appropriate to distribute the burden of population aging among age groups. However, some proposals, especially those aimed at increasing the working population, will create new major distributional conflicts if the demand for labor is not sufficient. The timetable for the introduction of various reform measures is of major importance, because the distributional conflicts can be aggravated and economic growth slowed if the right measure is introduced at the wrong time.

Until now, little has been said about the possibilities of improving labor productivity growth instead of increasing the working population. The level of future pensions also depends on the growth rate of wages and the total wage bill, and thus on economic performance. Moreover, distribution conflicts are less severe if the cake is bigger.

The Influence of Aging on Economic Performance

In most long-term labor market projections, two basic periods are distinguished: high unemployment until 2010 or 2020 and a quantitatively balanced labor market or even a labor shortage by 2020 at the latest. These projections normally only consider the supply of labor. The level and the structure of the demographic development determine

FIGURE 4-4. *Population, Employment, and GDP (1991 Constant Values), Western Germany, Selected Years, 1960–90*

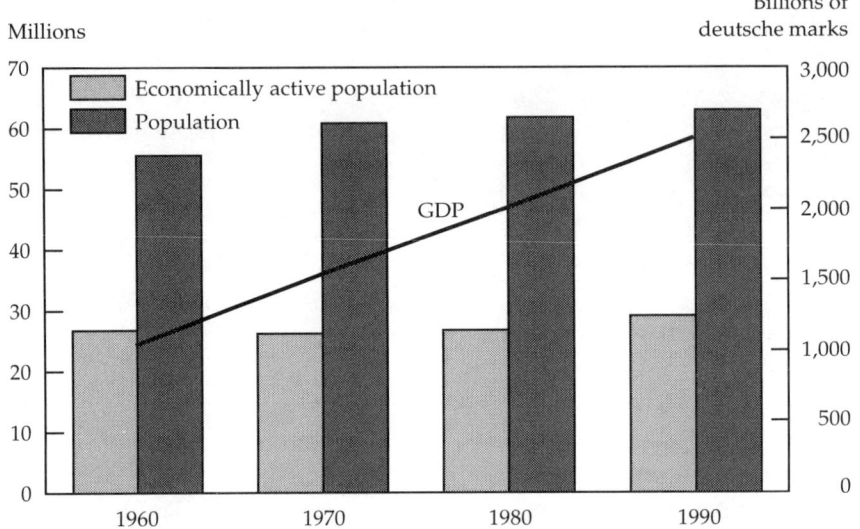

Source: Statistisches Bundesamt (1995).

the supply of labor and, to a certain extent, the supply of financial capital, whereby developments on international capital markets are very important. Additionally, the extent to which overall population development determines demand and economic performance must be addressed.

German economic development since World War II indicates that the driving force for economic growth has been the growth of labor productivity (figure 4-4). Between 1960 and 1994 GDP per economically active person in real terms grew by 250 percent.[69] But the growth rates of GDP and labor productivity have declined. Productivity growth has led to high growth rates of income and thus boosted consumption and capital formation, population having grown very slowly. These findings, however, do not demonstrate that demographics have no effect on aggregate demand, but clearly show the tremendous importance of productivity growth. In western Germany the

69. Statistisches Bundesamt, *Statistisches Jahrbuch* (1996, p. 41).

share of private domestic consumption in GDP has undergone only minor variations in the long term and amounted to 55 percent in 1994. Whether a changing age structure is affecting productivity growth is a matter of concern.

The impact of the changing age structure on domestic consumption affects the domestic economy and employment. Apart from domestic consumption by individuals, foreign demand has been instrumental in German economic development. The foreign trade balance has been positive since the 1960s, which entails a high share of domestic savings, making it crucial for capital accumulation. The share of exports in GDP has increased markedly since the 1960s and reached a peak in the mid-1980s. Over the past fifteen years it has varied between 22 percent and nearly 30 percent. In 1994 the share of exports in GDP amounted to 23 percent in western Germany, the export share of western German industry reaching 30 percent.[70] With regard to the export markets, demographics affects labor supply. However, it has to be noted that the average number of hours worked per week in western German industry has declined by a sixth.[71] This again reflects the effect of productivity growth on welfare because the average reduction in yearly working hours is regarded as an expression of welfare.

The Impact of an Aging Population on the Labor Market

I have already discussed the likely development of labor supply and related policy measures. The volume and the structure of labor demand can be partly derived from the demand in the domestic and foreign commodity and service markets. Moreover, labor-saving technological development is important in determining the demand for labor and the competitive position of Germany, which again affects total labor demand.

How might labor demand develop? The most important exogenous factor is the development of the worldwide economic outlook. The share of German exports in international trade will depend not only on the world economy but also on national factors such as cost trends, innovative capacity, marketing strategies, and currency stability.

70. Statistisches Bundesamt, *Statistisches Jahrbuch* (1996).
71. Statistisches Bundesamt, *Statistisches Jahrbuch* (1996, p. 41).

Domestic demand is divided into demand for imports and for German goods and services. The modal split is linked to relative prices, tastes, and especially to the demand for nontradable goods and services. The level of domestic demand depends on income development and the propensity to consume. Consumption as a share of income depends on income level and thus on the development of the export markets, age structures, values and tastes, and interest rates. In general, an increased demand for skilled labor is expected.[72] It is feared that labor scarcity will hinder growth. In the following discussion, cautious estimates for the long-term development of these factors and their effect will be given in light of labor demand.

FOREIGN DEMAND.   Despite the trend toward globalization, regional economic linkages retain their crucial importance. Trade within the European Union has intensified in the past few years. Nearly half of German exports were directed toward EU members in 1994. Since the enlargement of the EU in 1995, this share has increased (in 1994 some 15 percent of German exports were with European Free Trade Association (EFTA) countries.[73] Economic development in eastern and central Europe is becoming increasingly important for the economic outlook of the European Union, and especially for Germany. The volume of German exports to central and eastern Europe already passes that to the United States.[74] Although eastern European countries in geographical proximity to Germany (mainly the Czech Republic, Poland, and Hungary) seem to be managing the transformation to a market economy well, so that EU membership seems realistic in perhaps two decades' time, the economic performance of the former USSR is extremely uncertain. Additionally, the economic performance of North African countries and the Middle East might be of some importance to Europe.

A major challenge for Germany consists in how to ensure durable market shares in the fast-growing Asia-Pacific region. The future economic performance of China is uncertain, but China could be one of the new driving forces of the world economy. Despite a sharp increase of exports to the Asia-Pacific region in recent years, the export volume

---

72. Enquete-Kommission (1994, p. 207); and Klauder (1993a, p. 489).
73. Statistisches Bundesamt, *Statistisches Jahrbuch* (1996, p. 302).
74. See *Süddeutsche Zeitung* (July 19, 1996).

TABLE 4-20. *GDP Growth in OECD Europe and World Trade, 1960–92, 1992–2040*
Percent per year

Period	High variant		Low variant	
	OECD Europe	World trade	OECD Europe	World trade
1960–92	3.2	5.8	3.2	5.8
1992–2040	2.2	4.1	1.6	3.4

Source: Prognos (1995, p. 29).

is still low. In addition to political and economic instability, world trade might be hindered by restrictive trade policies of the leading economic world regions.

Owing to the number of uncertainties about world economic performance as well as the relative competitiveness of the German economy, projections of the development of German export markets yield contradictory results. According to both variants of Prognos's projection, export growth is assumed. European economic integration is still expected to lead to more economic growth. In the positive variant Prognos assumes that an offensive technology policy will be pursued that will ensure western European companies a leading position in international markets (especially in the ecological and communication sectors).[75] In its negative variant, lower gains from economic integration are assumed owing to distribution conflicts between poor and rich nations, delay of up to three or four decades in achieving a common currency, and the pursuit of a restrictive trade policy with the eastern European countries, which would slow down productivity growth within the European Union. Trade is intensified somewhat within the main world regions (NAFTA, Europe, Asia), but trade between regions grows slowly because of protectionist trade policy (table 4-20).

Earlier projections were somewhat more optimistic. According to the OECD's *Long-Term Prospects for the World Economy*, the economic outlook for the 1990s and the first decade of the next century is good. Widespread restructuring took place in the 1980s and new markets are emerging. Estimates for average growth in world output for the 1990s were about 3 percent. North America and OECD Europe were seen as likely to grow at between 2.5 percent and 3 percent a year, Japan at

75. Prognos (1995, p. 27 ff.).

between 3 percent and 4 percent, the Asia-Pacific as a whole at well over 3 percent, Latin America at around 3 percent, and Africa at a somewhat lower rate. The Asia-Pacific's share of world income could rise from 24 percent in 1989 to 35 percent in 2010 to more than 50 percent by 2040 (these numbers summarize a range of projections that were submitted in 1991). Estimates for OECD European growth rates are 3 percent to 4 percent for the 1990s and into the next century. This is mainly due to the gains from the Single European Market and further integration. In the long term the widening of the European Union to include central and eastern Europe could lead to considerable economic gains.

The growth rates for OECD Europe might well be overestimated. The gains from European economic integration could be moderated by the challenge of fiercer international competition for which countries of the European Union might be badly prepared. And taking the predicted shrinking and aging of the EU population into account, the positive prospects for German exports may be all the more doubtful. The restrictions on the demand side due to shrinking population might be reduced or even reversed if the purchasing power within the Union (and other highly advanced economies) grows. However, because it now seems questionable that income will grow sufficiently, it is even more important for Germany to enter the new markets, especially in Asia. Moreover, the consumption structure of the whole European Union may change as a result of the aging EU population and thus may hurt the German export markets if it is assumed that aging implies a growing demand for nontradable goods and services.

According to a special commission to the Federal Parliament, exports are not expected to increase because of international competition and an already high level of international trade involvement.[76] In the public debate, there is major concern about the future competitiveness of the German economy. In particular, the government, the employers' associations, and some academics insist that labor costs are far too high.

Demographics affect labor costs because of their effect on labor supply. Nonwage labor costs depend heavily on the financing of the public pension system. Wage costs depend additionally on labor demand and partly on the age structure (seniority wages) of the work

76. Enquete-Kommission (1994).

force. Moreover, nonwage labor costs indirectly depend on income taxes, because they affect collective bargaining. According to a study by the Ifo Institute, employment elasticity in regard to nonwage labor costs is about -0.3.[77]

In assessing the challenge of globalization, one must remember that in the past few years trade has intensified between the highly industrialized countries. Nevertheless, global competition may put pressure either on social standards or on the ratio of net wages to labor productivity. Because of its larger future share of elderly as compared with its main competitors, Germany might be particularly affected. In this context the extent to which increased interdependencies between nations will cause system competition and thus limit the capacity of a nation to shape a social system according its preferences is of major concern.

The supply of human capital is crucial for the innovative capacity of the economy and to improved productivity. Unit labor costs and capital costs together with the innovative capacity determine the international competitiveness of a highly advanced economy. A large part of the demand side on the export markets relies on this competitive position. Additionally, the development of the world economy is decisive (level effect). In regard to export markets, the domestic policy can react to aging's effects mainly on the supply side of the economy. (Monetary and exchange rate policy will not be analyzed in the context of population aging.)

One of the major future concerns is a relative decline in human capital. This might occur if the decrease in the size of the labor force coincided with less investment in human capital and if a harmful effect of an aging work force on productivity growth is assumed.

The options for Germany consist either in ensuring large investments in the domestic labor force or in importing labor. Other advanced countries will also be competing for labor, since they too will have aging populations. Long-term pitfalls of a selective immigration policy aimed at attracting skilled labor may involve a shortage of skilled labor in developing countries that would impede their long-term economic growth and thus hinder the development of new export markets for Germany and other advanced economies.

---

77. Vogler-Ludwig and others (1996, p.2 ff).

DOMESTIC DEMAND.   Demographic development affects aggregate demand. However, domestic demand depends not only on the size of population but on income. As long as population growth is linked to lower wages, the net effect is not clear cut. The share in consumption is negatively correlated with income. Thus the same product of income and inhabitants can have differing effects on consumption and capital formation. Consequently, the estimates of the impact of demographic change on total consumption vary significantly. According to Kessler, the effects of a shrinking and aging population on aggregate demand are not substantial—at least he could not find an automatically harmful effect.[78] According to a special commission to the Federal Parliament, private domestic consumption will increase, primarily because of dissaving by the older population, and thus boost economic growth.[79] However, a positive effect of aging on savings and thus reduced consumption is possible as long as incomes rise.[80] The different factors affecting the private demand therefore have to be considered separately.

The income of the elderly strongly depends on the state of the economy. In regard to the increasing financial burden of the public pension scheme, a relative reduction of the average pension is likely. The increasing amount of accumulated private wealth ensures additional income sources. Especially, the increasing share of housing owners increases the disposable income for all other goods significantly.

The consumption and the saving share depend on the motives for savings. Basically, there are three motives: to keep consumption at a constant level (saving during working life and dissaving once retired), to make bequests, and to accumulate contingency savings. Evidence for Germany shows that dissaving in retirement applies only up to a certain age; the oldest of the old are likely to consume less and save more. However, with the oldest old representing an increasing share of the elderly, new products and services may emerge to overcome age-related consumption constraints. A shrinking and aging population induces a greater share of consumption in total income. This effect might even be reinforced if saving to leave something to one's children

78. Kessler (1991, p. 94 ff).
79. Enquete-Kommission (1994).
80. Meier (1995).

diminishes with the decreasing birthrate. However, consumption might decrease and savings increase as today's younger people realize that their pensions will be relatively small. With smaller family units, they cannot rely as much on family for help. However, a considerable amount of wealth will be inherited in the next years. The high level of bequests will increase the ability to save a larger part of income, but the situation calls further savings into question. The people inheriting a huge amount of private wealth will already be in their fifties. The prospects of a lower pension level because of an aging population is likely to induce private saving for younger people, especially because they cannot rely on receiving the same huge bequests their parents did. This positive effect on savings will be reinforced by increasing life expectancy and reduced in case of a lengthening of the working life. However, expected increases in contribution rates might encourage the near-term propensity to consume because increasing contribution rates will reduce disposable income.

Shrinking household size also affects the propensity to consume. With smaller family units resulting from a declining fertility rate, consumption as a share of income is likely to decrease because income per household member is higher in households with fewer children or none. The decreasing size of elderly households will lead to an increase in single households and is thus more likely to have the opposite effect because maintaining a single household is relatively more expensive. The consumption volume, however, might decrease, since single households of the elderly are largely single women who receive smaller pensions and less income than they had while their husbands were alive. But the economic situation of elderly women will improve (in line with the increasing labor market participation rate of women). Both effects taken together, the shrinking household size will probably have at least a small effect on increasing consumption.[81]

The purchasing power of today's elderly is high, demonstrating the positive effect of population aging on consumption. However, the extent of this effect in the future depends on how the generational distribution conflict will be resolved. Arguments in favor of high future purchasing power for the elderly, or at least an important part of the elderly, refer to the large proportion of property owners, which is still

81. Kessler (1991, p. 139).

expected to expand, so that an increasing share of elderly will either have to pay no rent or will receive income from renting property. At the turn of the century a quarter of private wealth money and real estate will belong to persons aged 65 and older.[82]

The generally assumed higher propensity of the elderly to consume, at least until they reach a certain age, may not be beneficial only for Germany. Some of this purchasing power is expected to be used abroad because the share of pensions paid to people living abroad will rise from 2 percent in 1992 to more than 8 percent in 2040 as the share of eligible emigrants increases.[83] These purchasing power losses may even be underestimated if more retired people choose to live, at least for a good part of the year, in cheaper or more attractive regions in Europe or outside Europe. (The current trend of increased mobility and traveling abroad indicates a possibly different consumption behavior of future elderly as compared with today's.) It is tremendously important for the German economy whether the purchasing power of the elderly will benefit German industry and the service sector.

Not only the level of consumption but also the share of consumption of nontradable goods as well as public expenditures such as investments in infrastructure is important for the domestic economy. The consumption of domestically produced tradable goods and services is also a matter of concern. In general, the share of services in individuals' consumption expenditures increases with age. Whereas in 1988 persons younger than 35 years old spent 30 percent of their consumption budget for services, those aged between 65 and 70 spent 35 percent and those older than 70 spent 40 percent. The share of consumed services of the different age groups has grown 10 to 16 percent since 1978.[84]

Consumption patterns are related to education, income, and lifestyle. The lifestyle of today's elderly, especially of the so-called young elderly, is more consumption oriented than that of previous generations.

Future generations of elderly will have higher levels of education. The share of men 60 and older with university entrance qualifications will increase from 11 percent in 1991 to 16 percent in 2010 and

---

82. Rürup amd Sesselmeier (1993, p. 10).

83. See Prognos (1995).

84. See income and expenditure samples in Statistisches Bundesamt, *Einkommens- und Verbrauchsstichprobe* (1978, 1988).

22 percent in 2030. The share of women 60 and older with such qualifications will increase from 4 percent in 1991 to 7 percent in 2010 and 16 percent in 2030. The share of elderly men with university degrees will increase from 9 percent in 1991 to 14 percent in 2010 and 15 percent in 2030. For women the shares will rise from 2 percent in 1991 to 5 percent in 2010 and to 9 percent in 2030.[85] Middle class professionals often go to the theatre and concerts, eat out, and travel abroad. Consumption is oriented more toward services than goods. The share of future elderly in this consumer group will increase.

The consumption of today's elderly with intermediate educations and relatively high incomes is very much focused on their houses and social environment. Consumption is housing related (furniture, appliances, and so forth) as well as security oriented, which benefits the insurance industry. The younger old, who retire early and are often relatively wealthy, show high consumption of typical leisure activities such as sports and culture as well as luxury goods.[86] All in all, they are consuming nontradable services less extensively than people older than 60, but they represent not only potential for the nontradable sector but also for domestically produced tradable goods and services. Future elderly will increasingly become part of this group. Aging is also likely to reinforce some present global trends affecting both demand for nontradable services as well as for tradable goods and services.

—The elderly could demand a better environment to increase life expectancy (expanding markets for ecological products).

—Population aging is likely to reinforce the trend toward the leisure society, even if working life is longer. As long as an extended working life is combined with gradual retirement, leisure activities might increase in the long run. This kind of activity is connected with the demand for goods (imported or not, such as sporting goods) and domestic services as well as services consumed abroad (traveling). The growth prospects for the market for domestically consumed nontradable services are good.

—Demand for telecommunication and information goods and services will increase because of increased time off as well as reduced

85. Höhn (1994, pp. 252, 259).
86. Müller (1995).

mobility of the very old. The small size of their households will also increase demand.

Aging implies a growing demand for health care and related services, even assuming a relative reduction in public health care expenditures.[87] Because of increased time off, higher incomes (assuming a growing economy with an initially stagnating and then shrinking population), and aging, catering to the elderly is going to expand. Prognos expects the demand for transportation to decrease. However, the mobility of future elderly might increase, as it has already increased for younger and middle-aged groups. In particular, the demand for public transportation can be expected to rise. Because of rationalization and concentration, trade will decrease slightly in relative terms.[88]

Market potentials are expected in the media related to the ongoing privatization and market liberalization of radio and television as well as to a focus on small consumer groups, reflecting the trend toward individualization. Growing markets for education (implying a shift of the consumer structure from young to old), culture, and entertainment are expected.[89] However, not all of the demand for these services will be directed to nontradable services because both culture and especially entertainment have international dimensions. The share of international supply of entertainment and related services is likely to increase markedly because of the expansion of new telecommunication technologies and new media.

An increasing labor market participation rate is likely to boost the demand for nontradable services. Policy measures to increase the labor market participation rates of women and the elderly can be expected as a reaction to an aging population.

In tradable services aging will primarily have an impact on the financial sector, including the insurance sector. The expected growing demand for financial services will be connected to increasing private pension provisions and the accumulation of wealth.[90] The employment effects are not clear, since the banking and insurance sectors will face fiercer international competition. There is enormous potential for ra-

---

87. Hacker (1996, p. 191); and compare Prognos (1995).
88. Prognos (1995, p. 63).
89. Prognos (1995); and Rürup and Sesselmeier (1993).
90. Prognos (1995).

tionalizing these sectors, primarily from new telecommunication and information technologies.

The future elderly may consume more sophisticated durables as well as technologically advanced products of the entertainment sector.[91] This kind of demand represents potential for the German economy, but whether it can be realized will depend on Germany's international competitive position. However, as compared to younger generations, the elderly already have many durables and their taste for more technologically advanced products is less pronounced.

The demand for better housing and more living space depends heavily on income. In the past the demand was partly due to the trend toward individualization and the decreasing average household size. Per capita living space increased by nearly a third between the end of the 1960s and the end of the 1980s. The annual growth rates have now declined.[92]

Aging may increase again the share of single households. In light of the seventh population projection of the Federal Statistical Office, the share of elderly living on their own will increase in the first decades of the next century. This trend will mainly affect older women, but will also affect men and women in their sixties, as the share of elderly who have never been married or who are divorced expands (current trends for younger age groups can be partly projected into the future). The population 60 and older living alone as a share of all elderly might increase from 46 percent in 1991 to 54 percent in 2030.[93] Already the share of elderly living in single households is greater than for other age groups.[94] As the elderly grow in number, the number of single households will increase, so the average square meters inhabited per head can still be expected to increase.

Additional factors will work in the same direction. Compared with other countries, especially the United States or the United Kingdom, the German housing market is inflexible, and it is expected to remain so in regard to individual needs.[95] Thus the elderly might stay in houses or flats that could be too large for them, a result of the length-

91. Rürup and Sesselmeier (1993).
92. Bucher and Gatzweiler (1996, p. 30).
93. Höhn (1994).
94. Höhn (1994, p. 219).
95. Heunwinkel, Kujath, and Bergman (1996).

ening of working life, a desire to keep one's standard of living (staying in the same home is regarded as being part of the attained living standard), the expected increase in property values so that staying in the same home is perceived as being free, and finally the locally established social network. Many elderly people are likely to stay in the flats and houses they may have bought in middle age; some are likely to move to special housing for the elderly; and finally some will move into smaller quarteers to save money.

Increased life expectancy in itself could create demand for half a million dwelling units within the next ten years, corresponding roughly to a quarter of the capacity of the German construction industry.[96] Longer stays in the family home by the older generation mean fewer dwellings will be transferred to younger people. According to recent projections of the Federal Office for Spatial Planning, the overall consumed space for housing in Germany is expected to increase by 25 percent during the 1990s and the first decade of the twenty-first century. Between 1968 and 1987 occupied square meters increased about 60 percent.[97]

The elderly entering retirement at the turn of the century will still benefit from relatively high pensions. Sixty-three percent of those born between 1935 and 1945 are now living in their own housing.[98] The huge cohort born in the 1960s is expected to reach the peak of their housing needs in the next ten to fifteen years.[99] They will retire between 2020 and 2040. Their pensions will probably be relatively smaller than those of the generation before, but the share who own their housing is likely to be greater, perhaps 73 percent. The expectation of smaller public pensions could set incentives for an even greater share to invest in housing during working life. Moreover, an increasing number of houses and flats will soon be inherited.

A market is emerging for new forms of housing that integrate age-related services within building complexes. The elderly often prefer living on their own. But with increasing age, they may need some help. Because more and more elderly are also childless, the demand for special age-adapted housing and services might increase.

96. Börsch-Supan (1991, pp. 105, 123).
97. Bucher and Gatzweiler (1996).
98. Heunwinkel, Kujath, and Bergman (1996).
99. Heunwinkel, Kujath, and Bergman (1996).

As long as one assumes increased income and private wealth together with increased time off, there will be a demand for more housing, especially in eastern Germany. Moreover, demand for a second flat or house may grow. As income and wealth disparities among the elderly increase, important differences in housing standards can be expected. An increasing share of future housing investment will be for renovation and modernization, not new buildings.

The volume of future investment depends on foreign and domestic demand as well as on technological development. In its high population variant, Prognos assumes private investment will grow an average of 2.5 percent a year for the whole projection period (up to 2040); the low variant assumes about 1.1 percent. The share of GDP represented by public and private investment, including housing, is projected to be stable in western Germany up to 2040. In Germany as a whole, investment will decrease, especially in eastern Germany as compared with 1992.[100]

The direct effects of aging on investments will mean an increasing demand for such age-related facilities as hospitals and nursing homes. This effect will probably be accompanied by decreasing child- and youth-related investments.

However, a decline in investments might occur in the face of shrinking population. Even assuming that shrinking population does not adversely affect total consumption expenditures, a decline of investments is feared due to wrong expectations.[101]

Indirect effects of aging on investments are related to the assumed impact of aging on productivity growth and labor costs. Labor shortages related to demographic change raise wages. As long as this effect induces higher labor market participation rates and immigration, the shortage will be less severe and wages will grow less. Scarcity of labor may induce investments to substitute capital for labor.

GLOBAL TRENDS AND TECHNOLOGICAL DEVELOPMENT. New telecommunication and information technologies represent major structural trends, the net effects of which on total employment for countries like Germany are not yet clear. The technological developments are rein-

---

100. Prognos (1995, p. 56).
101. Schneider (1990, p. 560).

forcing the trend toward economic globalization. Globalization and fiercer international competition will lead to further restructuring in industry and will continue to shift employment toward the service sector.[102] The technologies are enhancing this trend on the consumption side, and the demographic development will reinforce the trend toward globalization.

According to a labor market projection by the Labor Market Research Center of the Federal Employment Office, by 2010 nearly three-quarters of all employed persons are expected to work in the service sector as compared with less than two-thirds in 1985.[103] Activities that demand high-level skills are especially expected to expand (from 22 percent of all employed persons in 1985 to 35 percent in 2010). These activities mainly include education and training, consulting, organization and management, and research and development. The share of employment within more standardized types of services is expected to decrease, while the share of trade-related services will remain constant. In industry, only the maintenance of investment goods will create employment in relative terms; the share of the other activities will decrease considerably.

Most important, the new technologies will create new challenges for the service sector because they will make a number of services tradable. A trend toward greater specialization in the service sector is therefore probable. Growing international trade will lead to more specialization in the industrial sector.

It is feared that with globalization the productivity margin, and thus the basis for Germany's living standard, will narrow. In contrast with past years, productivity in some sectors in the newly industrializing countries (for example, software developers in India) is high while wages are still comparatively low. Some observers argue that by combining low costs and high levels of human capital these new competitors will represent a serious threat to economic development in Germany (and other comparable economies) and will put wages and social standards under serious pressure. It is also doubtful that wages will converge over the world within a few decades.

Human capital is a decisive competitive factor, but not the only one.

102. Prognos (1995, p. 62).
103. Klauder (1993b, p. 26).

A country's infrastructure, for instance, is also important. Past developments have also demonstrated that productivity growth has not been impeded by trade. Most of Germany's foreign trade takes place with highly industrialized countries. Foreign investments are mainly motivated by entering the domestic markets rather than primarily by lower production costs.[104] Undeniably, the periods of strong economic growth in Germany, as in other advanced economies, are over. To remain on the achieved growth path, considerable effort will have to be put into realizing productivity growth and keeping a leading position in technological development.

Technological development and especially process innovations will lead to a continuously growing demand for skilled labor, and the skills needed will undergo rapid changes. At the same time, the level and the structure of the labor supply is crucial for the innovative capacity and competitiveness of the economy. According to a projection of the Labor Market Research Center of the Federal Employment Office at the end of the 1980s, the share of the required work force with a higher-education degree (*Universität* and *Fachhochschule*) will increase from 11 percent in 1985 to 18 percent in 2010, and the share with a degree from a technical college (*Fachschule*) will expand from 8 percent to 11 percent.[105] The share with a completed apprenticeship will remain at 58 percent, while the share having no vocational training will decrease from 23 percent to 13 percent.

Structural change and technological development will also necessitate greater creativity and flexibility. Rather than very specialized knowledge and skills, broadly based and more interdisciplinary basic skills and knowledge will be needed. Broad-based curricula will be increasingly necessary to meet labor market demand.

The fundamental question to be addressed in the face of the demographic change is whether an aging work force could impede productivity growth. In the past two decades, economic restructuring has been connected to youth-centered personnel policies. Consequently, unemployment among those 55 and older has been disproportionate and early retirement common. At the same time, compared with other European countries Germany has kept youth unemployment in check.

---

104. Wilhelm (1996).
105. Klauder (1993b, p. 28).

For many years, early retirement represented a widely accepted social contract in regard to distributing the labor market risks.

Youth-centered personnel policies can be found more often in the expanding service sector than in industry.[106] The findings of a case study of product innovation in microelectronics show that within their research and development programs companies are reacting primarily by recruiting and training rather than contracting out or other measures.[107] The economic restructuring in eastern Germany is strongly linked to youth-centered personnel policies.

The trend toward early retirement does not only reflect structural economic change but also strategic personnel policies of some firms. A personnel manager may dismiss elderly staff because of

—the fear that elderly workers lack innovative capacity,[108]

—the desire to avoid deteriorating performance connected to increased health risk,

—the desire to use human capital and the most up-to-date skills without having invested in the company's staff, and

—the desire to create career opportunities for the younger staff.

Moreover, given the possibilities for various forms of early retirement, dismissing the elderly on a large scale is cheaper for companies than dismissing younger workers.[109] More recently, youth-centered personnel policies have been eased by the large size of cohorts entering the labor market, implying relatively lower wages for younger workers.

The trends suggest the following questions: does the evidence of the past years indicate a "natural" decline in the performance of the elderly? To what extent are the observed trends driven by policy? From a comparative perspective, early retirement is particularly widespread in Germany (as well as in the Netherlands and France).[110] However, because of the increasing financing problems of the public pension plan resulting from the aging population, this type of social contract cannot be a model for the future. Companies operating in Germany are particularly poorly prepared to cope with the challenge of an aging work force.

106. Köchling (1995, p. 442).
107. Brasche (1993, p. 152).
108. Bäcker and Naegele (1995); and Schneider (1990, p. 562).
109. Bäcker and Naegele (1995).
110. Rosenow and Naschold (1993, p. 139).

In general, two contradictory effects of aging on individual performance can be identified:

—because of accumulated skills and experience, the productivity of the elderly is greater than that of younger age groups, and

—performance declines over the whole working life for a number of reasons, mainly related to health, and declining flexibility.[111]

Some findings indicate that the effect of experience may be twofold because it may restrain creativity and adaptability to new developments.[112] Nevertheless, experience is important for a wide range of functions in a company, and labor market analysts contend that elderly workers are doing particularly well at project management, coordination and planning, communication within the firm and with clients, tasks requiring a strong sense of responsibility, and jobs in some highly specialized areas. According to case studies, different age groups of workers can be matched with the production of different type of products, depending on how traditional or on how innovative the process is.[113] In the service industries a differentiation of types of skills needed can be made as well. For example, the elderly can be very productive in carrying out activities that require skills based on methods that do not change much. Consequently, firms are beginning to regard some of the elderly staff as a potential benefit. At the same time they are assigning easy and standardized tasks demanding few skills to the less efficient part of their elderly staff.[114] According to labor market projections, the numbers of these jobs will decrease, thus causing problems for attempts to lengthen working life.

One of the major risks related to aging is commonly perceived as lack of skills. The risk of unemployment is strongly linked to this lack. Half the unemployed aged 55 and older have not completed any vocational training.[115] Within the next decades required skill levels are expected to increase. In 1991 about 16 percent of all men and 47 percent of all women 60 and older lacked vocational training. According to projections on the basis of the Federal Statistical Office seventh pop-

111. Kessler (1991); and Hacker (1996, p. 182).
112. Kessler (1991, p. 146); and Barkholdt, Frerichs, and Naegele (1995, p. 427).
113. Köchling (1995, p. 444).
114. Köchling (1995).
115. Bäcker and Naegele (1995).

ulation projection, this share will shrink to 10 percent for men and 35 percent for women by 2030.[116]

However, increased formal education and training does not necessarily sufficiently lower the risks of an aging population because specific knowledge and skills, especially in high-technology industries, lose their value within a few years. Risks in regard to skills and experience-based human capital of older workers consist in down-skilling. Highly specialized, firm-specific qualifications can represent a risk as well.[117] With economic restructuring and technological change, the risk of down-skilling will increase.

At present, workers 50 and older are underrepresented in retraining.[118] Employers and elderly employees consider the return on investment too low. But both will have to change their view about the effectiveness of training for the elderly as companies face recruitment problems and workers a longer working life. Continuously adapting the skills to technological development by emphasizing lifelong learning will be inevitable to help avoid the deleterious effects of aging on economic performance.

The dynamics of future investments will depend on the rapid spread of new, or at least more sophisticated, technologies. According to Prognos's projection, productivity will grow 2.6 percent a year per hour worked in the high-population variant and 2.2 percent in the low-population variant. The difference between the two stems from assumptions concerning the speed with which new technologies diffuse and innovations are adopted.[119] The growth rates will be higher before 2010 than in the following three decades. Labor productivity growth is expected to increase slightly in western Germany, while in eastern Germany growth rates are likely to be higher in the first period.

Flexibility and the speed of acquiring new knowledge and skills will be decisive. But although these factors deteriorate with a person's age,[120] future generations of the elderly will have a greater capability to learn because they will already have been forced to adapt their skills

---

116. Höhn (1994, p. 259).
117. Barkholdt, Frerichs, and Naegele (1995, p. 425).
118. Barkholdt, Frerichs, and Naegele (1995).
119. Prognos (1995, p. 30).
120. Hacker (1996); and Barkholdt, Frerichs, and Naegele (1995).

to technological development. But innovative capacity might still suffer because a decreasing share of the young in the labor force is generally regarded as a decrease in innovative capacity.[121] Regional mobility also decreases with age, and it is unlikely that this trend will be reversed.[122] But appropriate measures can be taken to improve job mobility during the whole working life, including the final period.

An additional risk related to the changing age structure is poor motivation of younger workers resulting from fewer immediate career opportunities because of the huge cohort of elderly workers blocking the interesting jobs. Even though continuity is often regarded as good for a company, a large share of elderly persons within a firm, especially in management, may impede reactions to markets that are changing quickly. Moreover, the incentive to work might be diminished by higher rates of contribution to the social security system.[123] A shrinking work force inducing a scarcity of labor, especially of young, highly educated workers, may create pressure for technological development. Productivity growth might even be so high that elderly workers will still be replaced.[124]

The Investment-Saving Balance and the Role of Capital Markets

An aging population is likely to reduce the share of income it saves. The impact of decreasing savings on domestic investments is not evident. A greater share of consumption, especially increasing demand for domestically produced goods and services, boosts domestic investment, while a scarcity of capital and accompanying high interest rates hampers investment.

The effect of the proposed partial change from a pay-as-you-go plan to a capital-funded pension system is a matter of controversy in Germany. On the one hand, with a pension fund system the capital stock could be greater. Moreover, the additional capital stock owned by the population living in Germany would have some importance as an additional income source. (However, this effect is only important if this income does not just substitute the former level of public pensions

121. OECD (1988b); Kessler (1991); and Buttler (1990).
122. Kessler (1991).
123. Langmantel (1996).
124. Brasche (1993, p. 150).

based on a pay-as you-go system.) On the other hand, before 2020 the creation of such a capital stock substantially lowers total consumption and consequently economic growth. Later on, there is the danger of rapid decapitalization and a severe slowdown of economic performance. Thus like the pay-as-you-go system, a capital-funded pension plan is susceptible to major demographic changes.

When discussing the impact of domestic savings on domestic investment, one must bear in mind that the external capital balance in Germany is negative, primarily because Germans direct more financial and direct investments abroad than foreigners invest in Germany. Consequently, the fundamental question for German economic performance is how to direct more investments toward Germany rather than how to increase the domestic savings. In this respect, the level of additional capital costs such as taxes and regulation play a major role beside labor market factors and technological development in determining Germany's competitive position.

From an international perspective, Germany's savings level is a matter of concern because together with Japan it has been a major net saver for many years. Declining savings in Germany and Japan thus could raise international interest rates. In the case of Germany, it was feared that the economic restructuring of the former East German states would absorb a huge amount of capital and thus greatly reduce the capital exported. Only when enough investments have been directed to the new Länder could Germany resume its role of world net saver.[125] Recent developments show that foreign investments by Germany are declining somewhat, but this is due to exchange rate effects and not to an absorption of German capital by German unification.[126] The level of private investment in eastern Germany has not fulfilled expectations. At the same time, claims on world saving are expected to increase.[127] Consequently, there is some fear of rising international interest rates, which may affect countries with weak economies, such as many developing countries.[128] Capital would be allocated primarily to the Asia-Pacific region, where relatively satisfactory returns on investments are achieved. But higher interest rates may boost the saving

125. OECD (1992, p. 21).
126. Deutsche Bundesbank (1996).
127. OECD (1992).
128. OECD (1992); and Masson and Tryon (1990).

rate, so that a shortage of capital for economic growth may not occur. However, the elasticity of savings in regard to interest rates might not be important enough.

Policy Options

There are some prominent policy options that could help lower labor costs, expand the work force, and reduce capital costs.

LOWERING LABOR COSTS.   Several policies directed toward reducing contributions to the social security system are currently being discussed. However, reform of the system's financial structure can only resolve parts of the problem because capital costs as well as nonwage labor costs need to be reduced. Thus a redistribution of the costs is not enough, and growth rates of expenditures of public pensions must decline.

COUNTERING A SMALLER LABOR FORCE AND IMPROVING PRODUCTIV-ITY.   A labor shortage may cause high labor costs and hinder economic growth.

—One way to cope with a smaller labor supply would be to import workers. But it is questionable whether this solution can be implemented because there will be increasing demand for workers in many countries, especially countries that are themselves facing aging problems.

—Investments in human capital will thus be necessary at several levels (investing in nonnationals and nationals during their whole working life will be crucial). Moreover, all policies oriented to boost labor market participation rates might be appropriate, especially if investments in education and training have already been made. Increasing the labor market participation rates will lead to higher returns on investment. To ensure that workers' skills are constantly adapted and improved, continuous training will be crucial for all workers, including the elderly. The training should be based on two strategies: integrating the training process into work organization and spreading more specific training periods over the working life, which calls for shaping suitable working-life models.[129] Where new knowledge has

129. Barkholdt, Frerichs, and Naegele (1995, p. 429).

been acquired throughout the working life, the elderly may have enough learning capacity. The training of these workers should also be oriented toward their experience. A work organization that efficiently deals with complex tasks will promote creativity and ease learning.[130]

—If gradual retirement programs are to be effectively introduced, personnel managers and workers will have to change their attitudes.

—Policies to improve labor market flexibility, especially the skill and job mobility of the elderly, must be pursued.

—Personnel policies will have to respond to aging workers. Measures to provide health care will become increasingly necessary. Long-term effects are important because working conditions during the early working period may influence health later on.

—Strong motivation and flexibility of elderly workers can be achieved by varying and mixing tasks in the early stages of working life. And new types of careers, for example those independent of the hierarchy, must be designed.[131]

OTHER RESPONSES.   To attract more investments, Germany is currently considering lowering capital costs such as taxes. To improve capital supply, an objective of government policy has been to promote private savings. However, the effects of boosting private savings are more important under the aspect of asset income of the elderly. Finally, to meet the Maastricht criteria, there must be reductions in public expenditures. The possibilities for cutting are more favorable now than they will be in the future when the problem of an aging population has become more serious. A wide range of reductions is currently being discussed, and some have recently been adopted.

Macroeconomic Scenarios

The key factor of macroeconomic developments is the wage level. Two contradictory effects of wages have to be distinguished. High wages may accelerate structural change, in which case they would induce productivity growth. However, high wages can also harm com-

---

130. Hacker (1996).
131. Barkholdt, Frerichs, and Naegele (1995, p. 431).

petitiveness and impede productivity growth. The same kind of argument applies to low wages: either they favor labor-intensive production and do not set enough incentives to boost productivity or they help ensure a strong competive position.

In each of the following scenarios it is assumed that the wealth and income level depends strongly on the international competitiveness of the economy. The world economic outlook is assumed to be relatively good. Growth rates for the European Union are estimated to range between 1 percent and 2 percent. Lower growth rates than in the past are also assumed for the United States and Japan. The Czech Republic, Hungary, and Poland are assumed to do well; the former USSR will not recover economically for a long time. The Asia-Pacific region will grow at a fast pace, but rates will gradually slow during the first half of the next century. There will be an increase in aggregate worldwide demand.

SCENARIO 1.   In addition to the assumptions already stated, one must make assumptions about policy reactions. In this scenario a restrictive immigration policy is pursued, and the total labor force will decrease, especially after 2010. In *variant 1* no special policies to treat the problem of aging and falling productivity are envisaged. In *variant 2* it is assumed that policy will concentrate on investing in workers and boosting labor productivity.

In variant 1 high wages due to labor scarcity would harm Germany's competitiveness in the first period. Instead of trying to boost productivity through process innovation and investment in the work force, companies would relocate production abroad. Exports, GDP (or growth rates), wages, and domestic demand would all decrease, initiating a downward spiral. If wages would fall in the following period, it might be extremely difficult for the German economy to regain the shares of the world market it lost.

Savings as a share of income would be comparatively low and old-age poverty widespread. Higher savings would aggravate declining domestic demand and slow economic performance further. The innovative capacity of the German economy would suffer, not only from the poor economic climate but also from the aging of the working population.

The effect on the intergenerational distribution conflict would be severe as factor prices, especially on total wage costs, come under strong pressure. The possibilities for restructuring the financing of public pensions through taxes would be restrained (capital costs as well as labor costs would have to fall), and net real wages would fall in any case. Policies to increase the number of pension plan contributors, such as increasing participation rates for women and lengthening the working life, would be possible only at the cost of higher unemployment among other groups and would consequently fail. A slow shift from public to private pension provisions would be linked to a wide range of problems.

In variant 2 a smaller labor supply combined with higher foreign demand in the commodity and service markets would boost wages. This would exert pressure for productivity growth, and the response would be positive. Most important, Germany's competitiveness would not suffer from the wage increase. Instead, it would profit from the high growth rates of the newly industrializing countries in the Asia-Pacific and from a recovery of the central and eastern European economies, which would expand Germany's exports. Because an increase of wages can be largely compensated by productivity growth, high wages would not exert distorting effects. Higher wages and increased profit due to rising exports would expand domestic consumption and savings.

Domestic markets would feel a beneficial effect from an aging population. As compared with the younger population, the elderly spend a higher share of their income and consume more health care, cultural activities, and other nontradable goods and services.

Younger people's share in consumption would decrease slightly because they would save more. Several effects augment the saving rates, primarily a positive income effect and expectations of low public pensions, which would induce more people to shift to more private pensions. Additionally, because the growing world economy would need a huge amount of capital, interest rates would likely rise, which might induce additional saving. This would at least partly offset the effect of dissaving by the elderly. The higher savings of the young would allow for capital accumulation abroad through increasing direct investments. Thus, the increase in average income would be even more important in the long run and benefits from capital investments would represent an important additional income source for some future elderly.

The economic outlook would still be good, assuming that productivity increases could prevent Germany's competitive position from slipping. Higher foreign demand combined with productivity increases (increased jobless growth) might just keep labor demand at a constant level. In this case, a shrinking working population would mean falling unemployment and no labor shortage to hinder economic development. Decreasing unemployment would induce slight wage increases, so that there would still be incentives to increase productivity. However, a quantitatively balanced labor market would not solve the problem of mismatch in the labor market. Economic performance might suffer from a labor shortage in some market segments because the substitution of capital for labor would not be technologically possible in all cases.

Over time, the living standard of the elderly could remain at a high level, but the intergenerational distribution conflict would persist, and it is not clear how much the elderly would participate in economic development. The distributional conflict could impede economic growth if labor costs rose exorbitantly because bargaining power was strong enough to offset higher contribution rates with higher wages.

SCENARIO 2.   The scenario assumes that population and labor supply are increased by selective immigration policy, rising fertility rates, and improved labor force participation rates of women and the elderly.

Contrasted with scenario 1, the larger labor supply would lead to smaller wage increases or even falling wages. Consequently, there would be fewer incentives to substitute capital for labor and productivity growth would be slower than in scenario 1, variant 2. Export competitiveness would be improved because of lower wages but productivity growth would be slower. The net effect is ambiguous.

The more balanced age structure of the working population due to selective immigration and adoption of an appropriate integration policy would boost productivity and strengthen the innovative capacity of the German economy. Beneficial effects on the export sectors can be assumed. As in scenario 1, productivity increases would largely depend on investment in human capital.

The effects on the domestic demand would be positive if population growth offset the effect of relatively lower wages (higher propensity to consume, but lower per capita purchasing power). The average wage level would also be influenced by Germany's productivity growth and its international competitive stance.

A segregation of the labor market (by nationality) might occur, so that in some areas cheap labor for the production of nontradable goods and services would be available. In this case nontradable goods and services would be relatively cheaper, which would decrease imports and increase domestic demand for nontradable goods and services. Higher demand would not result in higher wages because immigration policy can react flexibly to changing labor demand.

The saving rate would be lower than in scenario 1 (lower average income and fewer incentives to contribute to private pensions because the number of contributors would not be decreasing, or at least would be doing so less dramatically). However, total savings might be at the same level as in scenario 1 or even above that level because the total population, and especially the number of younger people in the labor force, would be greater.

As the number of contributors grew, the intergenerational distribution conflict would be perceived as less pronounced than in scenario 1. Whether the living standard of the whole population would become higher than in scenario 1, variant 2, would depend on the possible difference in productivity growth.

Conclusions

A major challenge for Germany's economic performance is a possible shortage of labor. Importing skilled workers will be a more difficult problem than a shortage of unskilled labor, which can easily be resolved by immigration policy.

If Germany does not decapitalize because of an already high level of accumulated private wealth and certain cultural factors, the share of interest as an income source could increase, especially if other advanced industrial countries decapitalize more and if there is a demand for capital from the newly industrializing and the developing countries. A changing level of savings, and thus a changing supply of capital in Germany, will primarily affect the country's level of foreign financial and direct investment.

Economic growth does not necessarily imply higher employment: in fact Germany's jobless growth is a matter of concern in light of the high unemployment figures in the medium term and the financing of the social security system in the long term.

Productivity growth can be regarded as a potential way to finance the public pension system in the face of a shrinking labor force. According to current estimates, the acceleration of productivity growth by 0.5 percent a year between 2010 and 2030 can offset half the decline in the labor supply without increases in immigration.[132] Whether such productivity growth can be achieved in an environment of an aging work force is doubtful, however.

The living standard of the elderly in the present system is directly related to the improvement of labor productivity. As long as the public pension program includes a yearly dynamization of pensions based on the average development of wages, an increase in labor productivity will not solve the intergenerational distribution imbalances. Contributions for the younger workers will still have to rise more than in a model with smaller labor productivity increases but more persons working. Politically, a higher contribution rate is probably less acceptable than lower wages due to lower productivity growth rates but higher employment figures.

Productivity growth as the driving force for Germany's international competitiveness and thus for economic growth must be regarded as complementary to rather than a substitution for other policy measures such as increasing the number of contributors. However, there are some interdependencies between the number of contributors and productivity growth. Labor scarcity is likely to boost the incentives to improve productivity. However, if the labor shortage in some key sectors is too great, economic growth and the capacity of productivity growth could be compromised. Furthermore, an overall danger for economic growth is that productivity growth would not be great enough to compensate for wage increases. But a policy of expanding labor supply without worrying about productivity growth and trying to compete merely on the grounds of lower wages is likely to fail.

A combination of policy measures would be appropriate to cope with aging. A selective immigration policy should be pursued. At the same time, continuous training and the adaptation of training and personnel policies to an aging work force should be provided, as well

132. Klauder (1993a, p. 489).

as additional measures to boost productivity. A lengthening of the working life combined with gradual retirement seems inevitable. It is likely that future elderly will receive lower public pensions compared with those that are received now.

References

Achenbach, Klaus, and Eva Hanaberg. 1995. "Rentenversicherung: Ermutigende Zukunftsperspektiven." *Bundesarbeitsblatt* 11: 5–11.

Andrieu, M., W. Michalski, and B. Stevens. 1992. "Long-term Prospects for the World Economy: Overall Outlook, Main Issues and Summary of Discussions." In OECD, *Long-term Prospects*, pp. 7–25.

Bäcker, G., and G. Naegele. 1993. *Alternde Gesellschaft und Erwerbstätigkeit. Modelle zum Übergang vom Erwerbsleben in den Ruhestand*. Köln: Bund-Verlag, HBS Forschung, Band 11.

———. 1995. "Ältere Arbeitnehmer zwischen Langzeit-arbeitslosigkeit und Frühverrentung." *WSI-Mitteilungen* 12: 777–84.

Barkholdt, C., F. Frerichs, and G. Naegele. 1995. "Altersübergreifende Qualifizierung—eine Strategie zur betrieblichen Integration älterer Arbeitnehmer." *Mitteilungen aus der Arbeitsmarkt- und Berufsforschung* 3: 425–34.

Bernsten, Roland, and Doreen Blossfeld. 1995. "Rentenversicherungsbericht 1995. Trotz hoher Lasten solide." *Bundesarbeitsblatt* 9: 13–23.

Beyer, Jürgen. 1994. "20 Jahre Betriebsrentengesetz. Wo stehen wir heute?" *Bundesarbeitsblatt* 12: 10–18.

Blau, H. 1996. "Entwicklung und Reformansätze im Gesundheitswesen." *Ifo-Schnelldienst* 17-18: 26–37.

Blum, Norbert. 1996. "Regierungserklärung. Vertrauen in die Rentenversicherung." *Bundesarbeitsblatt* 3.

Börsch-Supan, Axel. 1991. "Aging population: problems and policy options in the US and Germany." *Economic Policy* 12 (April).

———. 1992. "Saving and consumption patterns of the elderly: The German Case." *Journal of Population Economics* 5: 289–303.

Brasche, A. 1993. "Sind Produktinnovationen mit mehrheitlich älteren Arbeitnehmern möglich?" In H.-J Bullinger and others, eds., *Alter und Erwerbsarbeit der Zukunft*, pp. 150–55. Berlin: Springer-Verlag.

Bucher, Hansjörg, and Hans Peter Gatzweiler (Bundesforschungsanstalt für Landeskunde und Raumordnung). 1995. *Perspektiven der regionalen Bevölkerungsentwicklung in Deutschland*. Beitrag für den ARL-Arbeitskreis Bevölkerungsentwicklung und Siedlungsstruktur. June.

Bullinger, H.-J., and others, eds., *Alter und Erwerbsarbeit der Zukunft*. Berlin: Springer-Verlag.

Buttler, G. 1990. "Arbeitsmarktreserven bei schrumpfender Bevölkerung." In B. Felderer, ed., *Bevölkerung und Wirtschaft*, pp. 441–53.

Das Parlament. 1996. *Sonderheft zu: Senioren heute.* March 1.

Davis, E. Philip. 1995. *Pension Funds: Retirement-Income Security, and Capital Markets. An International Perspective.* Oxford University Press.

Deutsche Bundesbank. 1993. "Zur Vermögenssituation der privaten Haushalte in Deutschland." *Monatsbericht* (October): 19–32.

———. 1995. "Zur Finanzentwicklung der gesetzlichen Rentenversicherung seit Beginn der neunziger Jahre." *Monatsbericht* (March): 17–31.

———. 1996. "Neuere Entwicklung des deutschen Netto-Auslandsvermögens und der Kapitalerträge." *Monatsberichte* (January): 31–54.

Deutscher Bundestag, Referat für Öffentlichkeitsarbeit. 1994. *Zwischenbericht der Enquete-Kommission "Demographischer Wandel."* Bonn: Herausforderung unserer älter werdenden Gesellschaft an den einzelnen und an die Politik.

Deutsches Zentrum für Altersfragen. 1993. *Expertisen zum ersten Altenbericht der Bundesregierung, III. Aspekte der Lebensbedingungen ausgewählter Bevölkerungsgruppen.* Berlin: "Weise Reihe" des DZA.

DIW. 1995. "Alternde gesellschaft. Zur Bedeutung von Zuwanderung für die Altersstruktur der Bevölkerung in Deutschland." *DIW Wochenbericht* 33: 579–89.

———. 1996. "Immobilienvermögen der privaten Haushalte." *DIW-Wochenbericht* 4/96.

Dresdner Bank. 1995. "Demographische Entwicklung erfordert Reform internationaler Rentensysteme (Teil 2: EU)." *Dresdner Bank Trends* (October).

Dudey, S. 1996. "Vorausschätzungen der Kostenentwicklung in der GKV— unter Berücksichtigung des demographischen Wandels für Gesamtdeutschland bis zum Jahr 2030—aufbauend auf Kranken- und/oder Rentenversicherungsdaten." In Enquete-Kommission "Demographischer Wandel," Bd. I: 279–341.

Enquete-Kommission. "Demographischer Wandel." Deutscher Bundestag (Hrsg.). 1996. *Herausforderungen unser älter werdenden Gesellschaft an den einzelnen und die Politik; Band 1 und 2.* Heidelberg: R.v. Decker's Verlag, Hüthig GmbH.

Felderer, B., ed., *Bevölkerung und Wirtschaft, Jahrestagung des Vereins für Socialpolitik in Wien 1989. Schriften des Vereins für Socialpolitik Band 202.* Berlin: Duncker & Humblot.

Fischer, W. 1990. "Bevölkerung und Wirtschaft in historischer Perspektive." In B. Felderer, ed., *Bevölkerung und Wirtschaft,* pp. 29–49.

Forum Demographie und Politik. 1995. Zuwanderung steuern. Hans-Ulrich Klose über Einwanderer, notwendige Auswahlkriterien und deutsche Interessen. Interview von Michael Jach Ulrich Reitz; Heft 7 (February): 30–34.

Gimbal, A. I. 1994. "Die Zuwanderungspolitik der Europäischen Union: Interessen—Hintergründe—Perspektiven." In W. Weidenfeld, ed., *Das europäische Einwanderungskonzept.*

Hacker, W. 1996. "Erwerbsarbeit der Zukunft—Zukunft der Erwerbsarbeit:

Zusammenfassende arbeitswissenschaftliche Aspekte und weiterführende Aufgaben." In W. Hacker, ed., *Erwerbsarbeit der Zukunft - auch für Ältere?*, pp. 175–93. Zürich: vdf Hochschulverlag AG an der ETH und Stuttgart: B. G. Teubner.

Heuwinkel, D., H. J. Kujath, and K. Bergman. 1996. "Entwicklung des Wohnens und Wohnumfelds älterer Menschen bis zum Jahr 2030." In Enquete-Kommission "Demographischer Wandel," Bd. II: 619–827.

Hofmann, Claus F. 1995. "Soziale Sicherung. Weiterhin arbeitsorientiert." *Bundesarbeitsblatt* (7-8): S. 5–9.

Hofmann, Herbert. 1994. "Szenarien der Arbeitskräfteentwicklung im Europäischen Wirtschaftsraum bis zum Jahr 2020." *Ifo-Schnelldienst* 25-26: 8–18.

———. 1995. *Long Term Labor Force Scenarios for the European Union. Final Report.* Scenarios prepared for the Statistical Office of the European Union. Munich: Ifo Institute for Economic Research.

Höhn, Charlotte. 1994. *Die Alten der Zukunft—Bevölkerungsstatistische Datenanalyse, Forschungsbericht im Auftrag des Bundesministeriums für Familie und Senioren Bundesinstitut für Bevölkerungsforschung, Schriftenreihe Band 32.* Stuttgart: W. Kohlhammer GmbH.

Kessler, H. 1991. *Arbeitsmarktpolitische Implikationen eines Bevölkerungsrückgangs in der Bundesrepublik Deutschland.* Frankfurt am Main: Verlag Peter Lang GmbH.

Klauder, W. 1993a. "Zu den demographischen und ökonomischen Auswirkungen der Zuwanderung in die Bundesrepublik in Vergangenheit und Zukunft." *Mitteilungen aus der Arbeitsmarkt- und Berufsforschung* 4: 477–94.

———. 1993b. "Ausreichend Mitarbeiter für Tätigkeiten von Morgen." In H.-J. Bullinger and others, eds., *Alter und Erwerbsarbeit der Zukunft*, pp. 22–31.

Köchling, A. 1995. "Wie Betriebe heute mit Altersstrukturen (nicht mit Älteren) umgehen—Anforderungen an die Zukunft." *Mitteilungen aus der Arbeitsmarkt- und Berufsforschung* 3: 437–53.

Koll, R., W. Ochel, and K. Vogler-Ludwig. 1992. *Die Auswirkungen der internationalen Wanderungen auf Bayern.* Munich: Ifo Institut für Wirtschaftsforschung.

Lampert, H. 1994. *Lehrbuch der Sozialpolitik.* Berlin.

Lang, O. 1996. "Die Einkommens- und Vermögensverhältnisse künftiger Altengenerationen in Deutschland." In Enquete-Kommission "Demographischer Wandel," Bd. 1, 57–278.

Langmantel, E. 1996. "Halbierung der Arbeitslosenquote bis 2000? Eine Modellrechnung." *Ifo-Schnelldienst* 17-18: 9–13.

Lesthaeghe, R., H. Page, and J. Surkyn. 1991. "Sind Einwanderer ein Ersatz für Geburten?" *Zeitschrift für Bevölkerungswissenschaft*, Jg. 17, Heft 3: 281–314.

Leibfritz, Willi, and Deborah Roseveare. 1996. "Aging Populations and Government Budgets." *OECD Observer* 197 (December 1995–January 1996): 33–37.

Masson, Paul R., and Ralph W. Tryon. 1990. "Macroeconomic Effects of Projected Population Aging in Industrial Countries." *IMF Staff Papers* 37 (3): 453–85.

Meier, C.-P. 1995. "Demographie und Ersparnis." *Zeitschrift für Wirtschaftspolitik,* Jg. 44 H. 1: 85–110.

Müller, Stefan. 1995. "Zielgruppe Senioren. Zwischen Markt-und Medienrealität." *Absatzwirtschaft* (12): 42–47.

Müller, Horst-Wolf, and Ulrich Roppel. 1990. "Eine Abschätzung des Kapitalbedarfs bei einer vollständigen Kapitaldeckung der gesetzlichen Rentenversicherung." In B. Felderer, ed., *Bevölkerung und Wirtschaft,* pp. 425–38.

Munz, Sonja. 1996. *Ansätze zur Überwindung der Erwerbsbeteiligung von Frauen im Erwerbsleben.* München.

Neue Züricher Zeitung (1995), OECD-Studie über Einkommensverteilung. Reichere Reiche und ärmere Arme. Ausbau der Altersvorsorge beeinflaut Einkommensdiskrepanz. In: NZZ 28.10.1995

Organization for Economic Cooperation and Development. 1988a. *Reforming Public Pensions,* Social Policy Studies 5. Paris.

———. 1988b. *Aging Population: Social Policy Implications.* Paris.

———. 1992. *Long-term Prospects for the World Economy.* Paris.

Parsche, Rüdiger. 1996. "Derzeitige Besteuerung der Renten nicht Systemgerecht." *Ifo-Schnelldienst* 14: 9–10.

Prognos AG. 1995. *Perspektiven der gestzlichen Rentenversicherung für Gesamtdeutschland vor dem Hintergrund veränderter politischer und ökonomischer Rahmenbedingungen. Herausgegeben vom Verband Deutscher Rentenversicherungsträger.* Postverlagsort Frankfurt am Main: DRV-Schriften, Band 4.

Rentenversicherungsbericht. 1995. Bericht der Bundesregierung über die gesetzlichen Rentenversicherungen, ins besondere über die Entwicklung der Einnahmen und Ausgaben, der Schwankungsreserve sowie des jeweils erforderlichen Beitragssatzes in den künftigen 15 Kalenderjahren gemäa 154 SGB VI.

Ritter, U. P. 1995. "Thesen zur Überalterung, Lebensarbeitszeit, Altergrenze und ruhestand." In B. Schefold, ed., *Wandlungsprozesse in den Wirtschaftssystemen Westeuropas.* Marburg: Metropolis-Verlag.

Rosenow, J., and F. Naschold. 1993. "Die betriebliche Frühverrentungspraxis am Scheideweg." In H.-J. Bullinger and others, eds., *Alter und Erwerbsarbeit der Zukunft,* pp. 139–43.

Rothgang, Heinz, and Winfried Schmähl. 1995. "The Long-Term Costs of Public Long-Term Care Insurance in Germany." Zentrum für Sozialpolitik Universität Bremen ZeS-Arbeitspapier 9.

Rürup, B., and W. Sesselmeier. 1993. "Die demographische Entwicklung Deutschlands: Risiken, Chancen, politische Optionen." Aus Politik und

Zeitgeschichte, Beilage zur Wochenzeitung Das Parlament B44/93 (October 29): 3–15.

Schmähl, Winfried. 1992. "The flat-rate public pension in the German social policy debate—from the early 19th to the late 20th century." Zentrum für Sozialpolitik Universität Bremen ZeS-Arbeitspapier 6.

————. 1995. "Migration une soziale Sicherheit—Über die Notwendigkeit einer differenzierten Betrachtung: das Beispiel der gesetzlichen Kranken- und Rentenversicherung." Zentrum für Sozialpolitik Universität Bremen ZeS-Arbeitspapier 5.

Schmid, J. 1994. "Zuwanderung aus Eigennutz? Der demographische Aspekt des Einwanderungsbedarfes in den EU-Mitgliedstaaten." In W. Weidenfeld, ed., Das europäische Einwanderungskonzept.

Schmidt, P. 1995. Die Wahl des Rentenalters: theoretische und empirische Analyse des Rentenzugangsverhaltens in West- und Ostdeutschland. Frankfurt am Main: Peter Lang Verlag.

Schneider, H. K. 1990. "Folgen einer schrumpfenden Bevölkerung für die Wirtschaftspolitik." In B. Felderer, ed., Jahrestagung des Vereins für Socialpolitik Gesellschaft für Wirtschafts- und Sozialwissenschaften in Wien 1989, Schriften des Vereins für Socialpolitik Band 202, pp. 557–73. Berlin: Duncker & Humblodt.

Schwarz, Karl. 1990. "Demographische Wirkungen der Familienpolitik in der Bundesrepublik Deutschland nach dem Zweiten Weltkrieg." In B. Felderer, ed., Jahrestagung des Vereins für Socialpolitik Gesellschaft, pp. 495–518.

Seehofer, Horst. 1996. "Die dritte Stufe der Gesundheitsreform." Wirtschaftsdienst 1996/II: 59–62.

Statistisches Bundesamt. Various years. Wirtschaftsrechnungen. Einkommens- und Verbrauchsstichprobe 1973, 1978, 1983, 1988, jeweils Fachserie 15, Heft 4 Einnahmen und Ausgaben privater Haushalte. Stuttgart.

————. 1996. Statistisches Jahrbuch 1995. Stuttgart.

Steffen, Johannes. 1996. "Rentenfinanzen unter dem Einflau des Arbeitsmarkts." WSI Mitteilungen 4: 218–28.

Steinman. 1996. "Zusammenhang zwischen Alterungsprozea und Einwanderung." In Enquete-Kommission "Demographischer Wandel" Deutscher Bundestag, 1–56.

Thon, M. 1991. "Perspektiven des Erwerbspersonenpotentials in Gesamtdeutschland bis zum Jahr 2030." Mitteilungen zur Arbeitsmarkt- und Berufsforschung 4: 706–11.

————. 1995. "Demographische Aspekte der Arbeitsmarktentwicklung—die Alterung des Erwerbspersonenpotentials." Mitteilungen zur Arbeitsmarkt- und Berufsforschung 3: 290–99.

Vogler-Ludwig, K. 1996. "Sozialpolitik, Beschäftigung und Wettbewerb." Ifo-Schnelldienst 17-18: 3–8.

Volgler-Ludwig, Kurt, unter der Mitarbeit von Christin Severin and Erich

Langmantel. 1996. "Versicherungsfremde Leistungen in der Sozialversicherung. Kurzstudie im Auftrag der SPD- Fraktion im Bayerischen Landtag." Munich: Ifo Institut für Wirtschaftsforschung.

Wagner, Adolph. 1994. "Demographisch bedingte Arbeitslosigkeit in Deutschland." *Ifo-Schnelldienst* 26-27: 19–22.

Weeber, Joachim. 1996. "Mehrwertsteuererhöhung zur Finanzierung von Sozialleistungen?" *Wirtschaftsdienst* 1996/II: 81–86.

Weidenfeld, W., ed. 1994. *Das europäische Einwanderungskonzept. Strategien und Optionen für Europa.* Gütersloh: Verlag Beterlsmann Stiftung.

Weidenfeld, W., and O. Hillenbrand. 1994. "Einwanderungspolitik und Integration von Ausländern—Gestaltungsaufgaben für die europäische Union." In W. Weidenfeld, ed., *Das europäische Einwanderungskonzept.*

Wenzel, B., and R. Flöter. 1993. "Produktivität durch Gruppenarbeit." In H.-J. Bullinger and others, eds., *Alter und Erwerbsarbeit der Zukunft*, pp. 47–49.

Wilhelm, M. 1996. "Motive deutscher und ausländischer Direktinvestoren." *Ifo-Schnelldienst* 16: 9–18.

Wirtschaft und Statistik. 1992. *Verfügbares Einkommen nach Haushaltsgruppen. Revidierte Ergebnisse der Volkswirtschaftlichen Gesamtrechnungen für die Jahre 1972 bis 1991* (July): 418–30.

———. 1994. *Entwicklung der Bevölkerung bis 2040. Ergebnis der achten koordinierten Bevölkerungsvorausberechnungen* (July): 497–503.

———. 1995a. *Geldvermögen und Schulden privater Haushalte Ende 1993. Ergebnis der Einkommens- und Verbrauchsstichprobe* (May): 391–99.

———. 1995b. *Grundvermögen privater Haushalte Ende 1993. Ergebnis der Einkommens- und Verbrauchsstichprobe* (June): 488–97.

Chapter 5

Population Aging and Japanese Economic Performance

Yukihiko Endo and Eiji Katayama

J APAN HAS one of the world's oldest populations, and during
the next quarter century it will grow even older at a very
rapid rate. This demographic change will have a major impact on
public programs and economic performance. The first part of this
chapter summarizes the demographic trends, explains the basic provisions of Japan's social security programs for the elderly, and provides
some projections of their future costs. In the second portion we evaluate some proposals for improving the financing and delivery of assistance services to the elderly.

Demographic Data

The Ministry of Health and Welfare (MHW) prepares demographic
projections for Japan every five years.[1] It uses three scenarios based
on different assumptions about fertility rates (other assumptions are
the same for all scenarios). The medium scenario is used to recalculate
the required premium or contribution rate for the public pension programs. All three scenarios for the 1992 projections indicate Japan's
rapid aging: the dependency ratio (the ratio of those older than age
64 to the number of those in the working population) increases from

1. MHW announced a new population projection in January 1997, revising the previous one downward (see the appendix for details). However, for this report we use the
previous projection because related numbers will not be revised until 1998, when a new
calculation for the public pension fund will be made.

FIGURE 5-1. *Aged Dependency Rate Based on Alternative Fertility Rate Assumptions, 1950–98, and Projected to 2020*

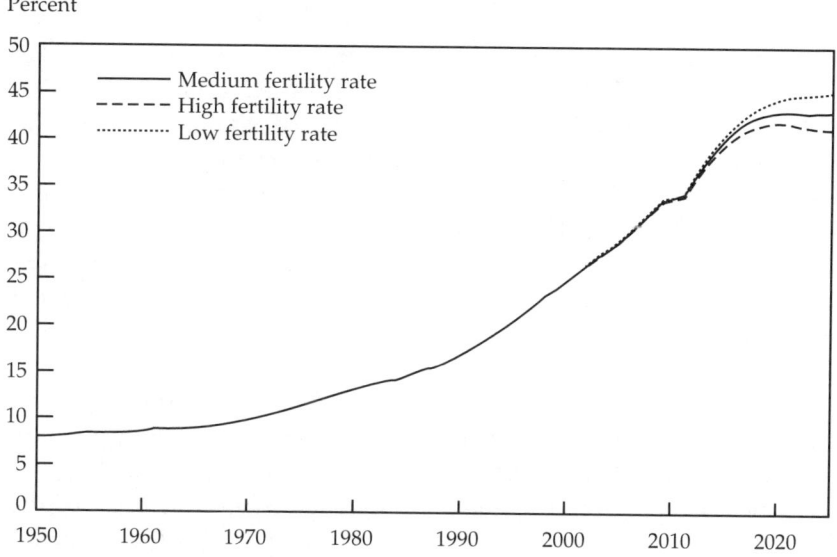

Source: Ministry of Health and Welfare 1992 estimates.

17.3 percent in 1991 to more than 40 percent in 2025 (figure 5-1).[2] The pace of demographic aging is unprecedented among the industrial countries, but many other Asian countries will face a similar situation in twenty to thirty years.

Life expectancy at birth, which is already the highest among the major countries, is projected to continue to increase; but the rapid pace of aging in Japan is primarily a reflection of a sharp drop in the fertility rate. The working population began to shrink in 1995. The 1992 MHW medium projection assumes that the total fertility rate will recover from a rate of 1.43 in 1995 to 1.80 in 2025 and 2.08 in 2090.

The fertility rate peaked at 2.14 in 1965, and its subsequent rapid decline has been due to varied factors. The average age for first marriage has shifted to the late twenties as more women go to college and

2. The aged dependency rate is defined as the ratio of the population over age 64 to the population aged 15–64.

enter the work force after graduation. The average age for first marriage for men rose from 26.6 in 1955 to 28.5 in 1995, and for women
from 23.8 to 26.2. The average age at which women bear their first
child is about 28, which is the oldest among the major developed
countries. It is also very difficult for women to fulfill the roles of worker
and mother at the same time because day care facilities and other
support services are in short supply. Cramped living conditions (in
major cities) have become a psychological deterrent to bearing more
children. The fertility rate for the Tokyo metropolitan area, for example, is only about 1.1. Finally, remaining single and other alternative
life-styles have become more socially acceptable. The ratio of unmarried men between ages 35 and 39 to all men increased from 3.1 percent
in 1955 to 19.0 percent in 1990 and the ratio for women from 3.9 percent
to 7.5 percent.

We do not foresee a fundamental change in these conditions and
therefore believe that the fertility rate assumption for the medium
estimate is high. The low estimate seems more realistic, implying an
aged dependency rate of 60 percent by 2050. However, because the
projections of public program costs are based on the medium scenario,
it is used in subsequent portions of this discussion unless otherwise
indicated.

Net immigration has a negligible influence on the age profile of
Japan's population. In recent years the large appreciation of the yen
has brought an influx of foreign workers. According to one estimate,
the total number of foreign workers (including illegals) is 425,000. Still,
this is just 0.5 percent of the working population in Japan. Japan has
never seriously considered immigration as a policy to moderate population aging, and the increase in net immigration is not taken into
account in the population projection.

The Economic Status of the Elderly

Although many still live with their children, Japan's elderly have
become more financially independent. Public pensions constituted
more than 50 percent of the income of the elderly in the mid-1990s,
but wage income is still relatively important (table 5-1). The averages
can be misleading, however. There are many nonworking old people

TABLE 5-1. *Sources of Income for the Elderly, Selected Years, 1977–94ª*
Percent

Year	Wage and salary earnings	Asset income	Public pension benefitsᵇ	Private pensions	Other sourcesᶜ
1977	42.8	10.4	34.1	n.a.	12.8
1980	44.2	7.8	40.3	n.a.	7.7
1985	39.6	6.8	47.2	n.a.	6.5
1990	33.9	10.5	49.7	n.a.	5.8
1994	36.0	6.5	54.8	n.a.	2.7

Source: Ministry of Health and Welfare, *Survey of Households* (annual).
a. Aged households are defined as those having only aged members or those with both aged members and unmarried members under age 18. The aged are defined as men older than 65 and women older than 60.
b. Includes employee pension insurance and mutual aid associations (for public employees, teachers, and others).
c. Includes social security benefits (other than the public pension) and private pension benefits.
n.a. Not available.

whose income consists solely of a pension; and income inequality is much greater among aged households than it is in other age groups.

The average income of the elderly is about half the average of all households, a ratio that has been constant for twenty years (table 5-2). The average income of households with a head 65 years or older and still working is about 80 percent of the average for all households. However, to understand the real financial status of the elderly, one has to take taxes into account, because the elderly benefit from several provisions of the tax system. The tax rate for pension income is lower

TABLE 5-2. *Income of Aged Households Relative to Other Households, Selected Years, 1977–93ª*
Percent

Year	Aged relative to all	Aged relative to non-aged, non–single parent households
1977	45.7	43.8
1980	49.3	47.0
1985	48.5	45.5
1990	48.6	45.0
1993	48.7	44.7

Source: Ministry of Health and Welfare, *Survey of Households* (annual).
a. See table 5-1 for definitions.

FIGURE 5-2. *Relative Income Pre- and Postadjustment, by Age Group*

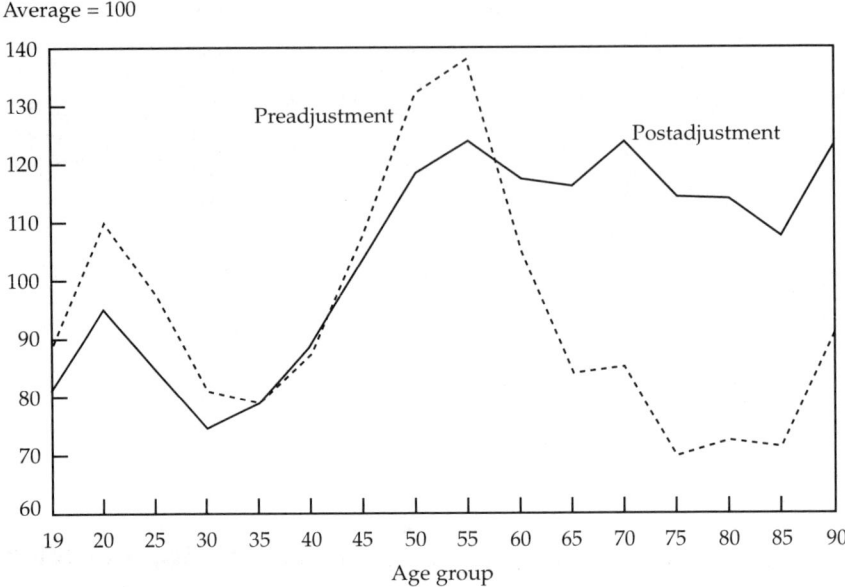

Average = 100

Source: Ministry of Health and Welfare.

than the general income tax rate. The elderly are also allowed a special deduction (¥0.5 million) for wage income on top of the general deduction (¥0.38 million). In addition, elderly people are entitled to use medical treatment, transportation, and other services free or for a nominal payment. One estimate indicates elderly people's personal income adjusted for taxes and noncash income would be 10 to 20 percent higher than the overall average, while for the group between ages 30 and 44 it would be about 20 percent lower than the average (figure 5-2). Finally, the elderly hold relatively large amounts of wealth, twice the average for the total population. Their major asset is real estate, which has experienced phenomenal price increases. Inequality of wealth, like inequality of income, is relatively great among the elderly.

Most of the elderly live with their children, and the proportion rises with age (table 5-3). Because families are still responsible for support-

TABLE 5-3. *Living Arrangements of People Age 65 and Older, Selected Years, 1975–95, and Projected to 2010*
Percent

	Alone	With spouse	With children	With other relatives	In institutions
1975	7.1	15.0	71.9	2.9	3.0
1980	8.3	18.1	67.4	2.6	3.6
1985	9.5	20.6	63.5	2.2	4.2
1990	10.9	24.1	58.5	2.2	4.3
1995	11.2	28.6	53.7	2.3	4.2
2000	11.6	32.5	48.6	2.3	4.5
2005	12.2	36.3	44.4	2.3	4.8
2010	12.7	39.7	39.9	2.4	5.3

Source: Ministry of Health and Welfare, *Projection of Living Arrangements of the Elderly in Japan, 1990–2010*, May 1995. Projections use MHW medium scenario.

ing the elderly in Japan, the roles of the government and the market are relatively small. At any given age, however, there is an increasing tendency for the elderly to live on their own. Government projections of how these living arrangements will change suggest that in 2010 the proportion of elderly people living with their children will be half that in 1975. The proportion of people living alone or in institutions will increase. This change suggests the need to reevaluate provisions for long-term care and other policies for the elderly.

Pensions and Other Public Programs for the Aged

Japan has a complex network of pensions, medical care, and other welfare programs that provide services for the elderly.

Pension Programs

The Japanese pension system is very fragmented, reflecting the piecemeal fashion in which it was developed. Although there has been universal coverage since 1961, the current system is not unified, and it has many differing provisions governing participation. A schematic outline is presented in figure 5-3. To begin with, the National Pension (NP) is a universal public program that provides a flat monthly payment to essentially all residents of Japan older than 60. Universal

FIGURE 5-3. *Pension System in Japan, 1995*[a]

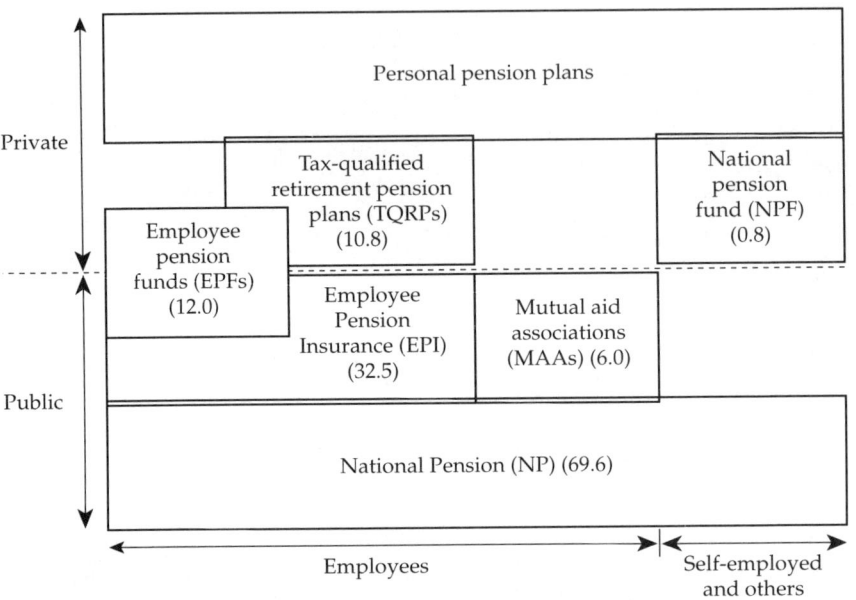

Source: Ministry of Health and Welfare.
a. Figures in parentheses are millions of participants.

coverage was achieved when the national pension program was extended to self-employed workers. It was transformed into a basic pension for all people in 1986.

A second earnings-related portion comes from several different funds. Private sector employees are covered by the publicly managed Employee Pension Insurance (EPI). But this portion (before inflation and wage increase adjustment) can be replaced by employee pension funds (EPFs). The EPFs are basically private corporate pension funds, but because they are used to replace the EPI, their tax treatment and other regulations are similar to those for the EPI.[3] Public workers,

3. Corporations can also choose to establish tax-qualified retirement plans. There are other private pension plans for the self-employed.

TABLE 5-4. *Pension Fund Participation, Selected Years, 1960–94*
Millions unless otherwise specified

Year	Total	National Pension (NP) only	NP and Employee Pension Insurance	NP and mutual aid associations	Working-age population	Coverage (percent of working population)
1960	17.41	0[a]	13.24	4.17	60.47	28.8
1965	43.35	20.02	18.42	4.92	67.44	64.3
1970	51.93	24.33	22.26	5.34	72.12	72.0
1975	55.46	25.88	23.89	5.68	75.81	73.2
1980	59.05	27.60	25.45	6.01	78.84	74.9
1985	58.24	25.09	27.23	5.91	82.51	70.6
1990	66.31	29.54	31.00	5.78	85.90	77.2
1994	69.55	30.96	32.74	5.85	87.13	79.8

Source: Ministry of Health and Welfare, *Annual Report*.
a. The national pension system started in 1961.

teachers, and others are covered by one of five mutual aid associations (MAAs). Rates of participation in the public programs are shown in table 5-4. The NP now covers about 80 percent of the working age population.

The minimum age for drawing a pension is currently 60, but it is being gradually increased to 65. This is not the "retirement age" indicated in many reports, however. Major companies have set the mandatory retirement age at 60, and a law enacted in 1994 made it illegal to set the age below 60 after 1998. We do not expect companies to raise their retirement age in the foreseeable future. Instead, we expect that people will change jobs around age 60 or will be reemployed by their former employer under a new, lower contract and keep working after the so-called retirement age. Furthermore, although workers can draw on the National Pension at age 60, benefits are actuarially adjusted for those who retire between the ages of 60 and 70.

The pension system has had a strong influence on increasing labor force participation. But in the aggregate, other factors, including the more frequent entry of women into the work force and the decline in self-employment (particularly in agriculture in the 1960s and 1970s), were more important. It is common in Japan for retirees to continue working beyond the retirement age, and earnings are an important

TABLE 5-5. *Labor Force Participation Rates, by Sex and Age Group, Selected Years, 1960–95, and Projected to 2010*
Percent

	Men			Women		
Year	Total 15 and older	Working age population 15–64	Elderly 65 and older	Total 15 and older	Working age population 15–64	Elderly 65 and older
1960	84.8	87.3	56.9	54.5	57.5	25.6
1965	81.7	83.9	56.3	50.6	53.6	21.6
1970	81.8	84.8	49.4	49.9	53.4	17.9
1975	81.4	85.2	44.4	45.7	49.7	15.3
1980	79.8	84.3	41.0	47.6	52.5	15.5
1985	78.1	83.2	37.0	48.7	54.5	15.5
1990	77.2	82.8	36.5	50.1	57.1	16.2
1995	77.6	84.5	37.3	50.0	58.5	15.6
2000[a]	78.0	86.0	38.9	49.8	59.5	16.4
2010[a]	76.6	87.4	38.4	48.2	60.6	16.6

Source: Statistics Bureau, Management and Coordination Agency, *Labor Force Survey*.
a. Figures for 2000 and 2010 are projected by Ministry of Labor using the medium scenario.

income source for the aged as a group. However, the increase in pension benefits in the 1970s did lead to reduced labor force participation among the elderly.

Ministry of Labor projections of the size of the labor force in 2010 assume a resurgence in participation among both the working-age population and those older than 65 (table 5-5). The projected increasing participation rate of the elderly is based on expectations that pension reforms undertaken in 1994 have reduced the retirement incentive: the pre-1994 pension system discouraged part-time work by the elderly. However, because the proportion of the elderly is rising, this greater labor force participation is not reflected in an increase in the overall rate when all age categories are combined. For women, the participation rate is expected to increase in all age categories from 1995 to 2010. But, again because of the aging effect, the overall labor force participation rate for women will decline.

CONTRIBUTION RATES. The National Pension requires a per capita contribution (currently ¥12,300 a month) of all participants. For those covered by EPI the contribution is 16.5 percent of monthly wages, half paid by employers. For those covered by corporate pension funds, the earnings-related contribution depends on the particular plan. There are two types of corporate pension funds, EPFs and tax-qualified retirement plans. Companies can choose neither, either, or both. However, the status of these plans in the public policies for the elderly is somewhat ambiguous. Because the EPF is a quasi-public system, it is burdened with many regulations. For example, the regulations bias asset allocation toward "safe" investments (fixed-income instruments such as government bonds) regardless of the maturity of each corporation's work force. And even tax-qualified plans must pay 1 percent of the accumulated fund as a special corporate tax every year (a heavy penalty for low-performing pension funds).

The government also pays about 95 percent of medical costs for those 65 and older. Currently, there is a debate over how to care for the elderly who are bedridden and require constant attention. The number of such people is expected to increase very rapidly (from 2 million in 1993 to 5.2 million in 2025, according to an MHW projection). It is becoming almost impossible for family members, who are traditionally supposed to support these elderly, to keep doing so. As a result, many are hospitalized even if they do not need medical treatment, which puts a financial burden on the insurance scheme. In response to these concerns, the introduction of separate, long-term care insurance is being planned.

DEPENDENCY RATIOS.   Table 5-6 compares the program dependency rates (PDRs) of the public pension programs with the aged dependency rates of the general population.[4] The PDR for the NP showed rapid aging until 1986. To accommodate self-employed workers, the government gave them special treatment, such as a shorter period for eligibility. And, because of the decreasing number of workers in agricultural sectors, the denominator for the program began to decrease in 1979.[5]

---

4. For the purpose of this comparison, the denominator of the ADR is the working population age 20 and older.

5. In 1986 the PDR for the NP had a new meaning. With the introduction of the basic pension system, both beneficiaries and covered workers include benficiaries who continue to work. The decline in the PDR for the NP from 1985 to 1990 reflects this reform.

TABLE 5-6. *Public Pension Program Dependency Ratios (PDR) and Aged Dependency Ratios (ADR), Selected Years, 1970–95, and Projected to 2025[a]*

		PDR			
Year	ADR	NP	NP (excluding exempts)	EPI	MAA
1970	11.7	1.0	1.0	2.4	n.a.
1980	15.1	19.3	21.1	8.1	27.2
1990	19.6	20.1	20.8	15.1	36.0
1995	23.2	23.2	24.6[b]	16.8	40.5
2000	27.5	29.1	32.5	24.6	n.a.
2025	47.8	53.1	59.2	42.0	n.a.

Source: Ministry of Health and Welfare, *Annual Report* (1996).

a. ADR is the ratio of people 65 or older to those 20–64. PDR is the ratio of beneficiaries to covered workers.

b. Figure would be 25.4 if it excluded those people who are not paying premiums.

n.a. Not available.

Despite the recent reforms, the PDR for the NP will continue to exceed the ADR. Under the medium fertility estimate, the ratio of covered workers to the population aged 20–64 will increase to 90.5 percent in 1995, to 91.1 percent in 2000, and to 92.4 percent in 2025, reflecting the higher labor force participation of women and old people. Meanwhile, estimated beneficiaries will increase from 91 percent of the population aged 65 and older in 1995 to 96 percent in 2000 and 103 percent in 2025.[6]

The PDR for the NP is high for several other reasons. First, the proportion of people who are exempt from paying premiums rose from 10.6 percent in 1961 to 15.7 percent in 1993. Second, some people simply refuse to contribute. Third, the medium population projection that is used to compute the ADR has an optimistic fertility rate assumption.

Unlike the NP, the PDR for the EPI is not expected to exceed the ADR in the future. This is because of the increase in the age of eligibility for pension payments from EPI. The age for receiving a public pension will be increased from 60 to 65 over thirteen years beginning in 2001.

6. The last number results from some differences in the methods used to project the numerators of the PDR and the ADR, as well as rising participation.

TABLE 5-7. *Replacement Rate of Pension Benefit, 1960–95*
Yen unless otherwise specified

Year	NP	NP + EPI	Average monthly wage	Replacement rate (percent) NP/ average wage	Replacement rate (percent) (NP + EPI)/ average wage
1960	. . .	3,598	21,747	. . .	16.5
1965	. . .	7,718	36,752	. . .	21.0
1970	. . .	14,388	70,240	. . .	20.5
1975	18,737	60,156	163,229	11.5	36.9
1980	23,300	106,219	238,175	9.8	44.6
1985	28,372	127,618	285,371	9.9	44.7
1990	32,555	145,827	329,443	9.9	44.3
1995	43,000	168,000	362,510	11.9	46.3

Sources: Ministry of Health and Welfare, *Pension and Public Finance*, 1995; and Ministry of Labor, monthly wage statistics.

BENEFIT RULES.   To be eligible for the full amount of the basic pension (NP), recipients must be at least 65 and have paid into the program for at least twenty-five years. In addition, there are a number of special provisions. For the EPI, recipients must meet the eligibility requirements for the NP and have paid into the program for at least one month.

The combined public pension (NP plus EPI) is paid to retirees based on the following basic formula:

Fixed portion:
¥65,000 × adjustment factor. The adjustment factor is 1 for recipients who have contributed for a full forty years, and for others it is a function of their contributions.

Wage-related portion (for employees):
Career average monthly real earnings × (7.5/1,000) × number of months covered under EPI.

Subsequent benefit payments are fully indexed to the CPI. As mentioned, actuarially reduced benefits from the NP can be received as early as age 60. Since 1973 the policy target has been to provide a benefit of about 60 percent of the monthly average wage of men for a fully qualified worker. The actual average payment level is about 45 percent (table 5-7) because of the immaturity of the system.

TABLE 5-8. *Total Medical Costs and Cost for Caring for Elderly, Selected Years, 1970–95, and Projected to 2025*

	National medical costs (Trillions of yen)	Medical costs for the elderly	
		Trillions of yen	Percent of total
1970	2.5	n.a.	n.a.
1975	6.5	0.9	13.8
1980	12.0	2.1	17.5
1985	16.0	4.1	25.6
1990	20.6	5.9	28.6
1995	26.7	8.5	31.8
2000	38.0	13.0	34.2
2010	68.0	28.0	41.2
2025	141.0	71.0	50.4

Source: Ministry of Health and Welfare, *Annual Report* (1996).
n.a. Not available.

The government refers to this pension scheme as a "semi-funded system." But it is actually a pay-as-you-go system. One-third of the basic pension payment comes from the general budget. Recently, the government has begun to interpret the public pension as a way for younger generations to support the elderly.

The Medical Programs

Public medical insurance programs cover essentially all people in Japan. Like the pension programs, they are somewhat fragmented. The medical insurance program for the elderly has a special status and is operated independently of other programs, but financially it is supported by the other programs and government funds.

When people reach age 70, they are exempt from paying for medical care except for an initial minor fixed fee. Free medical service for the elderly was started around 1970 by local governments. Political pressure forced the national government to introduce a similar program at the national level in 1972.[7]

Between ages 60 (the mandatory retirement age set by many big corporations) and 70, people are transferred from their employer's programs to the national medical insurance program, which is pri-

7. Campbell (1990).

TABLE 5-9. *Growth of National Medical Costs, by Contributing Factor,*
Selected Periods, 1993–2025
Average annual growth rate

Factor	1993–2000	2000–10	2010–25
Total	6.5	6.0	5.0
Population growth	0.3	0.2	−0.2
Aging	1.6	1.2	0.7
Others	4.5	4.5	4.5

Source: Ministry of Health and Welfare, *Annual Report* (1996).

marily for the self-employed. But even after the transfer, their costs
are financed by the employer's program.

National medical costs have increased rapidly (table 5-8), with a
consequent deterioration in the financial condition of the medical insurance programs. The national employer programs will go into deficit
in 1998. The reform of the system has become inevitable.

The growth rate of medical costs for the elderly is especially high,
and by 2025 the elderly will account for more than 50 percent of total
national medical costs. However, the biggest factor contributing to the
increase in medical costs is not aging, but general medical care cost
increases (table 5-9). Medical care payments are adjusted every two
years based on the change in personnel costs in the medical industry.
The future role of aging may be understated because of the optimistic
assumptions that underlie the medium population projections.

Other Programs

There are many other welfare programs, such as day care, that
provide services for the elderly. The public costs are still relatively
small—¥367 billion in 1985, ¥575 in 1990, and ¥817 in 1993, according to the Social Development Research Institute—because most services are provided informally, especially by family members. But as
living arrangements and family structure change, this informal support will become unsustainable. There is an active debate in Japan over
whether to introduce a public long-term care insurance program. Thus
public expenditure on these other programs can be expected to increase very rapidly in the near future. In addition, about ¥400 billion

TABLE 5-10. *Social Security Benefits as a Share of National Income (NI), 1995, and Projected to 2025*[a]

			2025					
	1995		Assumption A		Assumption B		Assumption C	
Benefit	Trillions of yen	Percent of NI	Trillions of yen	Percent of NI	Trillions of yen	Percent of NI	Trillions of yen	Percent of NI
Pension	34	9.0	139	15.0	104	15.5	93	15.5
Medical	24	6.5	96	16.5	96	14.0	96	16.0
Welfare	7	2.0	43	4.5	33	5.0	29	36.5
Total	65	17.5	278	29.0	233	34.5	218	36.5

Source: Ministry of Health and Welfare, *Annual Report* (1997).
a. Growth rate assumptions for national income.
A: 3.5 percent annually until 2000, 3.0 percent thereafter;
B: 1.75 percent annually until 2000, 2.0 percent thereafter;
C: 1.75 percent annually until 2000, 1.5 percent thereafter.
All scenarios assume the introduction of a long-term care insurance program that increases welfare spending but saves medical care costs.

of public funds are being spent annually on nonwelfare programs for the elderly. These are mainly for education and housing.

The Financial Outlook

Using various assumptions about the long-term growth of the economy, table 5-10 projects expenditures for social security (pension, medical care, and other care) in 2025. The total costs will rise rapidly, reaching about 30 percent of national income under the most optimistic economic assumptions and as much as 36 percent under the most pessimistic. The cost increases are heavily affected by the increase in the aged dependency ratio, but they also reflect the very generous benefits paid to old people compared with their contributions. We also believe that the assumed economic growth rate, the population projection, and the other assumptions result in an optimistic bias. Even so, under least-cost scenario A, the sum of social insurance costs and government outlays for other programs will reach 49 percent of national income.

Policy Evaluation

So-called universal social coverage was achieved in 1961 with the introduction of medical insurance and a pension program for the self-employed.[8] But because of the time needed to qualify for full benefits, these programs did not provide quick solutions for the poverty experienced by some old people. The 1968 annual *Economic Survey of Japan* called for an increase in public benefits for the elderly because the "traditional support system, that is old people working and living under the umbrella of a big family, has changed as a result of shifts in industry and family structure."

The year 1973 is called "the starting year of the welfare state" because benefits were dramatically increased then. Medical treatment became free for people 70 or older to cope with "the worsening financial situation of the elderly."[9] For those having made full contributions, pension benefits were raised to the level of 60 percent of average income earned by the male working population and were fully indexed to the CPI. After a long period of high economic growth, the redistribution of the fruits of growth to the weak—the elderly, farmers, or people suffering from pollution—became a political issue.

However, the first oil crisis also began in 1973. The 1973 *Economic Survey* had already predicted that "rapid aging in Japan will lead to a level of tax and social insurance premiums similar to those in European countries." But with the massive issuance of government bonds to bolster a domestic economy in recession, the fiscal situation worsened. Many proposals called for reevaluation of the programs. For example, *The Current Situation of the Aging Problem*, a report compiled by the Management and Coordination Agency, described the rapid change in demographic patterns to be expected in the future and warned that "current pension benefits have reached a level comparable with developed countries. Given the fact that our program has an earlier starting age (that is 60 years old), future costs will become much higher." It also warned that "the medical insurance program for the elderly has created excessive demand for medical services and put a

8. The following discussion of the history of policies for the aged is drawn mainly from the annual *Economic Survey of Japan* (Keizai-Hakusho).

9. *Economic Survey of Japan* (1973).

strain on the whole medical insurance program." Cutting back benefits began in 1982 with the introduction of fixed initial medical care fees for the elderly (deferment of the starting age for pension benefits was discussed in 1980, but was not decided).

The 1985 *Economic Survey* devoted many pages to analysis of the aging problem. It projected future government outlays for pensions and medical care. It also suggested that the savings rate would decline and that high taxes and social insurance premiums would reduce the labor supply. It concluded, "The social security system in Japan is like a big ship sailing out gradually to a stormy sea called the aging society. Little time is left for turning the ship to avoid the storm." After the 1985 analysis, a number of policy changes were implemented. Those changes, except long-term care insurance, are reflected in the cost projections provided earlier in this chapter.

Pension Programs

In 1986 the National Pension was transformed from a pension for the self-employed to a basic pension (with a fixed benefit) for all people. Wage earners' spouses (mainly women) were granted their own vested interests. On the benefit side the concept of a full pension was introduced. A person contributing for forty years is entitled to a full pension; those contributing for less than forty years receive reduced benefits.

In 1994 additional cost containment measures were introduced. First, the starting age for drawing reduced benefits was scheduled to be gradually raised to age 65 beginning in 2001.[10] Second, the adjustment of the earnings-related portion of the benefit was based on disposable income (a change from before-tax income). The difference is the social insurance premium paid directly by workers. This maintains a fairer balance between contributions and benefits because the more covered workers have to pay for pension programs, the less the beneficiaries will get. Third, a special levy on bonuses was put into effect. Fourth, a new adjustment prevented people from drawing pension

10. Although workers between the age of 60 and 65 currently receive a reduced benefit under the NP, employees receive a separate special supplement that providies the full amount from age 60. The effective retirement age for the NP is being raised to 65. The transition will occur from 2001 to 2013 for men and from 2006 to 2018 for women.

benefits and unemployment benefits at the same time. Fifth, the benefit level was adjusted so that people are encouraged to keep working even when they become eligible for pension benefits. The former benefit formula encouraged early retirement. Sixth, as a means of promoting more childbearing, an exemption from the social insurance premium was introduced for workers on parenting leave.

Medical Care and Other Welfare Programs

A 1986 reform increased the fixed fee the elderly are required to pay for medical services. In the same year, health care institutions began to be built to accommodate elderly people who need assistance in daily life. The recent policy focus on this area has not been on cost containment but on the introduction of long-term care services.

In 1989 a policy referred to as the Gold Plan was devised to increase the supply of long-term care services. Its policy target was revised in 1993 (the New Gold Plan) and implementation has been accelerated. In 1991 services provided by visiting nurses were covered by the medical insurance programs.

Problems with Current Policies for the Elderly

In spite of the recent reforms, Japan's policies for the elderly still have many problems. Although the focus of attention has shifted from the inadequacy of welfare programs to cost-containment measures, recent efforts to contain costs have been overwhelmed by the generous commitments made years ago. The shift in focus is closely linked with the decline in the economic growth rate (both actual and projected); and there is a growing awareness that the current system is not financially sustainable.

To begin with, the demographic aging process is accelerating. Government estimates tend to have an optimistic bias, but even its projections show an increasing pace (table 5-11). Both longer life expectancy and lower fertility rates contribute to the acceleration. Changes in women's life style have made it difficult for them to bear more children, and government policies have not accommodated those changes until recently. For example, day care facilities for working mothers are very limited in number as well as services.

TABLE 5-11. *Comparison of 1976, 1992, and 1997 Projections of the Aged Dependency Ratio*[a]
Percent

Projection year	1960	1970	1980	1990	2000	2010	2020	2030
1976	**8.9**	**10.2**	13.2	16.2	21.7	26.6	30.3	28.1
1992	**8.9**	**10.2**	**13.5**	**17.3**	25.1	34.1	43.2	43.5
1997	**8.9**	**10.2**	**13.5**	**17.3**	25.3	34.6	45.2	47.1

Source: Ministry of Health and Welfare, *Annual Report* (1996).
a. Actual numbers are in boldface.

Dependence on services provided to the elderly informally (especially by family) is not sustainable. Current welfare programs assume that traditional family functions remain the same, but this assumption is unrealistic. It is true that most old people are still living with their adult children and that many wives are taking care of their parents-in-law as well as their own children. But these responsibilities put physical and psychological pressure on the providers. Japanese families are facing unprecedented experiences because life expectancy has increased (by ten years since 1960) and because medical technology has prolonged lives. Now it is not unusual for old people (even pensioners) to take care of their own parents. Within the so-called family life-cycle model, the period from parents' retirement until both have died, during which grown-up children cared for them, averaged 5.3 years in the 1920s. In 1991 the period had lengthened to 20.3 years.

At the same time, there is a need to improve the quality of life of the elderly. The suicide rate among them is the highest among the developed countries. When they need long-term care, they tend to be confined to bed and are not allowed any social activities. A lot of domestic violence cases against the elderly are reported. Institutions for the elderly do not provide a high enough level of amenities to be attractive. When a family cannot support its elderly members, they tend to be hospitalized for long periods of time. The supply of nursing homes is not adequate, and families prefer hospitals because hospitalization does not give the impression of abandonment. This kind of arrangement is not only costly but also demeaning and detrimental to the health of the elderly.

The opportunity costs of relying on informal family services are very large but not well recognized. To take care of elderly parents, children must give up work. If care is provided by a middle-aged woman, the opportunity cost is about ¥3.4 million a year ($25,000–$30,000). In 1993 a million old people were estimated to require some assistance in daily life. Assuming that half are in institutions and the other half are taken care of by middle-aged women, the total opportunity cost reaches ¥1.7 trillion. Moreover, as the total working population begins to shrink, the labor force participation of middle-aged women becomes more important to continued economic growth.

With the change in lifestyle and demographic patterns in Japan, we expect that informal services that have been provided by family members will have to be at least partly replaced with public or commercial services. That will increase the financial burden on social security programs.

Finally, some programs are inefficient. The pension and medical programs are collections of many plans. Coverage, contribution rates, and other features are different and very complicated with many phase-ins and exemptions. Some programs get subsidies, others do not. Administrative costs are 2.3 percent of annual benefit payments in the NP and 0.3 percent in the EPI. For the EPI the social insurance premium is withheld from salaries, but the NP spends a lot of money collecting its premiums. There is also an evident lack of coordination among the programs. The 1994 pension reform abolished dual benefits from old-age pension and unemployment insurance (effective from 1998), but there are still instances in which a single recipient is eligible for double or triple benefits.

The government argues that a social insurance mechanism is preferable to a social security tax system because the insurance funding method can maintain a better relationship between contributions and benefits and can control free riders. But this distinction is simply false: under any pay-as-you-go system, whether financed by taxes or social insurance premiums, current benefits can be tied to past contributions, but nothing more is implied. Under the medical insurance program, which is financed with earnings-related social insurance premiums, the level of contribution has nothing to do with the level of benefits or the degree of risk.

One of the merits of a mandated social insurance system is that it supposedly prevents adverse selection. But in reality, adverse selection is taking place in Japan and it costs a lot of money. The penalty for noncontributors is denial of benefits, which they do not expect to receive in any case.

Solutions to the Financial Problems

Four major approaches have been suggested for dealing with the financial problems of the social insurance system: cut benefits, increase contributions, introduce advance funding, or convert to a privatized system.

A quarter century after the 1973 reform in welfare benefits, the average benefit levels have become very high relative to the earnings of the working population. For example, in April 1995 new male pensioners received on average ¥206,900 a month, while the average monthly salary of a new college graduate was only ¥198,000. Some efforts to curtail benefit levels are in place. For example, the retirement age for the NP will be raised to 65. Still, further cutbacks are inevitable. One measure, which is being considered in Germany and Sweden, is to link the level of benefit payments to average life expectancy. Each year, the benefit would be adjusted to the average life expectancy of the retiring cohort. This feature gives people incentives to work longer because the later they retire, the larger the monthly benefits.

However, reducing benefits has its limits. Given the wide gap between income and wealth of the elderly, a benefit cutback may increase the need for means-tested assistance programs. That would be not only inefficient, but also detrimental to the integrity of the public pension system. Along with the reduction of public pension benefits, a system should be established to promote financial self-help among old people. One way is to enable them to use their real estate holdings to generate income (that is, reverse mortgages).

The second option is to increase the contribution rate. It is impossible to determine the precise level at which contributors will lose their incentive to keep paying into the system, but there seems to be a consensus that asking for a further increase in contributions is difficult. Still, there are some untapped sources for contributions. One would involve including bonuses in the measure of earnings used to determine contributions. Japanese workers earn annual bonuses equivalent to 2.56 months of salary on average. The 1994 reform introduced a special assessment of 1 percent of bonus income. This contribution rate should be raised to that for regular wages so that employers cannot vary the proportion paid as a bonus so as to reduce their social insurance premiums. Another way to increase contributions would be to tax the income of the elderly. Many elderly can live well without drawing benefits from the public pension program. Rather than introducing a means test, the government could require th elderly to contribute through indirect taxes (sales taxes) on nonessential items.

The third way to bolster the financial position of the social insurance system would be to turn it into a funded system in which workers would contribute to their own retirement costs through higher current contributions. By expanding current saving, capital formation, and the future income available to both workers and retirees, partial funding can soften the zero-sum situation implicit in arguments over benefit cuts and tax increases. As of March 31, 1997, the Japanese public pension fund had ¥126 trillion in assets. This entire sum was loaned to the Treasury Investment and Loans Program (TILP), which is a financial function of government-sponsored financial institutions. Like the investment in government bonds, these loans are safe but the return is relatively low.

The need for reform of the TILP has produced many proposals urging transfer to a funded system (including privatization). However, the government argues against a funded social insurance system because of the high cost of transition. According to an estimate prepared by the Ministry of Health and Welfare, the present value of the unfunded pension liability just for the earnings-related portion is ¥350 trillion, about 70 percent of GDP, or 1.4 times the total value of government bonds outstanding. This liability will have to be financed either through future contributions or tax increases, and it should not be an excuse for not undertaking reform. The government argues that during the transition to a funded system the working population would have to pay for retirees as well as for themselves. But without reform the tax on the future working population is also expected to double.

In any event, a funded system has finally become attractive. But there is no agreement as to whether the investment decisions of a funded system should be made by the government or private agents. One version would involve a shift from a defined benefit to a defined contribution system. As demonstrated by reforms in Sweden in 1994, it is possible to construct a defined contribution plan under the pay-as-you-go funding method by simulating the investment return with a proxy (for example, the growth rate of wages in the case of Sweden). A reserve fund is necessary only to absorb short-term fluctuations.

A defined contribution system is really just a form of forced savings. Should the government support such a system, especially when the national saving rate is as high as it is in Japan? The answer is yes, with some qualification. The government may not have to operate the system (collect contributions, invest, and disburse benefits), but a basic infrastructure (safety net) such as tax incentives and a regulatory framework would be required to prevent situations in which more people rely on welfare programs due to the lack of savings.

Finally, some argue for instituting a private social security system. Although many of the advantages of privatization can be achieved in a public system with some changes in the tax structure, privatization is preferable to a government-run funded system because it isolates the investment function from political pressure.[11] Presumably, fund managers in the private sector are better at making investment decisions than are government bureaucrats, and they can invest in equities for higher returns without any political difficulty.

Citing the British experience, some criticize privatization proposals on the grounds that marketing costs associated with private fund management are a waste of resources. But this may not be true. Even under the government system, the participation of private fund management companies is required (the public fund is just too big to be effectively invested by a single entity, and the influence on the capital market is also big) and some marketing expenses are incurred.

Suggested Changes in the Public Pension System

Given our analysis, we believe the following reforms should be implemented as soon as possible. First, the NP should be converted to a tax-financed system. The eligibility standard and the level of fixed benefits should be linked not with the years of contribution but with,

11. For a discussion of a public system's possible achievement of the advantages of a private system see Mariger (1997).

say, years of residence in Japan. In principle, the direct involvement by the government in the provision of social security should be limited to redistribution. Therefore, the NP should be operated by the government as a pay-as-you-go system. The funding scheme should be tax based, preferably through indirect taxes such as a sales tax, so that old people contribute according to their consumption level. Tax funding can reduce the inefficiencies associated with the current "social insurance" method.

Second, the earnings-related portion of the public pension should be privatized and shifted to a funded system. Although transition costs are high, the way the United Kingdom privatized its system in 1986 could be copied. Employees will have their own accounts. A part of their new contributions (a social security tax rather than premium) will be accumulated in the accounts and the rest will cover the transition costs. They can choose to stay with the government plan, contract out to employers' pension funds, or contract out to independent plans offered by private asset management companies. These plans can be either defined contribution or defined benefit.

Third, the retirement age should be deferred in principle to reduce the financial burden, but at the same time it should be flexible so that each employee can choose when to retire. And the benefit level of both basic pensions and earnings-related pensions should be linked to the life expectancy of the cohort of retiring people. In that way people will have more incentive to keep working.

Fourth, conceptually there are two ways to make the transition to a funded system. The first is to issue government bonds equivalent to the unfunded liabilities and use the bonds to transfer both prior commitments and new contributions to the private sector. The second is to privatize only the new contributions, as was done in the United Kingdom. Even if the amount of government bonds outstanding is more than doubled, there may not be any impact on capital markets because only "hidden" liabilities are recognized. But once the amount is determined, there is no room for reducing the burden. The United Kingdom did lower liabilities by changing the base of the indexation from the wage growth rate to the inflation rate while keeping the past commitment portion of the earnings-related pension (SERPS). Because the transition cost for Japan is much bigger, similar measures will have to be taken along with privatization.

Fifth, the role of the government should be limited to providing tax incentives, regulatory enforcement, and some reinsurance (for example, maintaining an insurance fund against the failure of asset management companies).

Implications for Other Social Security Programs

The risk event for a pension system (retirement) is more or less predictable. Self-help can be stressed and the government's role can be limited to supervising redistribution. But in the case of medical and long-term care plans, it is difficult to separate the redistributive function from the whole insurance mechanism. And because the reason behind the worsening financial balance of these programs is mainly cost inflation rather than aging, specific measures should be implemented to improve their financial condition.

Still, some principles discussed for pension reform can be applied to other programs.

—A minimum safety net such as the NP provides in the pension system should be maintained as a universal system. In a number of areas the introduction of a means test is not efficient.

—"Normalization" should be encouraged to enlarge the contribution base. Normalization of the pension system implies that more of the elderly should be able to work without losing their entitlement and so contribute to the system. Similarly, normalization of other programs implies that the length of hospitalization should be decreased and home care should be promoted, not only to lower costs but also to make patients contribute more quickly.

—Some of the reform effort should be targeted to changing systems such as the civil service to improve the care of old or handicapped workers.

—The government should be responsible for this kind of program improvement, but much of the actual provision of care should be outsourced to the private sector.

Appendix: The New Population Projections

The Ministry of Health and Welfare announced a new set of population projections in January 1997. The contribution rate, or premium,

TABLE 5A-1. *Comparison of 1994 and 1997 Population Projections, Selected Years, 1995–2050*[a]

Year	Total fertility rate		Life expectancy at birth				Total population (thousands)	
			Male		Female			
	1994	1997	1994	1997	1994	1997	1994	1997
1995	1.42	. . .	76.36	. . .	82.84	. . .	125,570	. . .
2000	1.60	1.38	77.30	77.40	83.77	84.12	127,385	126,892
2005	1.72	1.43	77.65	77.80	84.25	84.64	129,346	127,684
2010	1.78	1.50	77.82	78.12	84.47	85.05	130,397	127,623
2015	1.80	1.56	78.01	78.39	84.72	85.37	130,033	126,444
2020	1.80	1.59	78.19	78.61	84.96	85.62	128,345	124,133
2025	1.80	1.61	78.27	78.80	85.06	85.83	125,806	120,913
2030	. . .	1.61	. . .	78.96	. . .	86.00	122,972	117,149
2035	. . .	1.61	. . .	79.10	. . .	86.15	120,132	113,114
2040	. . .	1.61	. . .	79.23	. . .	86.27	117,290	108,964
2045	. . .	1.61	. . .	79.33	. . .	86.37	114,432	104,758
2050	. . .	1.61	. . .	79.43	. . .	86.47	111,510	100,496

Source: Ministry of Health and Welfare, *Population Projections for Japan*, October 1994 and January 1997.
a. Medium scenario projected by Ministry of Health and Welfare.

for the public pension fund will be recalculated in 1999 based on these new estimates. As table 5A-1 shows, the new estimates have been revised downward from the previous figures: the new medium-case scenario is now closer to the low scenario in the 1992 estimates. Based on the new estimate, each retiree will be supported by 2.2 workers in 2020; in 1995 it was 4.8. The burden of supporting old people will have doubled in just twenty-five years.

According to a preliminary calculation by the Ministry of Health and Welfare, if there is no change in the benefit formula, the monthly contribution for the NP will be raised from ¥12,800 (the 1997 rate) to ¥24,300, and the premium rate for the EPI will be raised from 17.35 percent to 34.3 percent.

References

Campbell, J. C. 1992. *How Policies Change: The Japanese Government and the Aging Society.* Princeton University Press.

Conference on Welfare in the Aged-Society. 1994. *21 Seiki Fukushi Vision* (*Vision of Welfare to the 21st Century*). Tokyo.

Economic Planning Agency. Annual. *Economic Survey of Japan*. Tokyo.

Hiroi, Y. 1996. "Iryo-hoken to Shakai-hosho no Shouraizou (The Future of Medical Insurance and Other Social Securities Program)." *Shakai-hosho Junpo* 1918, 1919, 1921.

Mariger, Randall P. 1997. "Social Security Privatization: What It Can and Cannot Accomplish." Federal Reserve Board, Finance and Economic Discussion Series. Washington.

Maruo, N. 1996. *Shijo-shikou no Fukushi Kaikaku* (*Toward a Reform of Welfare Programs Based on the Market Mechanisms*). Nihon Keizai Shinbunsya: Tokyo.

Ministry of Health and Welfare. 1995. *Nenkin to Zaisei* (*Pension and Public Finance*). Tokyo.

———. Annual. *Survey of Households*. Tokyo.

Murakami, Kiyoshi. 1997. "Pension Problems and Proposals for Future Reform in Japan." *Benefits & Compensation International* 26 (April): 14–21.

OECD. 1995. "Ageing Populations, Pension Systems and Government Budgets: How Do They Affect Saving?" Economic Department Working Papers. Paris.

Ohno, Y. 1996. "Kokumin Seikatsu no Antei ni Okeru Shakai-hoshou to Sijyou (Social Securities and the Market)." Keizai Seminar: 19–26.

Okamoto, Y. 1996. *Koreisyairyou to Fukushi* (*Medical Care for the Aged and Welfare Programs*). Iwanami Syoten: Tokyo.

Takayama, N. 1992. *The Greying of Japan: An Economic Perspective on Public Pensions*. Oxford Univesity Press.

———. 1994. "On Intergenerational Equality." *Bunken Journal* 109 (December): 31–66.

Chapter 6

Population Aging and American Economic Performance

Barry Bosworth and Gary Burtless

D URING THE NEXT quarter century, population aging will produce major changes in the structure of the U.S. economy. These changes will have an enormous impact on public spending. The elderly have consumption needs different from those of younger households—in particular, they face higher health care costs—and their consumption is disproportionately financed with public funds. Fortunately for the United States, the most serious consequences of population aging will not be felt for a couple of decades. This contrasts with the situation in Japan and western Europe, where the consequences will soon be visible in public budgets.

In 1996 the Congressional Budget Office published projections of the long-term budget outlook of the federal government under the assumption that current programs and tax rates would be maintained (table 6-1). The increase in the number of aged Americans eligible for social security, mecicaid, and medicare, combined with a sharp deceleration in the growth of the labor force, will boost the share of GDP devoted to federal spending by one-fourth between 1996 and 2025. If no action is taken to scale back outlays or increase taxes, public debt as a percentage of GDP will explode.

In this discussion we examine the magnitude of the economic prob-

We gratefully acknowledge the excellent research assistance of Sheryl Zohn. This paper was prepared for a Tokyo Club conference in Paris, October 10–11, 1996. The views are those of the authors and should not be ascribed to the Brookings Institution or the Tokyo Club.

TABLE 6-1. *Federal Budget Outlays and Revenues, Selected Years, 1960–95, and Projected to 2050*
Percent GDP

	1960	1980	1995	2015	2025	2050
Program outlays	15.7	20.5	19.5	20.8	24.0	28.1
OASDI[a]	2.2	4.3	4.5	4.7	5.8	6.9
Medicare[b]	0.0	1.3	2.5	4.4	6.0	8.4
Medicaid[c]	0.0	0.5	1.3	2.4	2.9	3.8
Consumption	9.7	7.7	6.3	5.0	5.0	5.0
Other programs	3.8	6.6	4.9	4.3	4.3	4.0
Interest	1.3	1.9	3.2	3.4	5.3	15.8
Total outlays	17.0	22.4	22.6	24.2	29.3	43.9
Receipts	18.4	20.2	20.4	19.7	19.8	20.4
Budget balance	1.4	−2.2	−2.2	−4.5	−9.5	−23.5

Sources: *Survey of Current Business*, various issues; and Congressional Budget Office, unpublished data, May 1996.
a. Old age, survivors, and disability insurance.
b. Medical care for the aged and disabled.
c. Medical care for the poor.

lems created by population aging in the United States. The first section briefly considers the demographic changes that can be anticipated in the next several decades and evaluates the economic status of the elderly. The next section describes the basic structure of the income transfer and health programs that provide support to the elderly. The third section reviews projections of growth in the aggregate economy and the financial outlook of the major public programs for the aged. We conclude by describing and evaluating recent proposals to reform programs targeted on the elderly.

Demographic Trends and Needs of the Elderly

Compared with other industrial nations, the United States has a relatively youthful population. The aged dependency rate, the ratio of persons older than age 64 to those aged 15 to 64, has increased only modestly in recent decades from 0.15 in 1960 to 0.19 in 1995 (figure 6-1). Another measure of dependency, the ratio of the elderly plus children to the working-age population, has dropped dramatically from 0.50 to 0.35.

FIGURE 6-1. *Aged Dependency Ratio, 1960–97, and Projected to 2070*[a]

Ratio

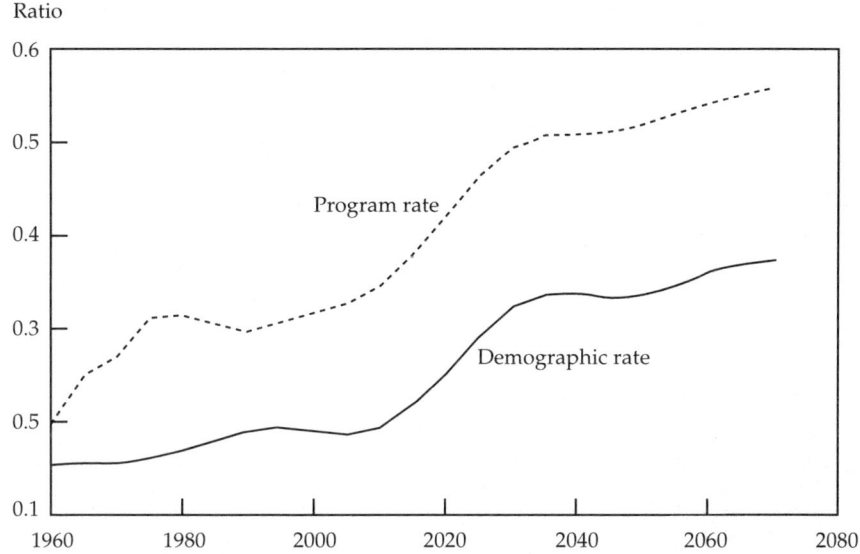

Source: Social Security Administration.
a. The program rate is the number of OASDI beneficiaries per covered worker. The demographic rate is the population older than 64 divided by the population aged 15–64.

Demographic Forecasts

The best known forecasts of the future U.S. aged dependency rate are published by the trustees of Old-Age, Survivors and Disability Insurance (OASDI). Popularly known as social security, OASDI is the main public program offering pensions to aged and disabled workers and surviving dependents of deceased workers. The annual report of the OASDI trustees contains detailed financial information on the current and future status of social security. The report evaluates the programs under three sets of assumptions, low cost, intermediate, and high cost, corresponding to optimistic, moderate, and pessimistic projections of the future solvency of social security. The forecast period extends for the next seventy-five years. The predictions of future revenue and costs are derived from a model that projects the number of people with given characteristics who are expected to contribute to the

TABLE 6-2. *Fertility Rates, Life Expectancy, and Population Age Distribution, Selected Years, 1960–90, and Projected to 2050*

Year	Total fertility rate[a]	Life expectancy at birth		Population distribution[b]			Elderly dependency ratio
		Male	Female	Youths	Working age	Elderly	
Actual							
1960	3.6	66.7	73.2	0.30	0.61	0.09	0.15
1970	2.4	67.1	74.9	0.27	0.63	0.10	0.15
1980	1.9	69.9	77.5	0.22	0.66	0.11	0.17
1990	2.1	71.8	78.8	0.22	0.66	0.12	0.19
Projected							
2000	2.0	73.0	79.7	0.21	0.66	0.12	0.19
2010	2.0	74.5	80.5	0.20	0.68	0.13	0.19
2020	1.9	75.3	81.2	0.19	0.65	0.16	0.25
2030	1.9	76.0	81.8	0.18	0.62	0.20	0.32
2040	1.9	76.6	82.4	0.18	0.62	0.21	0.33
2050	1.9	77.2	83.0	0.17	0.62	0.21	0.33

Source: Board of Trustees, *Annual Report* (1996).

a. Total fertility rate is the number of births that 1,000 women would have in their lifetime if, at each year of age, they experienced the birthrates occurring in the specified year.

b. "Youths" are aged 0–14; "Working age" is 16–64; "Elderly" are age 65 and older. Populations are estimations of the Social Security Area population.

social security program as well as the number who will be eligible for and will collect benefits.

Each projection is painstakingly derived based on extensive detailed assumptions about future economic and demographic trends. The most important can be summarized in terms of the long-run values of a handful of critical variables. The crucial demographic assumptions define future birthrates, mortality rates by gender at each age, age-specific disability rates, and net immigration into the United States (table 6-2). The critical economic assumptions describe the long-run trend in output per worker, annual price change, real interest rates, changes in labor force participation by age and gender, and the trend in untaxed fringe benefits as a percentage of labor compensation.

Figure 6-1 shows the trend in the aged dependency rate under the social security trustees' intermediate assumptions. Beginning in 2010, when the baby boom generation reaches retirement age, the rate will rise sharply to 0.32 by 2030 and then drift gradually higher in subsequent decades.[1] The effect of the population bulge associated with the baby boom is first to delay and then make worse an underlying gradual increase in the aged dependency rate. The cause of this trend is the steady increase in life expectancy combined with slow growth in the working-age population because of low fertility. The increase in longevity automatically produces an increase in the proportion of the average life spent in retirement if the retirement age does not change.

Although the future population of the aged can be predicted with some confidence, growth in the labor force is more uncertain because of potential changes in future birthrates and immigration policy. Perhaps surprisingly, the jump in the aged dependency rate over the next thirty years is due entirely to a slower rate of increase in the working-age population; there is no acceleration of growth in the population older than 64. The slower growth of the working-age population in turn reflects the 40 percent drop in the fertility rate over the past quarter century (table 6-2). U.S. fertility is projected to level out at a rate slightly below that required to maintain a stable population. Immigration is projected to continue at 650,000 legal immigrants and 250,000 illegal entrants a year.

Needs and Resources of the Elderly

The overwhelming majority of older Americans live alone or with their spouse (table 6-3) and rely on their own resources rather than transfers from relatives to support themselves. The percentage of elderly who live with other relatives is low and declining, although older women are more likely than older men to live with a younger relative. The proportion of aged Americans who live in institutions is extremely low until after age 75. Even among people older than 75 institutionalization is relatively uncommon.

Since 1960 there has been a dramatic improvement in the relative well-being of aged households. Their cash incomes have increased from 40 percent of the average for all households in 1969 to 57 percent by 1984, and the ratio has remained essentially constant in the past

---

1. The baby boom cohort refers to the population born during the post-World War II period of high birthrates, usually dated between 1946 and 1964.

TABLE 6-3. *Living Arrangements of the Elderly, by Sex and Age Group, 1980, 1990*
Percent unless otherwise specified

Living arrangement	Men		Women	
	1980	1990	1980	1990
	Age 65–74			
In institutions	1.8	1.5	1.9	1.6
Alone	11.8	12.8	33.4	32.7
With spouse	78.4	77.0	46.9	50.2
With other relatives	6.5	6.5	16.4	13.8
With nonrelatives	1.5	2.2	1.4	1.6
	Age 75 and older			
In institutions	7.2	6.8	12.5	12.9
Alone	18.5	19.4	41.8	47.1
With spouse	61.2	62.4	18.6	21.1
With other relatives	11.2	9.1	25.2	16.5
With nonrelatives	1.9	2.2	2.0	2.5
Number (millions)	10.3	12.8	15.2	18.5
Age 65–74	6.7	8.1	8.9	10.1
Age 75 and older	3.5	4.6	6.4	8.3

Source: Bureau of the Census.

decade (figure 6-2). The proportion of the aged living below the official poverty line has also fallen sharply from 35 percent to 12 percent between 1959 and 1994.[2] The reduction in the poverty rate was particularly large after 1970, dropping almost in half, and it occurred during a period when the overall poverty rate remained unchanged and the rate for children rose from 15 to 22 percent.

A focus on averages, however, does not reveal the diversity of economic circumstances among the elderly. Older Americans draw their income from labor earnings, public social security benefits, private pensions, and their own savings. Their labor force participation has decreased significantly in the past quarter century, reducing the importance of earned income. In addition, the proportion of men who

2. Committee on Ways and Means (1994, p. 1158); and http://www.census.gov/hhes/income/povsum.html. The U.S. poverty level is estimated using a multiple of three times the cost of an economy food plan with adjustments for family size. The poverty threshold for a family of four was $15,141 in 1994.

FIGURE 6-2. *Median Income of Aged Households, Relative to All Households, 1967–94*[a]

Ratio

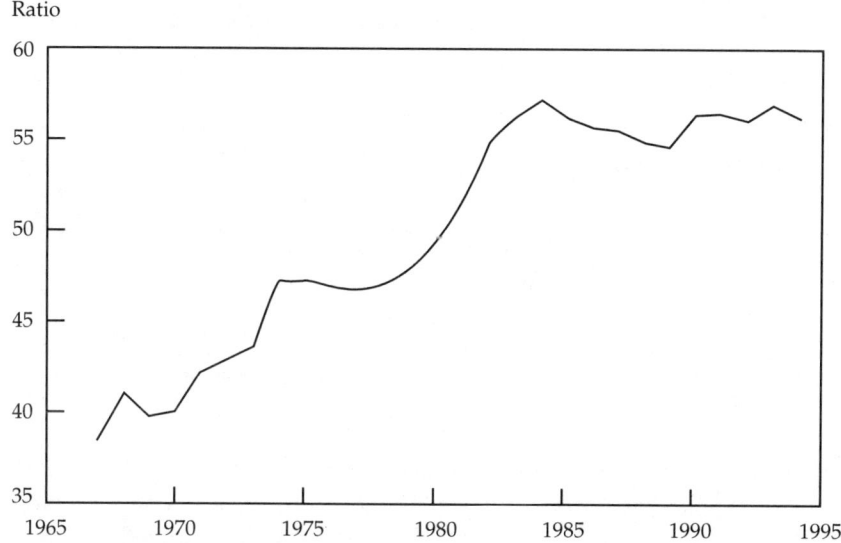

Source: Bureau of the Census.

a. Aged refers to householders older than age 64. The householder is the person in whose name the residence is owned or rented.

withdraw from the labor force before age 65, the age at which workers qualify for unreduced social security pensions, has expanded.

The elderly obtain somewhat more than 40 percent of their income from social security pensions, with the remainder roughly split evenly among labor earnings, private pensions, and income from their own savings (table 6-4). The proportion drawn from capital income is sensitive to interest rates, changing substantially from year to year. The relative importance of pensions has grown while that of earnings has fallen since the mid-1970s.

There are large differences in the composition of income at different points in the income distribution. In the lowest three quintiles of the distribution, social security exceeds 70 percent of total income (table 6-4). Private pensions and capital income are significant only for the top 40 percent of the income distribution, and earnings are important only for high-income family units. The small role of earned income at

TABLE 6-4. *Sources of Cash Income for Aged Family Units, 1974, 1984, 1993*[a]
Percent of total

Year	Earnings	OASDI	Asset income	Pensions and annuities	Other
1974	21.3	42.0	18.2	14.0	4.5
1984	13.3	40.5	28.2	15.0	2.9
1993	15.1	42.3	18.6	20.5	3.4
Quintile distribution, 1993					
1st	0.2	84.2	6.4	2.1	7.5
2nd	1.8	80.5	7.9	3.3	6.5
3rd	4.0	72.5	11.4	9.7	2.4
4th	8.7	49.9	15.0	23.0	3.3
5th	24.1	21.4	24.8	26.9	2.9

Source: Employee Benefit Research Institute (1995).
a. Aged family units include individuals age 65 or older plus married couples in which one spouse is older than 65.

the bottom of the distribution is particularly surprising. Under social security rules such retirees can earn significant wages without a reduction in their benefits. In part, the low labor income reflects the concentration at the bottom of the distribution of the very old and widows, two groups with low labor force participation rates. There is little evidence that younger retirees feel much pressure to augment their retirement income through part-time jobs.

Tabulations of cash income provide a very incomplete picture of the resources available to the elderly. A significant portion of the consumption they enjoy is not recorded as part of money income. Many live in homes or apartments they own. The flow of housing services that older people derive from owner-occupied housing is substantial, and it is typically ignored when statisticians compare the well-being of people who are older and younger than 65. In addition, the United States operates a program of national health insurance for the elderly, while working-age families must rely on private health insurance. Table 6-5 shows the monetary value of noncash income received by the elderly and nonelderly. Noncash income adds about 34 percent to the cash incomes of the elderly; it adds just 14 percent to the cash incomes of households without an aged member. The addition to cash incomes is even larger for low-income households. Among low-income elderly households, average noncash income is about 130 percent of

TABLE 6-5. *Noncash Income, by Type, as Percentage of Cash Income before Tax, 1992*

Income type	All income levels			Bottom quintile		
	All ages	Younger than 65	65 and older	All ages	Younger than 65	65 and older
Medicare	3	1	18	15	5	62
Medicaid	1	1	2	23	25	18
Employer contriutions to health insurance	4	5	1	3	4	0
Food subsidies	0	0	0	10	11	3
Housing subsidies	0	0	0	5	5	6
Return on home equity	8	7	13	30	27	42
Total	16	14	34	86	77	131
Capital gains	2	n.a.	2	0	n.a.	n.a.
Payroll taxes	−6	n.a.	−2	−3	n.a.	n.a.
Income taxes	−14	n.a.	−9	1	n.a.	n.a.

Sources: Radner (1994, table A-1); and Bureau of Census (1993). Includes all households with a member older than age 64. Zero denotes less than 0.5.
    n.a. Not available.

cash household income.[3] Thus, the relative income position of the elderly appears even stronger under an income definition that reflects taxes and in-kind transfers. When the broadest income measure is adjusted to reflect differences in family size, the median incomes of aged and non-aged families are essentially equal.[4]

Public Programs for the Elderly

The aging of the U.S. population will place heavy pressure on public budgets because a large percentage of retirees' consumption is paid for through public programs. In addition to the public OASDI, costly

3. Simple procedures to assess the value of in-kind benefits often overstate the income of low-income units relative to the poverty standard. For example, the valuation of health insurance benefits on a cost basis exceeds the value of insurance to recipients because the benefits are not fungible. That is, if the payments were offered in cash, recipients would almost certainly reallocate a significant portion to other kinds of consumption. The U.S. Census Bureau attempts to adjust for this problem by limiting the value of the medical in-kind benefits. The statistics in table 6-5 reflect this conservative assessment of the value of medical insurance benefits.
    4. Quinn and Smeeding (1993, p. 7).

tax incentives have subsidized the creation of private employer-based pension plans and tax-preferred individual retirement accounts (IRAs). Retirees also benefit under medicare, the publicly financed national health care system for the aged and disabled. The low-income elderly may also obtain health insurance under medicaid, a federal-state program that pays for doctor, hospital, and nursing home care for the indigent. Nursing home care for the elderly accounts for about one-third of medicaid outlays. Social security, medicare, and medicaid are the main public programs that will be affected by population aging in the United States.

Old-Age, Survivors, and Disability Insurance

Social security is a mandatory retirement and disability program that covers more than 95 percent of the U.S. labor force.[5] The percentage of the working-age population covered by the program has increased in line with the increase in female labor force participation (table 6-6). Social security actually consists of two separate programs, old-age and survivors insurance (OASI) and disability insurance (DI), but they are usually considered together. The programs are mainly financed by a flat-rate payroll tax, currently 12.4 percent of labor earnings up to a ceiling of $62,700, equally split between employers and employees. The earnings ceiling is indexed to the growth in economywide average wages.[6] In addition, the programs obtain a small amount of revenue from federal income taxation of part of OASDI benefit payments. Program revenues in excess of current benefit payments are deposited in the OASI and DI Trust Funds, where they are invested in nonmarketable U.S. government securities. Newly purchased securities earn a rate of interest equal to the average rate on marketable government debt with a maturity in excess of four years. A history of the basic provisions is provided in table 6-7.

For workers born in 1929 and later years, forty quarters (or about ten years) of covered employment is needed to qualify for retirement

5. The program covers private sector workers, federal government employees hired after 1983, and about 80 percent of state and local government employees. See Detlefs, Myers, and Treanor (1996, p. 5).

6. The wage indexation is based on the average wage with a two-year lag. The wage ceiling was about 2.6 times the average wage of $23,754 in 1994.

TABLE 6-6. *OASDI Coverage and Labor Force Participation, by Sex, Selected Years, 1960–90*
Percent

Age group	1960	1970	1980	1990
Covered workers as a percent of				
working age population[a]	64.0	68.3	71.9	78.1
Men	86.0	85.5	83.2	85.2
Women	42.7	51.6	60.9	71.1
Labor Force Participation Rates				
Men				
16 and older	83.3	79.7	77.4	76.1
16–64	90.4	87.3	85.8	85.4
55–59[b]	91.6	89.5	81.9	79.8
60–64[b]	81.1	75.0	61.0	55.5
65 and older	33.1	26.8	19.0	16.3
Women				
16 and older	37.7	43.3	51.5	57.5
16–64	42.0	49.3	59.9	67.8
55–59[b]	42.2	50.4	48.6	55.3
60–64[b]	31.4	36.1	33.3	35.5
65 and older	10.8	9.7	8.1	8.6

Sources: Board of Trustees, *Annual Report* (1996); and *Economic Report of the President* (1996).
a. Covered workers includes all individuals with any covered earnings during the year.
b. For age groups 55–59 and 60–64, LFPR data are from 1993.

benefits.[7] Computation of the benefits is performed in a four-step procedure. All benefits in the U.S. system are linked to the primary insurance amount (PIA), which is the pension for a single retired worker who begins to receive old-age benefits at the normal retirement age (currently 65, but scheduled to rise to age 67 gradually between 2002 and 2025). All other OASDI benefits are set equal to some percentage of the PIA.

The first step is the calculation of the worker's average indexed monthly earnings (AIME) in employment covered by social security. For workers who reached age 65 after 1993, the computation is based on the worker's earnings in the thirty-five years of highest earnings

7. Workers are credited with up to four quarters of credit for each year of covered employment. In 1996 one credit was recorded for every $640 earned during the year. Workers earning $2,560 or more received four quarters of credit.

TABLE 6-7. *OASDI Taxes and Benefits, Selected Years, 1960–95*

| | Taxable payroll as percent of | | | Tax rate[a] | | | OASDI benefits (percent wages) | | |
| | | | | | | | | | |
Year	Compensation	Wage and salaries	OASDI	Hospital insurance	Total	Low earner	Average earner	Maximum earner
1960	67.5	73.4	6.0	0	6.0	49.1	33.3	29.8
1970	65.4	73.3	8.4	1.2	9.6	48.5	34.6	29.2
1980	69.8	83.8	10.2	2.1	12.3	62.9	47.1	30.0
1990	71.2	86.6	12.4	2.9	15.3	58.1	43.0	24.4
1995	69.4	85.4	12.4	2.9	15.3	58.2	43.2	23.8

Sources: Board of Trustees, *Annual Report* (1996); National Income and Product Accounts; and Annual Statistical Supplement, 1994.
a. One-half paid by employers, one-half paid by employees.

up to age 62 or the age at which benefits are claimed. To determine the AIME, the Social Security Administration multiplies wages in each year of the earnings record by an index factor that reflects the growth of the economywide average wage since that year. For example, if the average wage when a worker was 30 years old is one-half of that when the worker reaches age 60, the worker's taxable wages earned at age 30 would be doubled for the calculation of the AIME. Wages earned at or after age 60 are not indexed.

The second step in benefit computation is the calculation of the PIA. The PIA is simply a percentage of the worker's average indexed earnings. In 1996 the PIA was

90 percent of the first $437 in AIME plus
32 percent of the AIME greater than $437 but less than $2,635 plus
15 percent of the AIME greater than $2,635.[8]

The dollar amounts in this formula—the so-called bend points—are adjusted each year to reflect the growth in economywide average wages. The formula is clearly redistributive because workers with low average wages receive pensions that are a higher percentage of past wages than workers with monthly incomes above $437.

The indexation of wages earned before age 60 and the annual adjustment of the bend points in the PIA formula ensure that average initial benefits rise at the same rate as average wages. Initial benefits increase in *real* terms if wages grow faster than prices and fall if prices grow faster than wages. The PIA is computed using the formula in effect when the worker was age 62, regardless of when he or she actually retires, and it is adjusted thereafter for increases in prices, not wages. This procedure ensures that the purchasing power of pensions remains constant after the benefit is claimed.

A third step in calculating retirement benefits is needed for workers claiming benefits before or after the normal retirement age. The earliest age at which workers can claim benefits is 62. Workers claiming benefits before the normal retirement age receive a permanently reduced monthly pension. For example, a worker who claims benefits at age 62 receives 80 percent of his PIA. Workers claiming benefits after

8. Board of Trustees (1996, p. 67). The comparable average monthly wage was $1,928.

the normal retirement age receive a delayed retirement credit. A worker reaching age 65 in 1996, for example, would receive a pension equal to 105 percent of his PIA if he delays claiming his pension until age 66.

The last step in the benefit calculation is the reduction in pension for workers who claim benefits while still earning substantial labor income. For people younger than 70, the social security pension is subject to an earnings test.[9] Starting at age 70 workers can receive a full pension regardless of the amount they earn.

In 1996 the average social security retirement benefit was $10,658, or 43 percent of the economywide average wage. A worker retiring at age 65 and earning half the average wage over his work-life received $6,459; a worker earning the maximum taxable wage received $15,013.[10] The Social Security Administration estimates that a worker claiming benefits at the normal retirement age who earned the economywide average wage throughout his career would receive a pension equal to 43 percent of his earnings just before retirement. A worker whose pay was one-half the average wage would receive a pension equal to 58 percent of his final pay; a worker who consistently earned the taxable maximum wage would receive 25 percent of his final pay.

Unlike most other countries, the United States provides a spouse benefit, equal to 50 percent of the retired worker's PIA. (Spouses who qualify for a retirement benefit based on their own earnings record would of course claim the retirement benefit if it is larger than the spouse benefit.) The U.S. system also provides a survivor benefit equal to 100 percent of the PIA for aged surviving spouses of deceased workers. Additional provisions are made for other kinds of dependents, such as minor children and surviving spouses under the age of 60 who care for minor children, but the total family benefit is limited

9. For retirees aged 62–64 in 1996 the earnings test applied to annual earnings in excess of $8,280; for retirees aged 65–69 the earnings test applied to earnings in excess of $11,520. Pensioners who were affected by the earnings test lost $0.50 in benefits for every $1.00 of wages in excess of the earnings limit if they were between 62 and 64; they lost $0.33 in benefits for every $1.00 of excess wages if they were older than 64.

10. Board of Trustees (1996, p. 184). The full distributional effects of OASDI are difficult to evaluate because low-wage workers tend to die at an earlier age, reducing their lifetime return. However, these workers are more likely to qualify for disability benefits, and their spouses and children are more likely to collect deceased-worker survivor benefits.

to a fixed multiple of the insured worker's PIA. (The family maximum benefit is usually between 1.5 and 1.88 times the PIA.)

Medical Care

Public medical insurance for the aged is provided primarily through two programs, medicare and medicaid. Medicare is divided into two parts. Part A, or hospital insurance (HI), is financed through a payroll tax on nearly all U.S. workers.[11] The combined employee-employer contribution rate for HI is currently 2.9 percent. Unlike the payroll tax for OASDI, the HI tax has no ceiling on taxable wages. Part B, supplemental medical insurance (SMI), obtains about 25 percent of its financing from premiums paid by beneficiaries and the remainder from general budget funds. SMI covers physician fees, outpatient hospital services, and some prescription drugs for the elderly and the permanently disabled. Most retirees also have a supplemental private plan to pay for services not covered by medicare and to finance part or all of the medical service charges that are not reimbursed by the program. People become eligible for medicare when they reach age 65, regardless of whether they have retired. In addition, nonelderly workers who qualify for disability insurance become eligible for medicare coverage two and one-half years after the onset of their disability.

Medicaid is a joint federal-state program that provides comprehensive health insurance to the indigent. Many old people in need of nursing home care can qualify as indigent and have their nursing home bills paid by the program. Medicaid also pays the medicare (part B) premiums for the indigent elderly.

Population aging will have a dramatic effect on overall health care spending. Medical costs rise sharply with age, and because the costs of the aged are disproportionately financed through public programs, public spending on health programs will grow dramatically after the baby boom generation reaches age 65. Average medical care consumption of people aged 65–74 is more than four times that of people 19–44 (figure 6-3). Half the medical consumption of the older age group is paid with public funds compared with less than a fifth that

---

11. Some state and local government employees hired before 1986 are not covered by the HI program.

FIGURE 6-3. *Medical Care Costs, by Age, 1995*

Dollars per capita

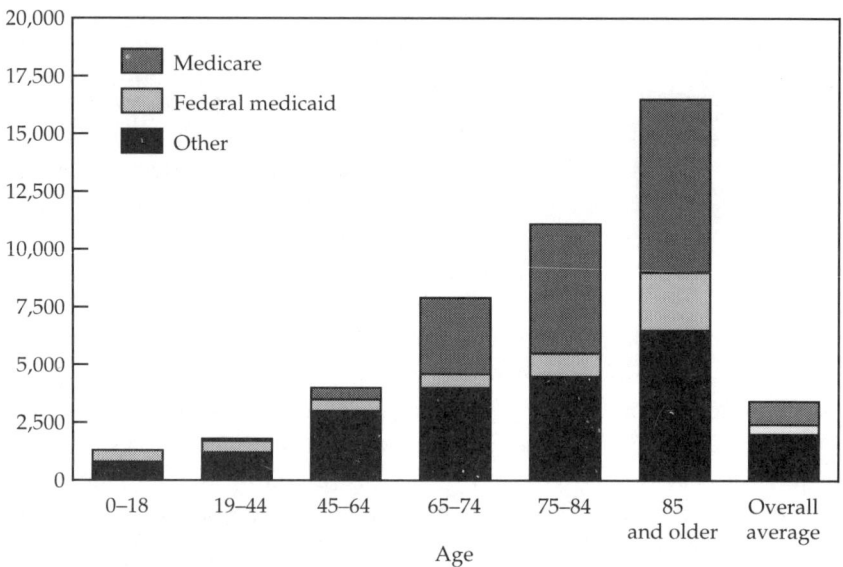

Source: Congressional Budget Office, and authors' calculations.

of the younger group. For people older than 85—a rapidly growing population—average medical consumption exceeds $16,000 a year, with more than $10,000 financed by federal government payments.[12] Surprisingly, private outlays on medical care do not decrease in retirement. Instead, the aged continue to pay for significant out-of-pocket expenses that are not covered by the government programs.

Other Programs

The U.S. government operates a means-tested Supplemental Security Income (SSI) program for aged, blind, and disabled people who do not receive adequate income from other sources. The aged represent about one-fourth of SSI recipients. Benefits under the program,

12. The medical care costs of the very old are overstated because nursing home care includes a large component of regular living expenses.

when combined with food stamp coupons provided under the food stamp program, assure elderly Americans of a modest income if they have little wealth and no other sources of income. Combined benefits under SSI and food stamps amount to 89 percent of the official U.S. poverty threshold for an aged person living alone. They provide 104 percent of the poverty threshold for an elderly couple.

The federal government and nearly all state and local governments also provide defined-benefit pension programs for their employees, many of whom were not covered by the OASDI program before the early 1980s. The state and local pension programs are designed as funded systems, but many have inadequate reserves to cover future claims. The old federal program was also a funded system, but its reserves consisted exclusively of federal debt. A new defined-contribution federal system was introduced in the 1980s when social security coverage was first extended to new federal employees.

Financial Outlook

The U.S. government prepares long-term actuarial projections for the OASDI and HI programs extending out for seventy-five years, and these forecasts are updated annually. The Congressional Budget Office has prepared a parallel projection of the medicaid program as part of its recent report on the long-term budget outlook.[13]

By 2025 the share of GDP devoted to OASDI, medicare, and medicaid will increase by two-thirds, rising to about 15 percent. Journalists and legislators frequently attribute that growth to a large increase in the elderly population. In fact, however, the more dramatic demographic change is the projected sharp slowing in the growth of the working-age population. The result is a much reduced rate of expansion
of aggregate incomes out of which the programs for the aged are financed.

Table 6-8 shows growth rates for some of the key demographic and economic determinants underlying the budget projections. The growth in total labor hours is expected to slow from an average of about 1.5 percent a year for the past thirty years to a few tenths of a

13. Congressional Budget Office (1996, pp. 69–95).

TABLE 6-8. *Projected Growth in Federal Outlays and Revenues,*
Selected Periods, 1960–95, and Projected to 2025–50
Annual percent change

| | Population | | | Economy | | | Budget | |
| | Age 15–64 | Age 65 or older | Labor hours | Output per labor hour | GDP | Revenues | Noninterest outlays | OASDI and health outlay |
Period								
1960–73	1.7	2.0	1.4	2.9	4.3	4.6	5.6	10.6
1973–85	1.2	2.2	1.5	1.1	2.6	2.8	3.3	5.4
1985–95	0.9	1.7	1.4	1.0	2.4	2.9	2.0	4.5
1995–2005	1.1	0.7	0.9	1.2	2.1	1.7	2.2	4.2
2005–15	0.6	2.2	0.6	1.2	1.8	1.9	3.1	4.3
2015–25	0.1	3.0	0.1	1.2	1.3	1.4	2.6	3.5
2025–50	0.2	0.8	0.2	1.1	1.3	1.4	1.7	2.0

Sources: Congressional Budget Office; and authors' estimates.

percent a year by 2025.[14] Under the assumption that output per worker grows at the average of the past quarter century, the resulting growth of GDP will be 1 to 1.5 percent a year. Meanwhile, spending on the major federal programs for the aged is projected to grow at an annual rate of 3 to 4 percent, more than twice the growth rate of the overall economy.

OASDI

Future cost trends in the social security system, as well as their financial implications, are most easily interpreted by focusing on the system's cost rate, the ratio of total benefit payments to taxable wages. The cost rate offers a direct measure of the pay-as-you-go tax rate required to finance the system in a given year. The cost rate is projected to slowly drift up between now and 2015 (figure 6-4). It will then rise sharply for the next twenty years as the baby boom population moves into retirement. The OASDI system is currently generating a surplus, but according to the most recent forecast of the social se-

14. Since 1960 the labor force has increased at an annual rate of about 2 percent, but this growth has been partly offset by the trend toward a shorter average work year. The social security actuary's projections assume a continued reduction in the length of the work year.

FIGURE 6-4. *Social Security Costs and Income, 1960–90, and Projected to 2070*

Percent of taxable wages

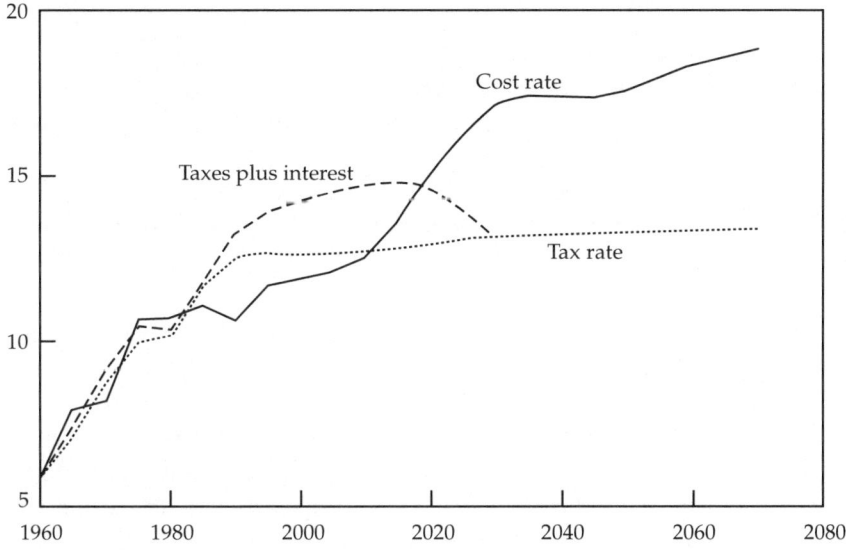

curity actuary, annual outlays will surpass revenues by 2020 and the reserve fund will be exhausted by 2030.

The cost rate (CR) can be further decomposed into two components, the program dependency rate (DR) and the benefit replacement rate (BRR):

$$CR = DR \times BRR.$$

The program dependency rate is the ratio of beneficiaries to active workers who pay taxes into the system. Variations in the dependency rate largely reflect the role of changing demographic patterns and retirement behavior. The benefit replacement rate is the ratio of the average pension benefit to the average covered wage. Trends in the replacement rate ordinarily reflect economic trends and changes in benefit legislation. Because both benefits and the ceiling for taxable wages are indexed, the American social security system is largely unaffected by variations in the rate of inflation.[15]

In the long run the system's cost rate is driven by demographic factors: fertility, immigration, and mortality. Thus the dependency rate (figure 6-5) rises by 50 percent between 1995 and 2025, and by another 20 percent by 2050. In contrast, the benefit rate is projected to fall about 8 percent by 2025.[16] The net result is a 50 percent increase in the cost rate, from 11.6 percent of taxable payroll in 1995 to 16.2 percent in 2025 and 17.5 percent in 2050.

The 1996 projections of the social security actuary show an actuarial deficit equal to 2 percent of payroll.[17] That is, however, only the tip of the iceberg because the simple passage of time requires additional tax increases as the valuation period extends further into the high-cost years of the next century. The tax rate has to rise by about 0.5 percentage points every ten years simply to maintain the standard of actuarial balance.

From one perspective, however, the increase in the cost rate greatly overstates the increased burden on future workers. The projections assume a continued erosion of the tax base as money wages fall in proportion to total labor compensation. An expanding share of compensation will flow into tax-exempt fringe benefit plans, such as employer-provided health insurance and private pensions. Furthermore,

15. Until recently variations in the interest rate also played a minor role in determining the financial condition of the system because social security was financed on a pay-as-you-go basis with no significant accumulation of reserves. The United States has recently moved toward a system of partial advance funding. Accumulated social security reserves are now about 150 percent of annual expenses ($500 billion). Reserves are expected to peak at about three times annual outlays after 2005. This makes interest income a significant financing component. The projections currently assume a real interest rate of 2.3 percent in the intermediate case. Under the pessimistic alternative the assumed real interest rate is 1.5 percent; under the optimistic assumption it is 3.0 percent.

16. The sensitivity of the dependency rate to alternative assumptions is reflected in the huge gap between the future rate under the high-cost and low-cost actuarial forecasts. For 2050 there is a 64 percent gap between the low- and high-cost projections of the dependency rate, while there is only a 12 percent gap between the high-cost and low-cost projections of the benefit replacement rate.

17. The actuarial balance is the present discounted value of the difference between future income and outgo, taking into account the initial reserves in the trust fund. In the past decade the extension of the forecast horizon and refinement of the estimates have caused the projected deficit to rise from 0.4 percent of payroll.

FIGURE 6-5. *Components of the Cost Rate, 1960–90, and Projected to 2070*

Percent

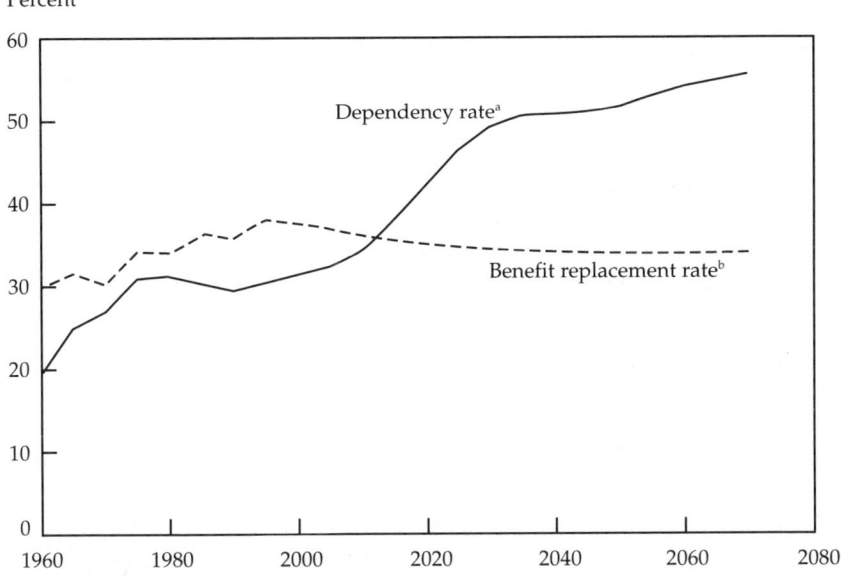

Source: Board of Trustees (1996).
a. Dependents as percent of workers.
b. Percent of average wage.

taxable wages currently represent only about 40 percent of GDP. If social security payments are measured as a share of GDP rather than as a share of taxable wages, the increased burden of social security appears far more manageable. Social security outlays rise from 4.8 percent of GDP in 1995 to 6.4 percent of GDP in 2025 and to 6.6 percent in 2050. To put this fifty-five-year trend in perspective, the change is actually smaller than the variation in U.S. defense spending between 1990 and 1995.

A major point to emphasize about the projections is the wide range of uncertainty. As noted earlier, the social security trustees' report provides three alternatives based on grouping the different demographic and economic assumptions in terms of their favorable or unfavorable impact on the trust funds. The intermediate projection, which we have used, is widely interpreted as representing the trustees' best guess of the future. Under the optimistic scenario, the fund would run surpluses throughout the seventy-five-year period, while the pessimistic assumptions imply that the OASDI trust fund will be exhausted as early as 2016.[18]

Medicare

The major problem in paying for the needs of the elderly will occur as a result of the spiraling cost of medicare and medicaid. The cost rate of the hospital insurance portion of medicare is projected to more than double by 2025 and to triple by 2070, rising from 3.4 percent of taxable wages in 1995 to 7.6 percent in 2025. Without additional revenues, the HI trust fund will be depleted by 2001. These projections are far more uncertain, however, than those for OASDI. This is reflected in the wider range between the low- and high-cost options, 4.8 and 12.3 percent, respectively, of taxable wages in 2025. Bear in mind that the eligible beneficiary population grows in line with that of OASDI. The faster projected cost increase in medicare is due to the steeper rise in costs per beneficiary. Unlike OASDI, medicare has no legislative link between contributions and future benefits. Benefit payments will rise at the rate of increase in medical care use plus medical care price inflation.

The Supplemental Medical Insurance program is operated on an annual basis with adjustment of premiums and financing from the U.S. Treasury as needed to cover each year's costs. As a result, SMI does not require the kind of long-term actuarial forecasts prepared for OASDI and HI. Estimates are made, however, of program costs for a ten-year horizon, and rough assumptions can be made to project costs over the longer term. SMI outlays are currently about two-thirds the size of those for the HI program. The Social Security Administration assumes that the costs per enrollee of SMI will decline to the growth of GDP per capita by 2020 and continue at that rate for the next 50 years.

Table 6-9 summarizes the cost trends in the medical programs.

18. The pessimistic and optimistic projections cannot be regarded as equally likely alternatives on each side of the mean, however. Several technical advisory groups have concluded that the probability that should be assigned to the pessimistic assumptions is far larger than the probability of the optimistic scenario.

TABLE 6-9. *Sources of Change in Medical Care Costs, 1980–95, and Projected to 2025–50*
Annual percent change, 1995 prices

Source	1980–95	1995–2010	2010–25	2025–50
Medicare				
Population growth	1.0	0.8	0.6	0.3
Age distribution	0.9	0.4	1.8	0.8
Intensity of utilization	5.2	4.8	2.0	1.1
Total	7.0	5.9	4.4	2.1
Medicaid				
Population growth	1.0	0.8	0.6	0.3
Age distribution	0.3	0.2	0.3	0.7
Intensity of utilization	7.3	5.8	2.0	1.3
Total	8.6	6.8	2.9	2.3

Source: Author's calculations from unpublished Congressional Budget Office data, 1996.

Costs are driven by growth in the total population, a shift in its distribution toward age groups with greater health care spending, and increases in per capita care utilization. In the table, expenditures are adjusted to exclude the effect of variations in general inflation, as measured by the price deflator for GDP. Although the demographic factors will contribute to a modest slowing of cost increases in the immediate future, the rapid aging of the population after 2010 will boost medicare spending substantially. Shifts in the age distribution are of less importance for medicaid. The projections for both programs appear highly optimistic in assuming a rapid slowing of the growth in per capita costs. On an age-adjusted basis, those costs slow from an average annual growth rate of 5.2 percent in the 1980–95 period to just 2 percent in 2010–25.

Proposals for Reform

Discussion of possible reforms to deal with the results of population aging has encompassed a great many proposals, ranging from simple benefit cuts or tax increases to drastic restructuring of the basic programs. The concern over future financing problems has also led to a reopening of the debate over the desirability of the public role in providing retirement income. Some Americans have always objected to the redistributional and coercive features of the OASDI and medicare programs. Young workers and more affluent voters often respond to the forecast of future financing problems by advocating a return to a system in which people rely on their own resources.

There are three basic options for responding to the future budgetary problems. The first two are obvious: benefit cuts or tax increases. These have dominated the public discussion for many years. The primary issue is perceived to be the division of a fixed amount of future resources between the young and the old. The choice is usually evaluated in isolation from the broader question of what determines the total amount of future resources. By now the list of potential changes is extensive, and the debate tends to revolve around the distributional and incentive consequences of specific reform alternatives.

The third option, advance funding of a portion of the future costs, represents a move away from the pay-as-you-go system. It is based on a dynamic growth perspective in which today's saving can provide the future income necessary to support the consumption needs of the elderly without reducing the consumption of younger workers. The implications of this option are less thoroughly understood by the public, however, and its advocates are divided as to whether the advance funding should take place within a public or a private system.

Although most of the reform proposals focus on social security, its financing problems are relatively modest compared with those of medicare. Within the next two decades, the medicare program will surpass OASDI in terms of total outlays, yet policymakers have advanced no comprehensive proposals for controlling its costs. The problems of financing medical care for the elderly are part of the problem of managing the soaring cost of national health spending in general.

Options under Pay-as-You-Go Financing

Under the intermediate assumptions about future economic and demographic trends, some combination of benefit cuts and tax increases totaling about 2 percent of taxable payroll, or 15 percent of benefit payments, will be required to bring the OASDI trust fund into actuarial balance.[19] Although Congress will be tempted to delay action until the financing problem becomes acute, there are persuasive arguments for enacting reforms as soon as possible, allowing workers ample time to adjust their saving and retirement plans. There is no particular economic reason for choosing between benefit cuts and tax increases, however. Benefit reductions, if phased in gradually, might be favored on efficiency grounds because they strengthen economic incentives to increase private saving and delay retirement. But reliance on benefit reductions alone would require a large scaling back of the programs.

The choice between benefit cutbacks and tax increases mainly involves matters of equity rather than economic efficiency. If taxes are hiked to avoid sharp cutbacks in benefits, the scale of the present redistributive public system will be preserved. Groups that benefit under the system will be protected; groups that lose under the present system will see their losses grow. But if future benefits are scaled back to keep the tax rate from rising, groups that receive net transfers from the system will see those transfers shrink.

These groups include low-wage workers and their dependents, married workers who have a nonworking spouse and child dependents, and workers who have long expected life spans. Groups that receive smaller net transfers or pay net taxes to the system include high-wage workers, single workers, dual-earner married couples, and workers who have a low probability of surviving until age 62. It is not always obvious which of these groups deserves special protection. A single worker with a short expected life span makes social security payroll contributions throughout his career but collects small lifetime benefits. Any reform that shrinks the present scale of social security would reduce this worker's expected contributions without appreciably affecting his expected lifetime benefits. Many observers might consider this outcome fair in comparison with a policy that hikes payroll taxes in order to protect the retirement incomes of workers who have very long expected life spans.

19. Actuarial balance is achieved when the sum of social security reserves and the present discounted value of expected future revenues is exactly equal to the discounted value of expected future outlays. The planning horizon for performing these calculations is seventy-five years.

BENEFIT REDUCTIONS.   The U.S. retirement system is often referred to as a three-legged stool, consisting of social security, employer-sponsored pensions, and individual savings. Retirement income from sources other than social security is significant only for the top two-fifths of the income distribution, however (see table 6-4). For most elderly Americans, social security is the principal source of retirement income. Furthermore, while the economic condition of the elderly has improved relative to that of active workers, a large percentage have incomes that are not far above the poverty level. The effects of reform on the income distribution are therefore an important aspect of the debate over changes in benefits.

The most straightforward benefit reduction is one that cuts the primary insurance amount for all new retirees.[20] The current long-term deficit in social security is about 15 percent of the summarized cost rate, implying that a 15 percent cut in benefits, if effective immediately and across the board, would eliminate the seventy-five-year imbalance. Congress is unlikely to impose a benefit reduction this large on people who are already receiving benefits, however. A benefit reduction that is restricted to new retirees would require time to have its full effect on total benefits, implying that a reduction of about 18 percent in the PIA, if phased in when new claimants begin to collect benefits, is needed to restore actuarial balance. Furthermore, the actuarial balance will continue to deteriorate as current surplus years are replaced with future years of deficit. If benefit reductions are delayed until 2025, the required reduction would be about 25 percent.

Some reform proposals would impose a disproportionate benefit reduction on high-wage workers by changing the replacement rate factors in the formula for calculating the PIA (currently 0.90, 0.32 and 0.15), or by adding a third bend point. This kind of reform would have only limited effectiveness in closing the financing gap, however, because the redistributional tilt in the present benefit formula is already pronounced. For example, if the Social Security Administration ignored all earnings above the second bend point when calculating the PIA, total benefit payments would eventually be reduced by just 7

---

20. Steuerle and Bakija (1994) evaluate a broader range of benefit changes in the social security pension formula. The focus of this section is on those changes that would improve the system's financial condition, as opposed to its equity or efficiency effects.

percent, or about half of the current long-term deficit.[21] Although a disproportionate benefit reduction for workers with high lifetime wages may protect retirees near the poverty line, it would reduce the already low marginal benefit received by high-wage workers, thereby increasing labor market distortions and pressures on employers to convert taxable money wages into untaxed fringe benefits.

The most common proposal to reduce social security benefits is to raise the normal retirement age, that is, the age at which full social security benefits (100 percent of the PIA) can be claimed. An increase in the retirement age from age 65 to 67, phased in over two decades beginning in 2002, is already scheduled to occur as a result of social security reforms enacted in 1983. Although the normal age of retirement has remained fixed at 65 since the program's inception, life expectancy at birth has risen almost 11 years for men and and 13.5 years for women since 1940. Life expectancy at age 65 has increased from 11.9 years in 1940 to 15.3 years today, and it is projected to rise by an additional 11 percent over the next 40 years.[22] Even though the normal retirement age will be increased to 67 by 2025, workers will remain eligible for actuarially reduced early retirement benefits that begin at age 62.[23] Under these circumstances, there may not be much practical difference between an increase in the normal retirement age and a reduction in the standard PIA. Both reforms scale back retirement and old-age survivors benefits across the board.[24] For a worker with the average life expectancy who retires at age 65, the increase in the normal retirement age from 65 to 67 is equivalent to a 15 percent reduction in the PIA.

A number of policymakers suggest that the phase-in of the higher retirement age should begin immediately and should be extended so that the normal retirement age is eventually lifted to 70. If the normal retirement age were increased to age 70 by 2030, about half of the current long-term deficit in social security would be eliminated. If the

21. The second bend point currently is set slightly above 50 percent of the taxable wage ceiling.

22. Board of Trustees (1995, table II.D2).

23. By 2025 the actuarial penalty for claiming benefits at age 62 will be 30 percent of the worker's PIA. The penalty for claiming benefits at age 62 is currently 20 percent.

24. For a discussion of these issues see Technical Panel on Trends and Issues in Retirement Saving (1995), especially pp. 70–103.

age of early retirement were increased at the same time from 62 to 67, the currently projected deficit would essentially disappear. (However, if mortality rates continued to fall after the end of the current seventy-five-year projection period, the deficit would eventually recur.)

Increasing the normal retirement age has been criticized on the grounds that while life expectancy has increased, the health condition of the elderly, and their ability to continue working, has not improved. The proposal may be acceptable to white-collar workers, who hold sedentary jobs, but is much less popular among workers employed in physically demanding jobs. To ease the burden on these workers, future workers might be allowed to apply for disability insurance under liberalized eligibility standards once they attain age 62. However, it is administratively costly to evaluate the health condition of prospective early retirees to determine whether they qualify for disability benefits. U.S. experience also suggests that the determination of health disabilities is inconsistent, leading to frequent legal and political battles over the determination process.

Although the debate over raising the retirement age usually focuses on the work capacity of people near the present retirement age, another equity issue is probably just as important. If the early retirement age were raised, workers with short life expectancies would suffer disproportionate losses in benefits. Workers can currently obtain actuarially reduced benefits starting as early as age 62. If the PIA is reduced or the normal retirement age is raised, but the early entitlement age is left unchanged, workers with short life expectancies would receive reduced benefits, but their retirement benefits would not be eliminated. However, if the early entitlement age were raised to age 67, workers with short life expectancies would suffer extremely large benefit losses. Liberalization of the disability insurance program would not, by itself, reduce these workers' losses. Many workers who have short life expectancies do not suffer disabling conditions until just before they die, so improvements in the DI program could not compensate them for the loss of early retirement pensions.

Another way to scale back social security outlays is to reduce indexation of benefits. This proposal is sometimes justified on the basis of recent claims that the consumer price index overstates inflation by failing to adjust fully for quality improvements in goods and services. The annual cost-of-living adjustment might be reduced so that it equals the rate of increase in the CPI less 1 percent. This proposal would have no effect on a worker's initial benefit, which would continue to be indexed to past growth in wages, but it would progressively reduce the real benefit of retirees as they age. If continued during every year of retirement, a 1 percent cut in the cost-of-living adjustment would reduce the pension of an eighty-year-old by 16.5 percent.

The short-run and long-run effects of reducing cost-of-living adjustments should be distinguished. If the reform were implemented immediately, current pensioners and workers who are about to retire (as well as all future retirees) would be forced to accept a reduction in benefits. Unlike most other proposals to reduce benefits, this one would force people who are already old to bear part of the burden of eliminating the long-term social security deficit. Because current pensioners would pay part of the cost of eliminating the deficit, younger workers and unborn generations would not have to pay as much. This outcome may seem equitable to some because the current generation of elderly has enjoyed an exceptional rate of return on its contributions to social security and medicare. Future generations can expect to receive much more modest returns.

The long-term effects of reducing the cost-of-living adjustment seem much less appealing. Few other forms of retirement income are indexed, so curtailing indexation in social security would exacerbate a pattern in which the relative and real income position of the elderly deteriorates as they age. Poverty and low income seem to be more serious problems among the very aged than they are among new retirees, so it is likely that a permanent reduction in the cost-of-living adjustment would increase poverty more than a cutback in the PIA that achieved the same long-term cost saving. The social security actuary has calculated that a cutback of 0.5 percent a year in the cost-of-living adjustment would reduce the long-term deficit in social security by 0.7 percent of taxable payroll.

Finally, it has been argued that social security benefits should be subject to a means test, reducing current benefits to affluent retirees. One option is to phase out social security benefits as family income (or wealth) rises above a certain threshold, say $75,000 a year. This proposal has a great deal of political appeal, but it is opposed by many economists who fear its effects on saving incentives. The redistributive PIA formula in the current system implies that benefits are already means tested, but the test is based on workers' lifetime earnings rather than their income during retirement. If the retirement benefit were to be calculated on the basis of workers' wealth or income at retirement, the means test would act as an additional tax on retirement saving.[25]

Means testing also raises other concerns. It may deprive social security of crucial political support by increasing the hostility of high-income workers and retirees, who will no longer benefit under the system. It may encourage retirees to shift assets to their children. It may also encourage overinvestment in assets such as housing that provide in-kind benefits excluded from the means test. Medicaid payments for nursing home care are now based on a means test, and concealment of income and assets is thought to be a severe problem in that program. Advocates of a means test argue that full-blown means testing is not very different from the 1983 decision to include high-income taxpayers' social security benefits in the federal income tax base. However, ordinary taxation of social security benefits probably represents an improvement in the fairness of the tax system. Outright elimination of pensions to a substantial minority of workers who have made large lifetime contributions to the pension system may not be regarded as equally fair.

MEDICAL CARE.   Like OASDI, the medical programs must provide for a greatly expanded population of beneficiaries, but in addition they are faced with a large increase in costs per beneficiary. Furthermore, because the programs deliver a service rather than simply providing cash, the debate over medicare and medicaid involves complex issues of price and quality that are absent from the discussion of social security. Much of the current American policy discussion of reductions in payments to health care providers reflects an erroneous view that recent increases in cost per beneficiary are simply the result of waste and inefficiency. Thus politicians sometimes promise large cost savings with little or no loss in the actual level of service delivered.

Most of the research on health care, however, concludes that the cost increases are driven in large measure by technological innovations

25. The very wealthy might actually face stronger incentives to save because a means test would eliminate the social security component of their retirement income, and they might attempt to replace some proportion of the loss.

that have broadened the range of potential medical interventions. Within the past few decades, organ transplants, bypass surgery, and other costly medical interventions have become commonplace. Furthermore, noninvasive and expensive diagnostic tests such as magnetic resonance imaging have become routine. Because they are less risky and painful, these tests are employed far more frequently than the procedures they replaced. The concentration of health care outlays on high-cost interventions also suggests that incentives to shop more wisely will have only limited effects. Similarly, proposals to move the aged into managed care plans may generate a one-time reduction in the level of spending, but continued large-scale saving is likely to involve limitations on patients' access to the high-cost interventions.

The budgetary problems of medicare and medicaid could be made more similar to those of OASDI simply by converting the programs to a voucher system that provided financial assistance for older Americans to purchase private health insurance. While such a change does not solve the broader social problem of rising medical care costs, it directly addresses the public budget issue. It does so, however, by shifting the problem from government to household budgets. It is not obvious how public welfare is improved if a significant fraction of the elderly chose to forgo insurance or to purchase private insurance that paid for very meager levels of medical protection. The financing problems of medicare and medicaid should be seen as part of a larger problem of rising health care costs for Americans of all ages.

REVENUE INCREASES.   The financing gap in social security and medicare could obviously be closed with a large hike in the payroll tax. But added taxes would probably accelerate the change in the composition of labor compensation away from taxable wages toward tax-exempt benefits. Already, more than one-third of the projected actuarial deficit in OASDI is due to a shift in labor compensation away from taxable wages and self-employment income.[26] Thus consideration must be given to some other changes in the structure of the U.S. tax system. These include raising the ceiling for taxable wages under the OASDI program (as has already been done for medicare), expanding

26. OASDI Trustees (1996, p. 189).

the definition of taxable wages, and taxing nonlabor incomes. Each alternative has advantages and disadvantages.

Without a change in the present social security pension formula, raising the taxable wage ceiling in OASDI will ultimately lead to an increase in the benefit paid to those earning wages above the current ceiling. Because of the redistributive tilt in the pension formula, however, the benefit increase would be small. Moreover, because of the long lag between the higher tax revenues and the extra benefit payments, the OASDI trust funds would enjoy a substantial net gain.

Only about 7 percent of workers have earnings above the ceiling, but eliminating the ceiling would have a very large effect on the marginal tax rate for these workers.[27] The distributional impact is similar to that of reducing the benefit for workers with high lifetime wages. Thus, the policy obviously favors low-wage workers in comparison with a policy to hike the payroll tax rate or other federal taxes. A ticklish political issue will eventually arise when workers who currently earn very high wages—sometimes in excess of $10 million a year—begin to claim social security pensions that may be substantially higher than average wages.

The trend in the composition of labor compensation toward untaxed fringe benefits might be reversed by broadening the tax base to include some compensation that is currently tax exempt. This proposal would eliminate some labor market distortions by treating all forms of payment in similar ways, and it would increase the relative tax on high-wage workers because of the greater importance of such benefit programs to them. Difficulties arise, however, in the assignment of a precise monetary value to some benefits, such as defined-benefit pension contributions and employer contributions to health insurance. It is nearly impossible to allocate fairly the costs of group health insurance to individual workers. The average contribution per insured worker grossly overstates the value of health insurance to young workers, who consume less expensive health services than older workers (see figure 6-3).

The inclusion of currently untaxed fringe benefits in the tax base

27. The proportion of covered earnings above the ceiling was 13.2 percent in 1993. See Social Security Administration (1994, p. 167). Currently workers above the OASDI wage ceiling face a marginal wage tax of 2.9 percent and those below it 15.3 percent.

raises an issue similar to that raised by eliminating the taxable wage ceiling. If the tax base is broadened, future benefit payments must also rise, because the pension formula is based on workers' covered earnings. Since untaxed fringe benefits are received by low- and average-wage workers as well as the highly paid, the additional benefit payments will be much greater than is the case when the ceiling on taxable money wages is lifted, a reform that only affects workers with earnings above the current wage ceiling.

A way to avoid these problems is to assess payroll taxes on employers for their contributions to employee health and welfare plans, but to exempt workers from making additional tax payments. Under this plan, employers may not need to allocate contributions to individual workers, since they are simply required to make tax payments based on their total contributions to employee benefit plans. Social security benefits would continue be calculated on the basis of earnings on which workers make contributions, but the trust fund would collect employers' contributions based on money wages plus employer contributions to private health and welfare plans. While this may be feasible in principle, it is not easy to implement as long as there is a ceiling on taxable earnings per worker. The employer would still need to determine whether the sum of money wages and contributions to fringe benefit plans exceeds the ceiling *for each individual worker.* The problem would disappear if the ceiling on taxable earnings were eliminated for purposes of calculating employer contributions.

That plan may raise serious questions of fairness, however. Even though policymakers maintain the fiction that the current payroll tax is imposed separately (and equally) on workers and their employers, most economists believe the full burden of the combined tax falls on workers. If this view is correct, it may be unfair to tax employers for contributions to worker welfare plans or for wages above the wage ceiling while calculating pensions on the basis of workers' money wages below the wage ceiling. In comparison with a worker who receives no company-provided fringe benefits, for example, a worker covered by a company welfare plan is implicitly required to make greater contributions for the same pension benefits.[28]

---

28. Some might argue that the higher contribution of the worker covered by a company-sponsored welfare plan is justified. That worker receives higher annual compen-

A final alternative is to look for additional sources of tax revenue. This is a strategy used by many social security programs around the world, where the national government is required to make annual contributions to the social security fund that are tied to the size of the taxable wage base or to contributions of employers and employees. The United States has been reluctant to finance social security and medicare part A benefits out of general revenues. (Medicare part B is financed out of general revenues and premiums charged to beneficiaries.) However, a portion of OASDI and HI revenues is derived from the application of the income tax to social security benefits. The use of the income tax has some appeal because it is administratively simple and would distribute the financing burden more broadly than a wage tax. In particular, the current elderly population, whose benefits have far exceeded past contributions, would be forced to help pay for a solution to the long-term financing problem. The elderly obviously avoid this burden if tax increases are concentrated solely on active workers and their employers. A broadening of the tax base would also reduce the size of the required tax hike, potentially reducing the distortionary effects of the additional tax. This change, however, would fundamentally alter the perception of social security as a publicly operated retirement program with earned rights. It would take on more of the characteristics of a simple transfer program, subject to annual modification.

Reliance on a broad tax base is more appealing in the case of medicare. Unlike OASDI, medicare benefits depend entirely on retirees' insured medical expenses, not on their contributions while they were at work. As a result, there is no strong reason to rely on a wage tax to finance a system that provides substantial medical insurance to retirees who may have made little or no past contribution to the system. Some analysts suggest that the medicare program would be better financed out of a broad-based value-added tax.[29] The original financing arrangement for SMI was actually based on the premise that annual program costs would be split equally between the retired, who are

---

sation than a worker paid the same money wage who is not covered by a welfare plan. Because social security is intentionally redistributive, it makes sense to require the worker receiving the higher compensation to pay more for each dollar of expected social security benefits.

29. Schultze (1992, pp. 310–14).

required to pay insurance premiums, and general federal revenues. But in response to political pressures, the premium payments of the elderly have fallen to just 25 percent of program costs. If the financing of SMI returned to the original division of costs, the long-run deficit in medicare would fall by about 0.3 percent of GDP.

Partial Funding

Proposals to resolve future financing problems by some combination of benefit reduction and tax increase are inherently divisive because the problem is viewed from the perspective of a zero-sum conflict in which any gains to younger generations must come at the expense of the old. These proposals do not change the fundamental nature of the problem, because the size of the future retiree population and their needs remain the same. The argument focuses on who is going to pay for the fiscal adjustment that is needed. People at the top of the income distribution advocate benefit cuts and greater reliance on individuals' own resources, while those with lower incomes may favor higher taxes, especially if the taxes are concentrated on high-wage workers or high-income retirees.

This kind of discussion diverts attention from alternative policies that could increase the total amount of future income out of which the consumption needs of both future workers and future retirees will be financed. The most obvious example is an increase in the saving of the current generation to finance an increased portion of its own retirement consumption. The added saving and capital formation would directly raise future capital income of retirees, but it would also increase the wages and taxes of future workers out of which the retirement benefits could be paid.[30] The expansion of saving could be accomplished under public or private auspices. Publicly, the current surplus of the retirement system could be expanded, either by an increase in the contribution rate or through a reduction in current benefits, and the added surplus set aside and allowed to boost national saving. Alternatively, the increased saving could take place within new or expanded private pension accounts. Whether the added saving is

30. Some aspects of partial funding were examined in Aaron, Bosworth, and Burtless (1989).

TABLE 6-10. *Net National Saving and Investment Balance, Selected Periods, 1960–95*
Percent of net national income

Category	1960–69	1970–79	1980–84	1985–89	1990–94	1995
National saving	11.9	9.2	6.4	5.2	3.5	4.9
Private	9.7	9.8	9.4	7.8	7.0	6.9
Households	5.6	6.3	6.7	4.6	4.1	3.8
Corporate	4.1	3.5	2.7	3.2	2.9	3.1
Government	2.2	−0.7	−3.0	−2.6	−3.5	−2.0
National investment	11.6	9.8	7.0	5.1	4.1	5.0
Domestic	10.9	9.6	7.7	8.2	5.3	7.2
Private	8.0	8.2	6.4	6.5	3.9	6.0
Government	2.9	1.3	1.2	1.7	1.4	1.2
Net foreign	0.7	0.3	−0.7	−3.0	−1.2	−2.2
Statistical discrepancy	−0.3	0.6	0.6	−0.1	0.5	0.1
Capital consumption allowance	12.0	13.0	15.3	14.1	13.6	12.9

Source: U.S. Commerce Department, revised national income and products accounts. State and local government employee pension accounts are moved from government to the household sector to match the treatment of private pension programs.

accumulated in public or private accounts, the crucial point is that the increase in retirement saving actually results in an increase in national saving. It cannot be offset by reduced saving in other public or private accounts.

Current interest in funding a portion of future retirement costs is fueled in part by the adverse trend in U.S. national saving. Rates of saving in both the public and private sectors fell sharply in the past decade (table 6-10). U.S. saving as a percentage of national income is less than half what it was in the 1960s. The net private saving rate dropped from an average of 9 to 10 percent of net national product (NNP) from 1950 to 1980 to just 7 percent in the 1990s. At the same time, the public sector deficit rose above 4 percent of NNP in the early 1990s. The nation has made recent progress in reducing the public deficit, but private saving is still far below its historical norm. The United States has come to rely on a steady inflow of foreign saving to finance domestic capital formation.

How large an increase in saving would be needed to finance the extra future budget outlays that will be required by population aging? Program outlays of the federal government are projected to increase from 19 percent of GDP in 1995 to 24 percent in 2025 (table 6-1). To fund those outlays at no cost to future workers, the United States would need to build up an added stock of assets, over a thirty-year period, sufficient to earn additional income equal to those outlays. Since 1960 the real return on physical capital in the United States, net of depreciation, has averaged about 6 percent, suggesting the need to increase the capital stock by an additional 80 percent of output.[31] In comparison, the national wealth of the United States in 1995 was estimated to be about $19 trillion, or 2.8 times GDP.[32]

The calculation of the additional saving that would be needed is complicated by a couple of factors. First, the expansion of capital formation, if the resources are invested in the United States, will drive down the return on both new and existing capital. Some of the decline is not a problem from a national perspective since it reflects a redistribution of income from the relatively less scarce factor of production (capital) to the more scarce factor (labor). The incremental gain to national income from an additional unit of investment, however, can be expected to gradually fall over the thirty-year period, increasing the required addition to the capital stock.

The probable decline in the return to capital could be moderated if the United States invested a portion of the increased capital abroad. Current national account estimates imply that U.S. residents make a return on foreign investments comparable to that available domestically. Thus, some of the decline in the rate of return could be avoided by investing in a larger global economy where the increment to capital would be relatively small.[33] Foreign investment, however, does raise other problems. Such an investment strategy would require the United States to shift from a net current account deficit with the rest of the world to a surplus during the period of capital outflow. Such a transfer of resources would involve an initial terms of trade loss. The price of exports would need to fall and that of imports to rise to accomplish the reallocation of trade flows.

Finally, not all of the increase in public outlays need be covered by

31. Bosworth (1996, pp. 98–100).

32. Board of Governors (1995). National wealth is domestic wealth minus net foreign liabilities.

33. This assumes that not all of the economies with aging populations will try to raise their saving and invest in the global economy.

saving in excess of current rates. The United States is entering an era of diminished growth in the labor force that will translate into a reduced need for additions to the capital stock. Thus a portion of the added spending can be accommodated out of reduced baseline investment. That is, the added capital formation should be viewed within the context of a slow fall in the "required" investment rate. In the long run, balanced growth dictates a rate of capital accumulation equal to the rate of growth in the labor force plus labor-augmenting technological change. For the United States this warranted growth of the capital stock has declined from 4 percent a year in the 1960s to about 2.5 percent in the 1980s (because of slower technology improvement), and in the Congressional Budget Office projection it slows to 1.3 percent for 2025–50 (because of slower labor force growth). The lessened capital needs will free up 2 to 3 percent of GDP from net investment.

Partial funding of future retirement obligations could be accomplished through either a continuation of the current public retirement system (OASDI and medicare) or by its conversion into a private retirement system. In each case there is a legitimate question of whether the increment to funding would really add to national saving and capital formation. Would the added retirement saving be offset by reduced saving in other accounts of the public sector or in reductions in private saving? We consider the advantages and disadvantages of the public and private alternatives in turn.

PUBLIC FUNDING.   Advance funding would be simplest to implement within the existing public programs because it would leave accrued benefit claims intact. The financing reform would require only some combination of an increase in the contribution rate or reduction of benefits to create a reserve, as well as a firm commitment to separate the surplus from other government accounts. From the perspective of the economic benefits to the nation, it matters little whether the reserve is invested in public or private securities. The economic benefits flow from the increased investment in real capital. If the social security fund purchased government debt, a larger proportion of private saving would go to finance private investment. If the fund were invested in private debt, a larger percentage of private saving would be used to cover the public sector budget deficit.

Investment of the increased social security reserves in private securities might be advantageous for two reasons. First, if the reserves were invested solely in public debt, there is a large risk that the additional retirement saving would simply be appropriated to finance spending in other government accounts.[34] This outcome was mandated in the balanced budget amendment to the Constitution proposed by congressional Republicans in 1995. Under the terms of the proposed amendment, social security was to be counted as part of the overall government budget. Any additional surplus in the social security account would therefore have the effect of making more funds available for current spending in other government accounts. If the added funds in the social security reserve were invested in private securities, as is done with state government retirement funds, Congress might find it more difficult to appropriate the additions to reserves to pay for other government operations.[35] Most proposals to invest social security reserves in private assets are based on the assumption that the money would be invested in large index funds and that fund managers would not be permitted to influence the operation of individual corporations.

Second, if the fund restricted itself to investing in government securities, most of the economic benefits of a high saving program would be concentrated in private incomes. The social security reserves would earn the comparatively low (but safe) return on U.S. Treasury debt, whereas a larger percentage of private saving would be held in higher-return private equities. The added private capital formation would boost the incomes of future workers, but it is doubtful whether future workers would recognize that their improved living standard was partly the result of increased saving and investment by past generations of workers and savers. They would remain as opposed as today's workers to any tax increase to pay for the heavier burden of social security benefits. Most of the increase in future capital income would accrue to private investors who bore the risk.

---

34. There is little reason to anticipate a change in private saving behavior because the promised future retirement benefit remains unchanged.

35. A variety of other suggestions have been made to increase the separation between the social insurance system and the rest of government. For example, social security is now an independent agency and its budget is reported separately from the rest of the federal government. However, the standard budget reports of the administration and Congress still include OASDI as part of the overall federal budget.

If the additions to the social security reserves were invested instead in a portfolio that included a substantial fraction of high-return private securities, the trust fund would earn a much higher future return, reducing the need for future payroll tax increases. Of course, this strategy would also increase the riskiness of the portfolio. However, concentrating all public retirement saving in U.S. Treasury debt is itself a highly skewed investment strategy that fails to take advantage of the benefits of portfolio diversification. Even though the social security reserves may face none of the risks of failure associated with private investments, they are highly exposed to political risks.

PRIVATIZATION.   Public management of a huge retirement fund has been questioned by many who suspect that investment decisions would be guided by political criteria rather than considerations of risk and return. Critics of a huge public retirement fund also challenge the assumption that voters and their representatives could be persuaded not to use the reserve as an offset to deficits in other government accounts. They therefore argue for partial privatization of the existing system by moving to individually owned and managed retirement accounts. Individual retirement accounts could reduce the political risks surrounding the current retirement system and would certainly offer people greater flexibility in managing their own retirement savings. In effect, proponents of partial privatization suggest moving to a two-pillar system comprising a small public component that provides a minimal poverty-level benefit—perhaps a flat benefit amount or one related to number of years of participation—and a defined-contribution pension with no redistributional element. Participants' funds in the individual accounts would be invested in a range of capital market assets, presumably directed by the individual contributors. This type of plan received wide and favorable notice after its successful introduction in Chile during the early 1980s.[36]

Critics of privatization note that the explicit separation of the redistributional component would result in strong pressure to reduce or eliminate it. Middle-class entitlement programs such as social security and medicare enjoy much broader political support than programs

---

36. See Diamond and Valdés-Prieto (1994) for a thorough discussion of the Chilean program.

such as SSI and food stamps in which benefits are explicitly redistributed toward the poor. Thus, some observers doubt that a partially privatized system would provide adequate old-age income security for workers with low lifetime earnings. Moreover, low-wage workers may also be poorly qualified to make good investment decisions.[37] Individual accounts also raise the problem of how to manage the conversion of the accounts to annuities when workers retire, become disabled, or (for those who leave survivors) die. If individuals were given the option of accepting lump-sum cash-outs, a private system for converting assets into annuities would encounter extreme problems of adverse selection because those with short life expectancies would choose cash. The price of annuities would therefore have to rise. This is not a problem faced by a national system of defined-benefit pensions, in which, by definition, there is universal and mandatory conversion to annuities. The U.S. government would also need to issue large amounts of public debt indexed to the CPI so that private firms could offer indexed benefits to annuitants. Privatization would inevitably involve higher administrative costs. The present universal public system is extremely efficient; its administrative costs are just 0.8 percent of annual benefit payments. No private insurance company or investment fund has administrative costs that are nearly this low. Private investment companies would also incur selling costs to attract retirement saving, and each company would have to establish a funds collection and distribution system.

Individual retirement accounts have obvious appeal to workers at the top of the income distribution. Private accounts have gained wider political support in a period when Americans are increasingly inclined to reject coercive, burdensome, and allegedly inefficient public redistribution schemes. Because an individual retirement account is effectively a defined-contribution pension plan, the establishment of tens of millions of such accounts eliminates the concern about the public sector costs of U.S. retirement programs because benefits are determined by contributions and market interest rates, not by government contributions. But there remain legitimate concerns about the consequences of such a system for low-wage workers.

37. Available survey evidence indicates that low-wage workers with IRA accounts make extremely risk-averse investment decisions, frequently choosing to put their funds in low-return bank accounts.

Conclusion

The expected future costs of public programs for the elderly are high, but with prudent public policy during the next three decades the costs should be economically manageable. The greatest problem for the United States is that the future liabilities of public retirement programs are mounting steeply in the face of decreasing propensity among Americans to save, both publicly and privately. The most effective policy to address the financing problem would be to move toward partial advance funding of the retirement programs. This would be a way to raise today's saving in anticipation of greater future consumption needs. But the policy would require a reduction in current U.S. consumption, either through a hike in taxes or an increase in private saving.

The controversial aspect of shifting to partial funding is whether the shift should occur within the framework of the present public system or a new privatized system in which workers own and control their own retirement accounts. The fundamental objection to a funded public program arises out of doubts that increased contributions to the public fund would truly be saved, add to national saving, and increase future national wealth. Privatization appears to reduce this risk because policymakers are less likely to spend the added saving if it is accumulated in millions of private accounts than if it is accumulated in a single, highly visible public account.

There are, however, many advantages to a public system that make it worth a major effort to preserve. The system is progressive in offering low-income workers larger benefits relative to lifetime earnings than are offered to high-income workers. Because public pensions are ultimately backed by the taxing power of the federal government, the system can credibly promise benefits that are indexed to inflation, a promise that is not as believable in a purely private system. As a result of the progressivity of the pension formula and benefit indexation, destitution among the American elderly has fallen remarkably in the past generation. In providing old-age annuities to all of the retired population, the public system avoids the high-cost problem of adverse selection present in private annuity markets. Social security administrative costs are substantially below those in any conceivable private plan. Many of the advantages of a public system are difficult or impossible to duplicate in a private system. Privatization has always appealed to those who dislike the coercive and redistributional aspects of the present public system. Growing interest in the idea of funding future retirement costs has introduced a new element to the debate over public versus private responsibility for retirement income planning.

References

Aaron, Henry J., Barry Bosworth, and Gary Burtless. 1989. *Can Americans Afford to Grow Old?* Brookings.

Board of Governors of the Federal Reserve System. 1995. *Balance Sheets for the U.S. Economy, 1948–94.* Washington.

Board of Trustees of the Federal Old-Age and Survivors Insurance and Disability Insurance Trust Fund. Annual. *Annual Report.* Government Printing Office.

Boskin, Michael J., Lawrence J. Kotlikoff, and John B. Shoven. 1988. "Personal Security Accounts: A Proposal for Fundamental Social Security Reform." In Susan M. Wachter, ed., *Social Security and Private Pensions.* Lexington Mass.: Lexington Books.

Bosworth, Barry. 1996. "The Social Security Fund: How Big? How Managed?" In Peter A. Diamond, David C. Linderman, and Howard Young, eds., *Social Security: What Role for the Future?* Washington: National Academy of Social Insurance.

Bureau of the Census. 1993. "Measuring the Effect of Benefits and Taxes on Income and Poverty: 1992." *Current Population Reports*, series P 60, no. 186RD. Department of Commerce.

Burtless, Gary. 1993. "The Uncertainty of Social Security Forecasts in Policy Analysis and Planning." Paper prepared for the Public Trustees of the Social Security and Medicare Boards of Trustees, Washington (December 28).

Committee on Ways and Means, U.S. House of Representatives. 1994. *1994 Green Book.* Government Printing Office.

Congressional Budget Office. 1996. *The Economic and Budget Outlook: Fiscal Years 1997 2006.* Washington: Superintendent of Documents.

Detlefs, Dale R., Robert J. Myers, and J. Robert Treanor. 1996. *Guide to Social Security and Medicare.* Washington: William M. Mercer.

Diamond, Peter, and Salvador Valdés-Prieto. 1994. "Social Security Reforms." In B. Bosworth, R. Dornbusch, and R. Lábán, eds., *The Chilean Economy: Policy Lessons and Challenges*, pp. 257–320. Brookings.

Feldstein, Martin. 1976. "The Social Security Fund and National Capital Accumulation." In *Funding Pensions: Issues and Implications for Financial Markets*, pp. 32–64. Boston: Federal Reserve Bank of Boston.

Hurd, Michael D., and John B. Shoven. 1985. "The Distributional Impact of

Social Security." In David A. Wise, ed., *Pensions, Labor, and Individual Choice*, pp. 193–215. University of Chicago Press.

Kotlikoff, Lawrence J. 1990. "The Social Security Surpluses: New Clothes for the Emperor." In Carolyn L. Weaver, ed., *Social Security's Looming Surpluses*, pp. 17–28. Washington: AEI Press.

Quinn, Joseph F., and Timothy M. Smeeding. 1993. "The Present and Future Well-Being of the Aged." In Dallas Salisbury, ed., *Pensions in a Changing Economy*. Washington: Employee Benefit Research Institute.

Radner, Daniel B. 1993. *An Assessment of the Economic Status of the Aged*, Studies in Income Distribution 16. U.S. Department of Health and Human Resources, Social Security Administration.

Schultze, Charles. 1992. "Paying the Bills." In Henry J. Aaron and Charles L. Schultze, eds., *Setting Domestic Priorities: What Can Government Do?*, pp. 295–318. Brookings.

Smeeding, Timothy M., Barbara Boyle Torrey, and Lee Rainwater. 1993. "Going to Extremes: An International Perspective on the Economic Status of the United States Aged," Cross-National Studies in Aging program project paper 13. Syracuse University, Maxwell School of Citizenship and Public Affairs.

Social Security Administration. 1994. *Social Security Bulletin, Annual Statistical Supplement*. Washington: Superintendent of Dcouments.

Steuerle, C. Eugene, and Jon M. Bakija. 1994. *Retooling Social Security for the 21st Century: Right and Wrong Approaches to Reform*. Washington: Urban Institute Press.

Technical Panel on Trends and Issues in Retirement Saving. 1995. *Final Report*. Washington: Advisory Council on Social Security.

Index

311